Ranking the World

Over the last decade, international rankings have emerged as a critical tool used by international actors engaged in global governance. State practices and performance are now judged by a number of high-profile indices, including assessments of their levels of corruption, quality of democracy, creditworthiness, media freedom, and business environment. However, these rankings always carry value judgments, methodological choices, and implicit political agendas. This volume expertly addresses the important analytical, normative, and policy issues associated with the contemporary practice of "grading states." The chapters explore how rankings affect our perceptions of state performance, how states react to being ranked, why some rankings exert more global influence than others, and how states have come to strategize and respond to these public judgments. The book also critically examines how treating state rankings like popular consumer choice indices may actually lead policymakers to internalize questionable normative assumptions and lead to poorer, not improved, public policy outcomes.

ALEXANDER COOLEY is Professor of Political Science at Barnard College, Columbia University in New York and Columbia's Harriman Institute. He has published commentaries and opinions in leading venues, including the *New York Times*, *Foreign Affairs*, and *Foreign Policy*, and serves on a number of international committees, advisory boards, and working groups engaged in global governance in the post-Communist region.

JACK SNYDER is the Robert and Renée Belfer Professor of International Relations in the Political Science Department and the Harriman Institute at Columbia University. He is a Fellow of the American Academy of Arts and Sciences and in 2012 received the International Security Studies Distinguished Scholar Award of the International Studies Association.

Ranking the World

Grading States as a Tool of Global Governance

Edited by

ALEXANDER COOLEY
Barnard College

and

JACK SNYDER
Columbia University

CAMBRIDGE
UNIVERSITY PRESS

CAMBRIDGE
UNIVERSITY PRESS

University Printing House, Cambridge CB2 8BS, United Kingdom

Cambridge University Press is part of the University of Cambridge.

It furthers the University's mission by disseminating knowledge in the pursuit of education, learning and research at the highest international levels of excellence.

www.cambridge.org
Information on this title: www.cambridge.org/9781107484122

© Cambridge University Press 2015

First published 2015
First paperback edition 2016

A catalogue record for this publication is available from the British Library

Library of Congress Cataloguing in Publication data
Ranking the world : grading states as a tool of global governance / edited by Alexander Cooley and Jack Snyder.
     pages   cm
ISBN 978-1-107-09813-8 (hardback)
1. Nation-state and globalization.   2. International relations – Statistics – Political aspects.   3. International economic relations – Statistics – Political aspects.   4. World politics – 21st century.   I. Cooley, Alexander, 1972– editor of compilation.   II. Snyder, Jack L., editor of compilation.
JZ1316.R36   2015
320.072–dc23

2014044750

ISBN 978-1-107-09813-8 Hardback
ISBN 978-1-107-48412-2 Paperback

Contents

Figures

Tables

Contributors

Rawi Abdelal is the Herbert F. Johnson Professor of International Management at Harvard Business School.

Nehal Bhuta is Professor of Public International Law at the European University Institute.

Mark Blyth is Professor of International Political Economy at Brown University.

Mlada Bukovansky is Professor in the Department of Government at Smith College.

Alexander Cooley is Professor of Political Science at Barnard College, Columbia University.

Seva Gunitsky is Assistant Professor of Political Science at the University of Toronto.

Samuel Schueth received his Ph.D. from the Department of Geography at the University of Minnesota and currently works as a professional social scientist and consultant.

Jack Snyder is the Robert and Renée Belfer Professor of International Relations in the Political Science Department at Columbia University.

Preface and acknowledgments

This project was made possible by a generous grant from Columbia University's Harriman Institute to the editors for the 2010–2011 core project on "Human Rights in the Post-Communist World: Strategies and Outcomes." For the project, the editors explored the theoretical, normative, and policy-related issues surrounding international attempts to introduce human rights standards and political reform in the post-Communist states. Rankings and ratings emerged as powerful tools of these international efforts, yet we soon discovered that while international legal scholars were now engaging with the topic of indicators and global power, international relations scholars had not assessed these practices, even as they have been embraced by policymakers, international governance actors, and the media.

The core project supported a number of key initiatives for us to assess and learn about the emerging power of international rankings. The Harriman Institute held a series of public panels and lectures featuring academics, policymakers, and NGO representatives that explored various rankings-related topics, including democracy promotion, international media freedom, international corruption, and illicit indicators and the contested politics of numbers. The project also supported an initial authors' workshop at Columbia in February 2012, featuring the contributors to this volume, along with Andrei Tsygankov, Lee Becker, and Tudor Vlad. We are thankful to Kevin Davis, Benedict Kingsbury and Sally Merry of NYU, whose work on indicators has been invaluable to our own understandings. The project also supported research visits to the headquarters of various rankings organizations, including Transparency International, the World Bank, Fund for Peace, Open Budget Partnership, Revenue Watch, Heritage Foundation, and Publish What You Fund. We thank these and other organizations for their cooperation and sharing of materials concerning the political issues we were interested in.

The typescript and ideas presented have been vastly improved from advice and feedback provided by two Cambridge University Press reviewers and participants at workshops held at Yale University, Columbia University's International Politics Seminar, Koç University, and Cornell University's International Law/International Relations Colloquium. The editors are especially thankful to Sarah Levine for her invaluable research assistance and to Audrey Greene for assistance in preparing the manuscript. Chapter 6 is an edited version of the article "Assembling international competitiveness: The Republic of Georgia, USAID, and the Doing Business Project," *Economic Geography* 87, no. 1 (2011): 51–77. We thank Wiley for granting permission for its inclusion.

Abbreviations

BPI	Bribe Payers Index
CAM	Coppedge, Alvarez, and Maldonado 2008
CAST	Conflict Assessment Software Tool
CDO	collateralized debt obligation
CPI	Corruption Perceptions Index
CPJ	Committee to Protect Journalists
CRA	credit rating agency
DBI	World Bank's Ease of Doing Business Index
DFID	Department for International Development (United Kingdom)
EIU	Economist Intelligence Unit
FDI	foreign direct investment
FSI	Failed States Index
GBCR	Georgia Business Climate Reform
GCI	Global Competitiveness Index
GNIA	Georgian National Investment Agency
IFI	international financial institution
IMF	International Monetary Fund
IO	international organization
MCC	Millennium Challenge Corporation
NGO	non-governmental organization
OECD	Organisation for Economic Cooperation and Development
PACL	Adam Przeworski, Michael Alvarez, Jose Antonio Cheibub, and Fernando Limongi
RRO	ratings and rankings organization
S&P	Standard & Poor's
SEC	Securities and Exchange Commission
SMRC	State Ministry for Reform Coordination (Georgia)
TI	Transparency International
UDS	Universal Democracy Score
USAID	United States Agency for International Development
USFfP	US Fund for Peace

1 The emerging politics of international rankings and ratings
A framework for analysis

ALEXANDER COOLEY

Introduction

On May 7, 2012, on his first day as once-again elected President of the Russian Federation, Vladimir Putin declared that he would make economic modernization the goal of his administration, vowing to take Russia from its current position as 120th on the World Bank's Ease of Doing Business Index (DBI) to 50th by 2015.[1] The remark was noteworthy for two reasons: First, the Russian President chose the DBI as an authoritative and credible outside judge of the endemic bureaucratic corruption and dismal investment conditions that still characterize the country. Second, Putin cited the DBI even while he and other Russian officials have consistently denied the authority of other international rankings of Russia, such as those measuring Russian democracy, civil liberties, or media freedoms. Given Russia's near obsession with guarding its sovereignty against the influence of Western external actors and non-governmental organizations, the Kremlin's public acceptance of the DBI seems even more striking.

Nine months earlier, the private New York-based credit rating agency Standard and Poor's announced that it was downgrading the credit rating of the United States for the first time ever from its "AAA" highest rating.[2] The downgrade came in response to the political brinksmanship displayed by the US Congress in the lead-up to its vote to raise the US debt-ceiling and spawned a host of media scrutiny and commentary. What gave this private company the right to judge, let alone downgrade, the powerful United States? What impact would this decision have on the world's

---

[1] "Russia's Putin orders investment, labour shake-up," *Reuters* May 7, 2012. Also see the speech from February 3, 2012 in which Putin made more favorable references to DBI at: http://www.bsr-russia.com/en/economy/item/2138-putins-speech-to-rspp-business-lobby-full-text-translation.html.

[2] www.standardandpoors.com/ratings/articles/en/us/?assetID=1245316529563

economic superpower? And what would the downgrade mean for global perceptions about US capacity to continue to exercise its traditional leadership role in world affairs?

These two anecdotes suggest that rankings are playing an increasingly important role in the domains of international relations and public policy, yet scholars and commentators have not yet fully appreciated their scope and impact on state behavior and global governance. Dozens of private actors, international organizations (IOs), non-governmental organizations (NGOs), and even governments have started issuing rankings, ratings, or other indicators that provide information about, measure, and assess the performance of states in world affairs. As tools of organizational power, these rankings are designed to exert normative pressures on states to promote change in a country's performance or improve some aspect of its domestic institutions or policymaking.[3] Taken cumulatively, Kevin Davis, Benedict Kingsbury, and Sally Merry observe that these indicators are even becoming a new and distinct "technology of global governance," creating and disseminating new forms of knowledge and embedding themselves in international institutions and administrative practices.[4]

Some of these ratings and rankings organizations (RROs) are relatively well known. The so-called "big three" credit rating agencies of Moody's, Standard and Poor's, and Fitch are the main private companies that evaluate and rate the creditworthiness of sovereign entities, while, since 1995, the Berlin-based NGO Transparency International has ranked states on their levels of public corruption in its annual Corruption Perceptions Index (CPI). The World Bank's DBI each year ranks countries according to a number of indicators that capture aspects of their regulatory environment, while the US-based NGO Freedom House releases annual democracy rankings that characterize countries as "Free," "Partly Free," or "Not Free."

We now have established global rankings that measure levels of human development,[5] quality of life,[6] hunger,[7] business

---

[3] Bauhr and Nasiritousi 2012.

[4] Davis, Kingsbury, and Merry 2012a; and Davis, Fisher, Kingsbury, and Merry 2012.

[5] United Nations Development Program, "Human Development Index," http://hdr.undp.org/en/statistics/hdi.

[6] Organisation for Economic Cooperation and Development, "Better Life Index," http://www.oecdbetterlifeindex.org.

[7] International Food Policy Research Institute, "Global Hunger Index," http://www.ifpri.org/publication/2011-global-hunger-index.

environment,[8] budget transparency,[9] aid transparency,[10] environmental performance,[11] democracy,[12] media freedoms,[13] civil society,[14] and economic freedoms.[15] Nor are international indices limited to political and socio-economic issues, as rankings and scorecards now also measure the likelihood that states will fail or collapse,[16] assess their compliance with international efforts to stem human trafficking,[17] evaluate the security of their nuclear materials,[18] judge their coherence and effectiveness as members of the European Union,[19] assess their levels of militarization[20] and propensity to wage war.[21] Appendix 1 identifies ninety-five of the international rankings, ratings, and indices that have emerged through the year 2013, and classifies them according to issue area.

State reactions to international rankings

Given the public statements by state leaders about RROs and their increasing prominence in the global policy sphere, it seems curious that

[8] World Bank, "Ease of Doing Business Index," http://www.doingbusiness.org/rankings.

[9] Open Budget Partnership, "Open Budget Index," http://internationalbudget.org/what-we-do/open-budget-survey.

[10] Publish What You Fund, "Aid Transparency Index," http://www.publishwhatyoufund.org/resources/index/2011-index.

[11] Yale University, "Environmental Performance Index," http://epi.yale.edu.

[12] Freedom House, "Freedom in the World," http://www.freedomhouse.org/report-types/freedom-world; and Economist Intelligence Unit, "Democracy Index," http://www.eiu.com/public/thankyou_download.aspx?activity=download&campaignid=DemocracyIndex2011.

[13] Freedom House, "Freedom of the Press," http://www.freedomhouse.org/report/freedom-press/freedom-press-2012.

[14] Civicus, "Civil Society Index," http://civicus.org/what-we-do-126/csi.

[15] Heritage Foundation, "Economic Freedom Index," http://www.heritage.org/issues/economic-freedom/index-of-economic-freedom.

[16] Fund for Peace and Foreign Policy Magazine, "Failed States Index," http://www.foreignpolicy.com/failedstates.

[17] United States State Department, "Trafficking in Persons Report," http://www.state.gov/j/tip/rls/tiprpt.

[18] Nuclear Threat Initiative, "Nuclear Materials Index," http://www.ntiindex.org/results/#1-0.

[19] European Council on Foreign Relations, "European Foreign Policy Scorecard," http://www.ecfr.eu/scorecard/2012.

[20] Bonn International Center for Conversion, "Global Militarization Index," http://www.bicc.de/our-work/gmi.html.

[21] Vision of Humanity, "Global Peace Index," http://www.visionofhumanity.org/gpi-data/#/2011/conf.

the topic has not received more attention from international relations scholars, even as legal scholars, development practitioners, and anthropologists have generated important theoretical insights and empirical findings.[22] States are now responding to these external rankings, but their concerns and reactions vary considerably. Some governments flaunt their improving performance on indices in glossy large ads in international publications such as *The Economist* and *Financial Times*, while elites, as typified by President Putin's speech, also use these rankings as focal points to identify areas of policy priority and launch new initiatives. Other times, states might even attack the very authority, credibility, and legitimacy of RROs, in an attempt to counter negative evaluations, as was the case with China's reaction to being ranked poorly in the World Bank's 2013 DBI survey or, as Abdelal and Blyth describe in this volume, when European Union officials during the Euro-crisis attacked credit rating agencies (CRAs) as counterproductive and even threatened to ban them from issuing downgrades.[23] Responding to RROs has become a common concern for policymakers across a wide variety of fields, especially as their visibility has increased over the last decade.

The extensive literature on international organization suggests two general approaches for explaining how states might react to these outside assessments: rationalist and socially driven responses. Proponents of rational bargaining approaches would claim that states are most likely to respond to those changes in rankings that exert material costs.[24] A number of these international rankings potentially can inflict economic damage upon recipients. For example, states that are downgraded by international CRAs usually have to pay higher rates on their bond issues, while states that do not meet benchmarks set by RROs on issues such as political rights or rule of law will not be eligible for assistance under the US Millennium Challenge Accounts. Just as with analyzing the effects of foreign aid conditionality, small states that are economically dependent on international donors or capital flows will

---

[22] See Merry 2011; and Davis, Kingsbury, and Merry 2012b. One exception is the international political economy literature on credit rating agencies. See Sinclair 2005; and Bruner and Abdelal 2005. Also see Rotberg 2014 and Kelley and Simmons 2015.

[23] "Doing in business at the World Bank," *Wall Street Journal* May 7, 2013. On the European reaction to CRAs, also see Klinz 2011.

[24] For representative examples, see Abbott and Snidal 1998; Koremenos, Lipson, and Snidal 2001; and Krasner 1982 and 1991.

care more about international rankings than states that are economically self-sufficient or relatively insulated from international lenders. On the other hand, external rankings that exert no material costs should be ignored.

A second strategic response by states might be to "teach to the test," or minimize actual institutional reforms by targeting the most malleable measures and indicators on which they are actually ranked, thereby improving their scores without adopting new norms or standards of behavior. Sociological research suggests that, over time, indicators inevitably become substitutes for the phenomena that they are measuring, rendering the indicator itself, not what it is measuring, the focus of social action. For example, in their study of the effects of the *U.S. News & World Report* law school rankings, Sauder and Lancaster find that university administrators have adopted a number of strategies specifically aimed at improving the indicators used to assess their rank.[25] As states become increasingly attuned to the importance of certain RROs, rationalists would expect them to design strategies to generate as quick improvement as possible, while generating the least political disruption possible.[26]

Taken even further, rationalists would also expect states to conform to the basic expectations of "Campbell's Law." In his 1970s study of the dynamics of standardized educational testing and teacher performance Donald Campbell observed, "The more any quantitative social indicator is used for social decision-making, the more subject it will be to corruption pressures and the more apt it will be to distort and corrupt the social processes it is intended to monitor."[27] Thus, gaming the system, attacking the credibility of rankings, and directly lobbying RROs for improvements in rankings (without accompanying behavioral changes) are all behaviors broadly consistent with rationalist approaches.

On the other hand, constructivist scholars and social theorists would emphasize that states would react according to the norms and social pressures generated by RROs. In extreme cases, states might be fully socialized by an RRO to accept its authoritative judgment and

---

[25] Sauder and Lancaster 2006.
[26] This may even be internalized. For example, the government of Rwanda has a special division housed within the Ministry of Foreign Affairs whose exclusive focus is on improving the country's place in international rankings.
[27] Campbell 1975: 35.

uncritically implement its prescriptions. For example, in response to the 2011 pilot index on aid transparency, published by Publish What You Fund, the Swedish International Development Cooperation Agency (SIDA) fully accepted the report's findings and even announced that it would adopt future versions of the index as a benchmark for assessing its performance on aid transparency.[28]

But short of socialization, work on the social dynamics of international groups suggests that RROs might still exert influence by impacting the recipient's social status. From this perspective, though states pay attention to their overall global standing on an issue, they will be especially concerned when an international ranking highlights their hierarchical standing, either through "naming and shaming" or by judging them against a peer state, rival, or regional grouping.[29] For example, Armenian officials are unlikely to be bothered if their country is compared in the area of corruption or democratization to Ecuador or Zambia; however, any unfavorable comparisons to neighbor and rival Azerbaijan are carefully noted and scrutinized. Work on stigmatization in international relations even suggests that, in certain cases, lower-ranked states might embrace their "deviant" status as a counter-stigmatization strategy designed to undermine the international normative and political order in which a ranking is embedded.[30] By exerting social influence, rankings appeal to the status of states and state leaders, offering positive reinforcement for their practices, opprobrium, or opportunities for normative contestation.

Framing an international relations research agenda on rankings

But exclusively focusing on state responses, and their drivers, to selected rankings does not capture the broader array of international impacts potentially generated by the rise of RROs. Because rankings have so rapidly become an increasingly accepted policy tool in the international arena, we are mandated to think more broadly about their role in global governance and international organization.

This introductory volume represents a first cut at exploring some of the important theoretical, methodological, and political issues raised

---

[28] Author's interviews with representatives of Publish What You Fund, London: May 2012. Published with permission of SIDA.
[29] Johnston 2001; and Bauhr and Nasiritousi 2012: 544–545.
[30] Adler-Nissen 2014; and Zarakol 2011.

by the proliferation of RROs in the study of international relations. It brings together a distinguished group of scholars to examine these issues across a wide range of international rankings and issue areas. Theoretically, we identify the different roles played by RROs in international relations and consider why certain actors acquire the authority to issue rankings about states, what common methodological issues ratings and rankings engender, and how rankings might reconfigure political relationships at both the transnational and domestic levels. Empirically, we consider the importance of RROs in a broad range of issue areas, including assessing the quality of democracy, controlling corruption, ensuring media freedom, evaluating the creditworthiness of states, and determining which states are the most likely to "fail." As we will see, RROs are growing in scope and relevance to the practice of global governance. They have the power to informally regulate global institutions and practices, to create specific normative understandings about issues like "corruption" or "failed states," to measure the openness of a state's media environment or political system, provide benchmarks for aid distribution and other policy decisions, and reconfigure political networks among international actors and domestic bureaucracies in their efforts to respond to ranking pressures.

Though the proliferation of rankings and ratings is a global phenomenon, many of our contributions focus upon the experience of the post-Soviet states. Instructively, the rise of RROs has overlapped with the post-Communist states' so-called political and economic transitions. Born out of the assumption that the collapse of socialism would yield progress towards market economies and liberal democracies, the post-Communist transitions spawned new rankings such as Freedom House's *Nations in Transit* or the European Bank for Reconstruction and Development's transition indicators that were designed to measure, track, and highlight this political and economic progress.[31] Throughout the 1990s, such RROs provided upbeat assessments of these transitions and documented steady improvements throughout the world in the areas of democratic development, respect for political rights, and market-friendly economic reforms, theoretically reinforcing the assumptions in the Western policy community that the teleological transition model was broadly applicable, despite some laggards.[32] But

---

[31] For a critical overview, see Gianonne 2010.
[32] See, for instance, Karatnycky 1999; and Pilon 1993.

during the 2000s, under the assertive and often revisionist leadership of Vladimir Putin, Russia led a backlash in the region against RROs, criticizing rankings and ratings, and singling out Freedom House, as harboring clear biases serving the foreign policy agendas of the West.[33] This was part of a broader backlash against the perceived meddling of Western actors in the domestic politics and sovereignty of the post-Soviet states during which Russia and several Central Asian states expelled democracy and human rights monitors and enacted more restrictive laws against Western-funded NGOs. At the same time, other former Soviet countries such as the Baltic states and Georgia (after 2003), as Schueth documents in his chapter, openly embraced RRO judgments precisely to signal their desire to integrate with the West and be judged according to Western standards.

The political debates that we observe surrounding Western RROs in the post-Soviet sphere are reflected more broadly in emerging research about how global power relations are implicated in the information-gathering and the production of indicators in developing countries. Sally Merry's work suggests that UN statistical gathering procedures designed to produce generalizable indicators have been contested and accused of excluding southern inputs, while Morten Jurgen's research shows how the enduring inaccuracies of African statistics used as inputs in a broad array of indicators distort fundamental related policy actions such as foreign aid allocations, evaluations, and development policy.[34] And Seva Gunitsky's contribution to this volume suggests that the reliability of democracy rankings varies precisely in that category of "middling states," neither consolidated democracies nor authoritarian, that policymakers consider the most susceptible to external democracy promotion efforts and targeted projects.

The link between theory generation about RROs and the emerging policy context across different issue areas, then, is critical, and informs all of our chapter contributions, including this introductory chapter and the conclusion. The next part of this analytical overview examines the origins of the recent rankings frenzy, especially the proliferation of new rankings and indices in the 2000s. The chapter then outlines four different roles that RROs have come to play in global governance and

---

[33] Tsygankov 2012; and Lyudmila Alexandrova, "Reaction to Freedom House report in Russia," *ITAR-TASS Daily* February 2, 2007.

[34] Merry 2011; Jurgen 2013.

international affairs – as judges, sources of governmentality, advocacy tools, and as self-promoting organizations. The next section investigates three themes that inform the comparative study of rankings and the chapters of this volume – the authority of RROs, the methodological questions surrounding their construction, and their emerging ability to create new political configurations and networks, both transnationally and within states themselves. The chapter concludes with brief summaries of our contributors' chapters. Ultimately, our authors' use of a wide variety of social science theories, methods, and approaches to engage with the rise of RROs suggests a fertile new research area that is ripe for further theoretical development and practical scrutiny.

The origins of the rankings frenzy

Why this proliferation of international rankings and indices? Scholars of the development of the modern state have long noted how technologies to standardize accounting, measurements, coinage, and weights were critical in the expansion of bureaucratic reach and capacity and, in Hendrik Spruyt's account, determined the administrative superiority of the modern state over competing organizational forms such as city states or city leagues.[35] As James Scott has exposed, the modern state could only acquire true administrative capacity, or "get a handle on its subjects and their environments," when it reduced complex social and local practices into simplified new categories amenable to standardization, classification, and regimentation.[36] Similarly, historians and sociologists have noted how during the late nineteenth century quantification became critical for the development of public bureaus and state regulatory capacity.[37] The very exercise of modern public accounting, for budgeting, planning, and infrastructure development, was founded upon the modern state's ability to successfully measure and evaluate complex social practices.

Such accounts of the genealogy of indicators as a tool of statecraft are fascinating and obviously relevant, but by themselves are insufficient to explain the dramatic burst of new international RROs since the post-Cold War period. As Figure 1.1 suggests, of the total of ninety-five indices that we have identified in Appendix 1, eighty-three have appeared since 1990 and sixty-six since 2001.[38] These RROs are now

---

[35] Spruyt 1994.　　[36] Scott 1999.　　[37] Porter 1995.
[38] The criteria for included RROs are described in Appendix 1.

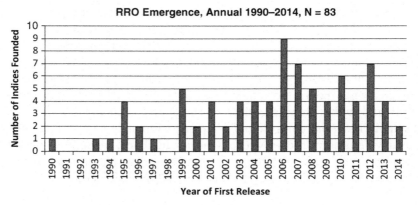

Figure 1.1 RRO emergence, annual 1990–2014, N=83

being produced explicitly in the international realm and targeting a diverse global audience of national policymakers, international bureaucrats, transnational activists, and media outlets.

The spectacular proliferation of international rankings seems to be the result of at least three related trends: the adoption of techniques of performance evaluation in modern political and social life, the strengthening of global governance networks, and the proliferation of new information technologies and open data sources.

First, the global practice of ranking and rating is part of a broader trend within social life over the 1980s and 1990s to develop tools for performance evaluation and assessment. Spawned by the neoliberal turn and demands for public sector accountability, and embodied in the dissemination of modern management techniques, assessment practices have now been adopted by most large public and private organizations, including corporations, bureaucracies, and not-for-profits.[39] Driven by the twin axioms of transparency and accountability, performance evaluation and internal risk management, in turn, require a set of standardized and comparable benchmarks, as well as appropriate scales for rendering judgments. As a result, star ratings, letter grades, scores, and ordinal rankings have all become common metrics in the assessment of individuals and organizations. Even in the social sphere,

[39] See, especially, Power's (2007) account of the rise since the mid-1990s of modern risk management and the adoption of internal controls in corporations and other organizations. On NGOs specifically, see Ebrahim 2003.

external rankings as measures of quality inform a broad range of our personal decisions including the selection of schools or universities, the evaluation of service providers, the comparison of consumer products in designated categories, and even decisions over leisure activities such as what hotels we stay in during our vacations and what movies we choose to watch.

In the political realm, demands for greater accountability and public sector reform accelerated the adoption of performance evaluation metrics and procedures through the 1990s.[40] Rankings and ratings have come to play an important role in assessing the provision of state services and the performance of elected officials, local governments, bureaucrats, and governing institutions.[41] For example, states are nationally ranked on how their students perform on standardized tests, the quality of their healthcare, their rate of taxation, and the number of jobs that they create in any given year. A growing number of advocacy organizations and citizens' movements issue "scorecards" to assess elected officials on their voting records on the environment, gun control, reproductive rights, or unionization.[42] Techniques of ranking and rating have become common tools of information gathering, judgment, and evaluation in political life, though their diffusion into the international realm as organizational practices has lagged their adoption domestically.[43]

Second, the rise of international rankings has coincided with the proliferation of global governance networks over the last twenty years and the emergence of new regulatory actors. As Avant, Finnemore, and Sell argue, global governance is performed across borders by a number of authoritative new actors who actively make rules, set agendas, classify phenomena, evaluate outcomes, and implement rules and programs.[44] Contrary to state-centric or functionalist

---

[40] Wholey and Hatry 1992. A more critical account is given by Sanderson 2001.

[41] See Cutler and Waine 1998, ch. 2. Saint-Martin (2004) argues that such new management techniques were introduced to the public sector by a cohort of consultants and accountants with previous experience in the private sector.

[42] See especially Humphreys and Weinstein (2007) for a field experiment that assesses the impact of scorecards as a mechanism for parliamentarian accountability in Uganda.

[43] Pistor (2012) traces how, during the mid- to late 1990s, the indicators generated by the once self-contained research and data-gathering divisions of international organizations such as the World Bank were transposed into normative benchmarks deployed by officials for policy purposes.

[44] Avant, Finnemore, and Sell 2010.

theories, these new "global governors" are active agents, forging relationships and pragmatic alliances, contesting policy terrains, and networking with a variety of actors to both exercise their authority and affect the transnational governance of their preferred issues. Importantly, this scholarship suggests that the state is not so much "retreating" as it is forging new types of relationships with new global actors, sometimes in partnership, other times delegated, and other times more adversarial.

Of particular importance in this era has been the development of global standards and best practices across a variety of issue areas as well as the proliferation of accompanying international regulatory bodies to oversee them.[45] As Tim Büthe has argued, private regulation has expanded transnationally in part because it is functionally better suited to dynamic, specialized, and complex emerging issue areas where national government regulation may lack the technical capacity and international governmental cooperation might be cumbersome or slow.[46] Moreover, he notes that NGOs, motivated by normative and social commitments to these specific causes, now play an important monitoring or watchdog role across these areas to enforce these new private standards. From this perspective, RROs both provide the regulatory raw material to benchmark compliance, in the form of indicators (and rankings), and also act as monitors who track and assess compliance with these new international standards, norms, and expectations, thereby producing the very fabric of contemporary global governance.[47]

Third, with recent advances in information technology, data gathering, analysis, and dissemination, it is now far easier for individuals and organizations to research and compile indicators on a wide range of issue areas, as well as to present and share their findings. State statistical agencies, international organizations, and non-governmental organizations routinely collect, code, and present data in more transparent and easy-to-use ways, allowing for the generation and repackaging of indicators for a variety of different research and analytical purposes. Media outlets consume these rankings and indicators as authoritative background that validates a story about a particular

---

[45] See Mattli and Woods 2009; and Büthe and Mattli 2011.
[46] Büthe 2010a; and Büthe and Mattli 2011.
[47] Davis, Kingsbury, and Merry 2012b; and Buduru and Pal 2010.

country (e.g. corruption scandal in Uzbekistan) or become the focus of the story itself (Georgia's improved business climate as measured by the World Bank's DBI). As Peter Andreas and Kelly Greenhill observe, the ease of dissemination of statistics and numbers due to technological advances, coupled with media demand, has strengthened their credibility.[48] Many of these indices have also impacted scholarly understandings of these international issues, providing new measures and data sets for researchers to evaluate state performance and explore potential causal relationships across different issue areas.[49] At the same time, the incorporation of these indicators in new research has raised questions about how new types of global knowledge are produced and disseminated, as well as how transnational networks of peer review are mobilized to produce comparative rankings.[50]

What do international rankings and ratings do?

Though this volume examines both ratings and rankings, these practices formally differ. A rating assigns a discrete value, indicator, or grade to the performance of a state that is independent of the other rated units. For example, countries rated by the US State Department's Human Trafficking Report are placed into one of three categories (Tier 1, 2, or 3), while credit rating agencies assign grades to borrowers such as sovereign states that evaluate their perceived capacity to repay their debts. In theory, at least, ratings are calculated and assigned independently for each rated entity based on a discrete set of performance criteria and measurements.

In contrast, rankings are inherently relational, as states are assigned an ordinal ranking in comparison to each other. Ranking thus necessarily confers status on countries ranked highly and stigmatizes those ranked lower.[51] The distinction between the two practices is more than academic, as it often generates confusion and practical concerns among both observers and ranked states. For instance, in the realm of corruption government officials regularly complain that certain steps they have taken are not reflected in changes in their rankings, without fully appreciating that a ranking remains a relative measure, not an

---

[48] Andreas and Greenhill 2010: 13.   [49] Williams and Siddique 2008.
[50] On the politics and transnational networks of peer review, see Porter 2009.
[51] On how international institutions confer social status, see Johnston 2001.

indicator of individual progress.[52] In other cases, such as Freedom House's Media Freedom Index or the Open Budget Index, indices combine both rankings and ratings, providing an individual country score as well as a comparative ranking or assessment of the target state within the broader group of countries.

Rankings and ratings are also inevitably viewed temporally, often identifying trends. The DBI itself singles out its annual most improved "top ten" countries, while from 2007 to 2010 Freedom House surveys of democracy in the world all referred in some way to the steady erosion of global democracy. Capturing or even establishing trends appears to be a critical aspect of the public appeal of international ranking and ratings, as countries are rewarded or criticized based on their previous positions.[53]

With these distinctions in mind, we outline four critical roles that international rankings and ratings might play in contemporary world politics: they provide expert judgments about the performance of states; they provide mechanisms for global regulation and monitoring of states; they are used as advocacy tools; and they function as branding or "flag-planting" devices, used by NGO and IOs to assert their jurisdictional authority over specific issues. These roles are not mutually exclusive, though they do suggest that a ranking or rating may simultaneously play multiple roles in the global domain.

RROs as judges

At the most basic level, rankings provide specialized information about the performance of states on a number of issues. Rankings and ratings, as part of the growing universe of indicators, reduce complex phenomena into quantifiable indicators that can be used to assess the performance of states. Ideally, then, RROs reduce the information-gathering problems associated with particular international issues or categories of state practices, but they do so by divorcing these judgments from their local, cultural, and social context.

---

[52] Author's interviews with representatives of Transparency International, Berlin, November 2011.

[53] Whether the international community should be judging certain state behaviors, such as human rights compliance, on a curve is, of course, a related and an ethically fraught issue.

In some cases, states and other public actors have quite willingly ceded or delegated the function of information provision to RROs, either because they lack the necessary expertise and information-gathering capacity or because it is simply more cost-effective to allow an external organization to assume such functions. For example, despite widespread government complaints about international credit rating agencies and their failure to anticipate important financial episodes such as the East Asian financial crisis, the US mortgage-backed securities crisis, or the current European sovereign debt crisis, credit rating organizations still perform these rating functions, as governments have delegated this role and show no political will to assume these same duties.[54]

Of course, like all actors that issue judgments, RROs are constantly open to criticism regarding the appropriateness, accuracy, and neutrality of their measures, assessments, and working assumptions. The very ease through which rankings and indices quantify and simplify, or as Sally Merry describes it, "their capacity to convert complicated contextually variable phenomena into unambiguous, clear, and impersonal measures," also leads to accusations of selectivity and bias.[55] All indicators embody a standard or rule that is used for measurement.[56] Thus, evaluation cannot be removed from the standards and assumptions that allow measurement to take place, while the reduction of complex and even ecological relationships to standard and simplified categories relates to the broader spread of the modern practices of governmentality and planning or, in Scott's phrase, the pathologies of "seeing like a state."[57] Globally, the production of such standards or rules is further embedded in and produced by transnational political relationships, despite their outwardly "technical" nature.[58]

Consider those RROs that measure business-related legal reforms and rank countries according to the quality of their regulatory and investment climates. Legal scholars examining the World Bank's DBI surveys have found that nuanced or sector-specific legal norms may not be amenable to standardized measurement,[59] while economists have found that the index's focus on eliminating formal institutions and regulatory barriers may actually yield their substitution by informal

---

[54] See Bruner and Abdelal 2005.   [55] Merry 2011.   [56] Büthe 2012: 29.
[57] Scott 1999.   [58] See Büthe 2010b; and Büthe and Mattli 2011.
[59] Davis 2004; and Davis and Kruse 2007.

practices.[60] Moreover, the publicly contested and evolving content of legal practice is itself replaced by an external drive for impersonal standardization. As Galit Sarfaty observes, "when indicators translate legal norms into quantifiable metrics, there are unintended consequences," and warns, "[s]ince indicators carry scientific authority, they mask potential conflicts of interest among technical experts and leave little room for contestation."[61]

Numerical judgments may be complemented by a high-profile classification or label assigned to the country. Sometimes labeling accurately and neutrally describes the degree of what is being measured, such as the labels of "Extensive Information" or "Minimal Information" that the Open Budget Index assigns to its composite scores about how much information governments provide about their national budgeting formulation.[62] But classifications can also themselves cross the line to become pejorative judgments, such as when RROs judge countries to be "Not Free" (Freedom House), "Slackers" (European Foreign Policy Scorecard), "Critical" (Failed States Index), or "Highly Corrupt" (Transparency International). In fact, in many cases, it is the classification or labeling of their country by RROs that state officials find more objectionable than the country score itself.

The assumptions, classifications, and judgments embodied by rankings also can disseminate new international norms that, in turn, frame policy choices in terms that favor powerful states and limit alternative forms of knowledge and practice, what Barnett and Duvall have termed "productive power."[63] As Mlada Bukovansky points out in her chapter, the rise of the CPI and the Transparency International (TI)-led anti-corruption regime has defined international anti-corruption efforts primarily in terms of focusing on the quality of internal institutions of individual states as the key to development failure, rather than the transnational context that facilitates rigged tenders, capital flight, and money-laundering. In the security realm, as Nehal Bhuta explores, the rise in various Failed State indices, both within and outside of the US government, appears to be predicated on the widely held post-9/11 assumption that failed states constitute an immediate security risk as they may destabilize regions and provide shelter and a home base for

[60] Arruñada 2007.   [61] Sarfaty 2013.
[62] See http://internationalbudget.org/what-we-do/open-budget-survey/rankings-key-findings/rankings.
[63] Barnett and Duvall 2005: 3.

terrorists and militants with transnational aspirations. Such indices reinforce the prevailing assumption about the security risk "state failure" supposedly implies, though some empirical studies question this formulation.[64]

RROs as global regulators and sources of governmentality

Beyond issuing expert judgments, rankings and ratings have increasingly become integral to the fabric of global governance and in emerging global administrative law and regulatory practices.[65] In some cases, the use of rankings and ratings has remained informal, while in others their role has been formalized and embedded within actual international regimes and governmental decision-making. Consequently, RROs are increasingly blurring distinctions between private and public functions and now have the potential to alter the forms, exercise, and even distribution of power in certain areas of global governance.[66]

The last two decades have seen the rapid rise of private actors playing governance functions such as setting standards, resolving disputes, and framing appropriate international responses to common challenges.[67] RROs can be considered a part of the rise of such privatized governance, even though these actors themselves might deny that they play such formal "governing roles." For example, though senior officials at Transparency International deny their role as a source of global regulation, TI has been the central actor in the spawning of a new transnational anti-corruption advocacy network, especially within the OECD.[68] Similarly, Moody's and Standard and Poor's officially state that their ratings are meant to be impartial assessments of creditworthiness, but neither official nor private actors can access contemporary capital markets without obtaining a rating for a bond issue. Accordingly, as Timothy Sinclair argues, ratings organizations in practice function as *de facto* bond-issuing licensors.[69]

The Foucauldian perspective on governmentality draws our attention to the assortment of practices and tools through which social

---

[64] See Patrick 2006.   [65] Davis, Kingsbury, and Merry 2012a, 2012b.
[66] Davis, Fisher, Kingsbury, and Merry 2012: 4.
[67] See Avant, Finnemore, and Sell 2010; Büthe 2010a; Büthe and Mattli 2011; and Mattli and Woods 2009.
[68] Bukovansky 2006.   [69] Sinclair 2005.

power is constituted and reproduced in everyday institutional interactions, not just hierarchically transmitted through formal lines of authority. Scholars have suggested that indicators and rankings, because of their simplifying judgments, decontextualized assumptions, and embeddedness in various sites of global power, also function as hidden and powerful tools of governance that reproduce structural inequalities and biased policy agendas.[70] Similarly, much of the "New Public Management" literature draws distinctions between how international organizations such as the European Union have employed standard-setting as substitutes for "old-style" problem-solving strategies and overt political bargaining.[71] Instead, the introduction of standard-setting in the EU and other international organizations has necessitated, in turn, benchmarking and the collection of data for measuring these established thresholds. Like the use of "best practices," rankings are increasingly used in these allegedly responsive "bottom-up" monitoring systems. For example, the EU's Open Method of Coordination has been cited as exemplifying the "new-style" public management techniques of cyclical coordinating, monitoring, benchmarking, and surveillance.[72] From the "governmentality" perspective, rankings, ratings, and indices not only act as judgments, but function as subtle regulatory tools.

At the same time, as scholars of international regimes have long observed, the findings and agendas of RROs are not immune to state-led or structural power politics and may even be directly influenced by them.[73] The US reaction to the World Health Organization's 2000 first ranking of global health systems is an important case in point. After the US was ranked 39th in the world in the pilot WHO study, which considered factors such as inequality in healthcare access and universal coverage, US official and media criticism was so intense that the WHO Executive Board recommended dropping the ranking practice in future surveys.[74] Similarly Abdelal and Blyth in their chapter suggest that the rankings of credit rating agencies have provided both political cover

---

[70] Davis, Fisher, Kingsbury, and Merry 2012; Löwenheim 2008.
[71] Van der Vleuten and Verloo 2012.
[72] Borrás and Jacobsson 2004. Though see Schäfer (2006) on how surveillance techniques and data-gathering are also being employed by "old-style" institutions such as the OECD and IMF.
[73] See Keohane 1984; Krasner 1982; and Wade 2002.
[74] See Fisher 2012: 236–238.

and useful weapons for powerful states, especially Germany, to implement their preferred austerity agendas over other possible solutions to
the Eurozone debt and banking crisis. Thus, RROs and their agenda-
setting and social pressure may reconstitute international regimes and
governance procedures in more hidden ways that favor powerful states
and their capacities.

RROs are also integrating themselves with global and national regulatory regimes and procedures in more formal ways. Under the Basel II
and Basel III accords on capital adequacy and banking regulations, the
ratings issued by credit rating agencies were deemed an important
component for assessing a bank's capital holding requirements for its
risk portfolio, while individual states may require that pension funds or
other domestic financial vehicles only be allowed to hold assets above a
certain rating (e.g. AAA only). Bhuta suggests that international donors
such as USAID and DFID now use failed states indices to allocate
resources, while these same indices are now poised to become the
bedrock of the new monitoring regime of failing states established by
the Responsibility to Protect (R2P) doctrine and the institutionalization of a number of UN-based early warning mechanisms.[75]

One of the most important developments in the evolving regulatory
role of RROs came in 2004 when the United States government established the Millennium Challenge Corporation (MCC), an aid account
designed to reward countries for demonstrating progress on a number
of social and political areas. From its inception, the MCC delegated
evaluations of candidate state performance to RROs; it currently relies
on seventeen different indicators.[76] For example, the democracy NGO
Freedom House's criteria are used to measure a country's "Civil
Liberties" and "Ruling Justly," the World Bank's indicators measure
"Rule of Law" and "Control over Corruption," and the Heritage
Foundation's Economic Freedom Index is used to assess a country's
openness to trade.[77] And although DC-based US State Department
officials rarely intervene or attempt to interfere in the production of

---

[75] See the pleas in United Nations Secretary General 2010 to prioritize development
of standardized criteria and enhance information-gathering capacities as part of
the early warning effort.
[76] See "Guide to the MCC Indicators" at http://www.mcc.gov/documents/reports/
reference-2011001066102-fy12-guide-to-the-indicators.pdf.
[77] www.mcc.gov/documents/reports/report-2010001039502-selection-criteria-and-
methodology.pdf.

these indicators, it is not uncommon for the RROs used by the MCC to receive direct inquiries from US embassy representatives in MCC candidate countries about a country's relative standing and prospects for meeting the necessary threshold.

RROs as advocates

In other cases, RROs establish rankings and ratings primarily to advance their transnational advocacy efforts on particular issues. The external criticism of a state's practices by an RRO can become an important focal point for both domestic and external activists to strengthen their information campaigns, frame proposed solutions, and mobilize for change.[78]

Ratings labels can further reinforce these social judgments, functioning as a classical advocacy tactic of "naming and shaming."[79] For example, in the second iteration of the European Foreign Policy Scorecard, its authors created new labels of "leaders" and "slackers" to characterize member countries' support for EU policies, designations intended to elicit responses from individual country missions about their performance.[80] Kyrgyzstan's steady democratic erosions under President Kurmanbek Bakiyev were most dramatically highlighted when Freedom House's 2010 index downgraded the country from "Partly Free" to "Not Free," spawning a series of articles on the political backsliding of the small Central Asian country from the media and human rights organizations.[81]

Many of the more recent rankings, especially in the area of promoting transparency in governance, were initially designed as advocacy tools to pressure governments to improve practices. The 2010 Revenue Watch Index ranks forty-three countries in their management of revenues from natural resource sales, while since 2006 the Open Budget Initiative Index has issued a biannual ranking on the transparency of government budgeting procedures.[82] In 2011, the NGO Publish What

[78] Keck and Sikkink 1998.
[79] On naming and shaming, see Keck and Sikkink 1998. On its efficacy as a human rights promotion strategy, see Hafner-Burton 2008.
[80] Author's communications with scorecard researchers. See European Council on Foreign Relations 2012: 21.
[81] See, for instance, Bruce Pannier, "Kyrgyzstan relegated to the back of the class," *Radio Free Europe/Radio Liberty* January 12, 2010.
[82] See Revenuewatch 2010 and International Budget Partnership 2010.

You Fund released its inaugural Aid Transparency Index, assessing the availability of information regarding aid allocation on the part of both international financial institutions and bilateral donors. All three of these new transparency indices were funded, at least in part, by the New York-based Open Society Foundations (OSF), a foundation dedicated to promoting transparency.[83] For the World Bank, too, a publicly stated driving purpose behind the production of indicators such as the Ease of Doing Business and its Global Integrity Index has been to identify certain areas of governance to target for reform and to improve decisions about aid allocation.[84]

In some cases, and consistent with social approaches to international institutions, RROs strategically compare and contrast the performance of states to their neighbors and regional rivals. For example, the Open Budget Index deliberately holds the rollout of its biannual reports in regional groupings, so as to encourage competition among individual Ministers of Finance over their ranking.[85] This finding is consistent with international relations scholars who have found similar regional patterns of diffusion in other global governance practices such as commitments to human rights treaties.[86] And, much like Mlada Vachudova's account of how EU conditionality and judgments spurred political activists in East Central European candidates to demand greater accountability of national governments that were not meeting accession benchmarks, external RROs can generate focal points for domestic actors within states to advocate for reforms within their particular issue domain.[87]

RROs as organizational branding exercises

An NGO or IO might also use rankings and ratings to "flag-plant" or brand themselves as the pivotal organizations advocating a particular cause or global concern. Generating a ranking, rating, or index about that issue can be an invaluable tool in staking the organization's claim to govern that issue and advance the solutions to the problem in question.

---

[83] Author's communications with OSF senior administrators.
[84] Arndt 2008: 280–284.
[85] Author's interviews with Open Budget Index representatives. Washington DC: Open Budget Initiative, October 2010.
[86] See, for instance, Simmons 2009.   [87] Vachudova 2005.

Branding is especially necessary in what is now a crowded market for advocacy organizations.[88] Although NGOs may retain strong normative commitments to their advocacy cause, they nevertheless remain organizations that must fight for their survival and secure funding. In turn, this not only necessitates ensuring a steady stream of funds and operating revenues, but it also forces NGOs to distinguish their particular advocacy efforts from those of possible competitors. To this end, creating a unique index or ranking can establish the credibility of a particular NGO in an issue area and can be a critical vehicle for external fundraising.[89] In this respect, the subscriber-based funding model of the credit rating agencies, where sovereigns and private actors pay to be ranked, distinguishes them from other RROs that must raise external funds for their activities.

Once an organization generates an initial index, it becomes a signature "calling card" activity and it is very difficult not to keep producing it. Transparency International itself claims that, "the annual Corruption Perceptions Index (CPI), first released in 1995, is the best known of TI's tools. It has been widely credited for putting TI and the issue of corruption on the international policy agenda."[90] Notwithstanding both external criticism about the CPI's methodology and internal debate regarding its utility as a policy tool, TI remains committed to producing the index as its annual flagship publication. Every year the publication generates an intense global media spotlight and crystallizes the organization's international reputation as the world's leading anti-corruption watchdog.[91] As Figure 1.2 suggests, the international media spotlight on the anti-corruption watchdog increases dramatically in December when the new CPI is released.

The role of rankings and indices as branding devices seems especially important for think tanks and policy institutes. Over the last decade, policy institutes such as the Heritage Foundation (Economic Index), Brookings Institution (Rule of Law), International Food Policy

---

[88] See Bob 2002 and 2005; Cooley and Ron 2002.
[89] On NGO strategies and the pursuit of credibility, see Gourevitch, Lake, and Stein 2012.
[90] www.transparency.org/policy_research/surveys_indices/about.
[91] Moreover, Arndt (2008: 286) has also identified intra-organizational "flag-planting" as a possible motive for generating high-publicity indices, as when the rise of the Ease of Doing Business indicators elevated the importance of the World Bank Institute and the International Financial Corporation (IFC) within the bank.

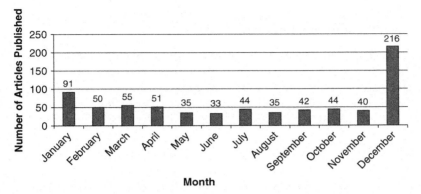

Figure 1.2 Monthly media coverage of Transparency International's CPI, 2012 (Proquest)

Research Institute (Global Hunger Index), Hudson Institute (pilot Philanthropic Freedom Index), Fund for Peace (Failed States Index), and European Council on Foreign Relations (European Foreign Policy Scorecard) have all housed new indices or international rankings that have bolstered their public image as centers of information-gathering and expertise. Perhaps not surprisingly, since 2005 global think tanks themselves have been ranked according to their international prominence and policy impact.[92]

Self-branding and high-visibility launches of new indices also raise the issue of RRO accountability. Though RROs may be committed advocates to their causes, these NGOs, according to Robert Keohane and Ruth Grant's distinctions of the sources of international accountability, are neither accountable through participatory mechanisms nor, with the exception of the credit rating agencies, through delegated authority, but rather principally rely on their reputational standing.[93] As the international media publicizes and reproduces their findings, new RROs become accepted authorities on their issues, often with little organizational scrutiny. As the following section will show, the pursuit of legitimacy and authority are of enormous importance to RROs and the broader impact of their rankings practice.

[92] See McGann 2008.　　[93] Grant and Keohane 2005.

Three framing issues: Authority, methodology, and reconfiguring political relations

Our contributors focus on three sets of issues critical to assessing these varied roles of RROs in international politics: the authority of RROs, the methods they employ, and how rankings and ratings reconfigure political relationships domestically and transnationally.

Political authority

First, we explore how RROs acquire, maintain, and wield their authority when issuing judgments in their particular policy domains. Following Avant, Finnemore, and Sell we define authority as the ability to induce deference in others and regard RROs as "authorities who exercise power across borders for the purposes of affecting policy."[94]

What gives RROs the authority to render judgment and why have some of these rankings become embedded in global administrative law and governance institutions? In the international sphere, authority can be acquired via a number of mechanisms including delegation, technical expertise, hierarchy, and competence.[95] For example, according to Barnett and Finnemore authority in international organizations is generated from the expertise imputed to their members and technocrats.[96] Even if their bureaucratic power was originally delegated by states, the organizations retain the ability to classify, categorize, and change meanings (e.g. who is a refugee, what is poverty) in ways that can profoundly influence the international policy agenda. Similarly, NGOs that successfully have launched globally recognized indices usually assert some form of expert authority, derived from their professional reputation as an organization working on the particular issue and/or their channeling of outside expertise into the production of the rating or index.

But our authors also suggest that RROs have assumed other types of authority. Abdelal and Blyth's account of CRAs emphasizes that their role as arbitrators and de facto judges in international financial

---

[94] Avant, Finnemore, and Sell 2010: 2.
[95] On the importance of authority in legitimating different forms of hierarchy in international politics, see Lake 2009. On private authority, see Hall and Biersteker 2002.
[96] Barnett and Finnemore 2004.

markets has been delegated by states, despite the complaints and protests of government officials about CRAs' purported lack of accountability and bias. Schueth's exploration of the World Bank's Doing Business Index points to the hierarchical authority of the Bank, especially when dealing with small and relatively poor states such as Georgia. In fact, Schueth's chapter shows how the DBI, despite obvious flaws and inconsistencies with other rankings of the business climate, was itself uncritically accepted by a network of other actors, including US foreign aid officials, as critical evidence of Georgia's commitment to market-led reforms.

The problem of authority becomes even more politically charged when RROs are perceived as serving the naked interests and geopolitical agendas of certain states. The refrain that RROs represent the United States and powerful Western countries is becoming an increasingly popular criticism in the politics over indicators and indices. As Andrei Tsygankov has explored, Freedom House's partial funding by the US government and the presence of former and current US officials on its Board of Directors has eroded its authority as a "neutral" arbitrator of democratic standards and, instead, has rendered it vulnerable to accusations that it is a tool of the US foreign policy establishment.[97] The often-cited US State Department's country rankings on human trafficking as presented in its annual Trafficking in Persons Report (since 2001) have been regularly criticized for favoring US allies, while the US Government Accountability Office (GAO) itself has noted that bureaucratic infighting within the State Department about individual country assessments has undermined the credibility of its rankings.[98] The credibility of an RRO, as Gourevitch, Lake, and Stein observe about NGOs more broadly, is therefore critical to its ability to be globally accepted, so it is no surprise that RROs are often criticized for their political or methodological bias.[99]

Further, Sally Merry has explored how differential capacity in the developed and developing world has politicized the use of indicators in global governance and precipitated increasing demands for countries themselves to play a more active role in the production of statistics.[100] Some countries have even undertaken projects to spawn different

---

[97] Tsygankov 2012.   [98] Friman 2010.
[99] On the determinants of NGO credibility, see Gourevitch, Lake, and Stein 2012.
[100] Merry 2011.

indices as an alternative to Western RROs.[101] Nevertheless, the effort to de-Westernize certain rankings and introduce new, regionally produced alternatives seems only likely to accelerate over the coming years, creating the potential for increased competition among RROs. For example, in the area of credit ratings, China, Russia, and Egan Jones, the world's fourth-largest rating agency, plan to create a Universal Rating Agency, to be based in Hong Kong, that will offer an alternative source of credit ratings to the US-based Moody's and Standard and Poor's.[102]

Another related issue is why some issue areas feature one authoritative global RRO, while others lack it. For example, why has Transparency International's CPI become accepted, despite its admitted flaws, as the main global authority on corruption rankings, while in other areas such as media or democracy, rankings remain relatively fragmented and dispersed among multiple actors? In turn, the structure of the RRO "market" may also have important consequences for the behavior of RROs and the impact of the rankings themselves. In quasi-monopoly situations such as corruption rankings, NGOs that seek to distinguish themselves from TI must find alternative products and activities if they are to survive. For example, for 2011 the DC-based anti-corruption organization Global Integrity dropped the publication of its global country rankings, in favor of producing more detailed country-specific reports and sectoral assessments.[103]

On the other hand, the presence of multiple rankings in any particular issue may dilute the ability of any single RRO to successfully "name and shame" countries. For instance, Becker, Vlad, and Nusser find that over 100 organizations worldwide are engaged in some type of media freedom assessment, the most prominent of which are Freedom House, Reporters without Borders, IREX, and the Committee to Protect Journalists (CPJ).[104] In such a market structure RROs may have incentives to generate some product differentiation in their rankings, even within the same issue area. In their study of private regulation Büthe and Mattli suggest that private actors who are

---

[101] See Stone 2012.

[102] See "A Different Rating," *Global Times* May 7, 2013.

[103] Presentation by Nathaniel Heller, Executive Director of Global Integrity. New York, Columbia University, October 2010. Also see public statement at: http://www.globalintegrity.org/node/792.

[104] Becker, Vlad, and Nusser 2007.

monopolist standard-setters domestically are also more likely to institutionalize their rule-making authority internationally.[105]

Methodology

Our second area of focus is the range of methodological issues that inform the production of rankings and ratings. Though criticizing the methodological rigor of RROs is increasingly a rhetorical tactic deployed by governments to discredit their findings, the unmistakable trend in established RROs has been towards increasing sophistication and transparency in their data-collection procedures and methods. All RROs can be scrutinized and compared on their data sources, conceptual validity, and reliability of measures.

First, the sourcing of data is a perennial source of methodological discussion and debate among RROs. Some RROs generate their own original indicators, whereas others cull them from the public domain and other organizations. Credit rating agencies, for example, publicly state that they do not conduct any research beyond what is publicly available so as to avoid being accused of concealing private information. But even data-gathering RROs employ widely varying practices and techniques for collecting information and making assessments. For example, in the area of international media rankings, the staff at Freedom House assigns a 30-point score to a country's media legal environment, a 30-point score to its economic environment, and 40 points to its political context, thus yielding a 100-point aggregate final score.[106] By contrast, the Paris-based Reporters without Borders (RSF) primarily relies on the results of a questionnaire that is sent to members of the domestic and foreign media in the target country, as well as some NGO monitors. The results are assessed in-house by RSF staff.[107] These RROs both contrast with the case of the New York-based CPJ, whose indices on press freedom and government impunity actually evolved out of the NGO's earlier activities as an information-clearing house about the safety of reporters across the world.[108]

---

[105] Büthe and Mattli 2011.
[106] Karin Karleckar presentation, February 2011. New York: Columbia University.
[107] For a comparative methodological discussion, see Becker, Vlad, and Nusser 2007.
[108] Presentation of Anne Nelson, former Director of the CPJ. New York: Columbia University, February 2011.

The question of whether RROs should rely on "subjective expert judgments" or "objective indicators" is also commonly debated. Both Freedom House's Survey of Freedom in the World and TI's CPI have been criticized for relying on expert opinions to assess the performance of countries, rather than "objective" measures.[109] Yet, perhaps because of these criticisms, both of these RROs now go to great lengths to publicize their data sources and aggregation methods, as well as to disclose the roles that external experts actually play in the evaluation process. To avoid the accusations of bias that accompany opinion-based measurements, many "newer" generation RROs, especially those focused on transparency issues, have conscientiously designed their rankings and measures around binary material indicators, thereby also allowing comparability across country and time.

Second, once data is collected, do the measures used by RROs validly measure or capture the concepts that they claim? Of course, the problem of conceptual validity is ubiquitous in the social sciences. Validity can be eroded either by relying on simplified data or measures – because they happen to be available – that really don't capture the phenomenon in question or, on the other hand, from multidimensionality or the mixing of different or even opposite concepts within a single measure. An example of the latter is in the Freedom House press freedom index, which does not distinguish between the greater availability of information in a country and increased attempts by the government to control media.

Aggregating multiple data sources is another common technique used to improve the accuracy of measures and reduce bias, with the latest TI CPI drawing on seventeen different surveys of corruption perceptions worldwide. However, the move towards aggregation and composite measures raises a host of other validity problems. First, using aggregate measures may actually make it difficult to pick up subtle changes or shifts identified by just a few indicators, as trends may be lost in averaging or, in the case of perceptions-based sources, may significantly lag. Second, as Stephen Knack argues, there is considerable reason to doubt the independence of various data sources, especially in perception-based issues such as corruption, given that RROs tend to consult with the same expert sources and reports.[110]

---

[109] On the validity problems of questionnaires and perceptions, see Andersson and Heywood 2009 and Apaza 2009.
[110] Knack 2007: 266–268.

Third, aggregating data sources only heightens the sensitivity of the coefficients assigned to these inputs, decisions that are rarely fully explained in the public domain. As Bhuta observes in his chapter, most failed states indices rely on second- or even third-order indicators, thereby making weighting decisions paramount for the generation of a country's final score. In cases where different policy objectives require aggregation, weighting decisions used for standardization and ranking may significantly underestimate or overestimate the importance that each state actually places in that policy area. For instance, a decision to weigh healthcare "responsiveness" more heavily than "equity of access" would positively increase the ranking of the United States healthcare system in comparison to its peers.[111] Deciding on the relative importance of each policy area is an inherently political, as well as methodological, choice.

In his contribution to this volume, Seva Gunitsky identifies yet another validity problem that informs democracy scores: the various components that constitute categories like "media freedom" or "civil liberties" may actually overlap or even be redundant. Consequently, Gunitsky finds in his empirical study of post-Soviet democracy trends that Freedom House scores tend to exaggerate the poles of the authoritarian–democracy continuum, both overestimating the degree of authoritarianism in states such as Uzbekistan and Belarus and also overestimating the democratic performance of states at the other end, most notably the Baltic states.

Another broad methodological concern for any RRO should be the reliability of the raters, or the extent to which a measuring procedure will reproduce the same assessments when repeated by independent observers. Do RROs have some internal process for assessing inter-coder reliability? Do they use multiple coders and/or expert judgments and, if so, what are the procedures for dealing with a coding disagreement? One particularly quirky approach to data gathering is embodied in the Fund for Peace's annual Failed States Index, published in conjunction with *Foreign Policy* magazine.[112] The core component of the FSI is the Conflict Assessment Software Tool (CAST), a content analysis program that sorts through hundreds of thousands of pages of reporting, news accounts, and documents produced within states, at the regional and local levels.[113] The CAST searches for key terms, phrases, and characterizations that

---

[111] Oliver 2012.   [112] See http://www.foreignpolicy.com/failedstates.
[113] See the CAST description at: http://global.fundforpeace.org/cewa.

historically have signified state weakness and/or deterioration in social conditions.[114] Though these trends identified by CAST are triangulated by statistical analysis (based on public sources) and the judgments of two expert country trends coders, the content analysis itself remains proprietary and not subject to outside verification or replication. Sometimes, a methodologically conscientious RRO might even sacrifice some conceptual validity in the interests of reliability. For the 2011 CPI, the senior research staff at TI bowed to pressures to make the index more reliably comparable across countries (something that the international media and governments were already doing despite the organization's disclaimers about not comparing countries) by *only* including data sources measuring perceptions that could be standardized.[115]

Despite a range of potential pitfalls, an overall assessment of the state of RRO methodology suggests that it is much improved compared to first-generation studies, which relied on small surveys or expert advice. Indeed, as the number of RROs continues to proliferate, new RROs look to other successful indices as models and consult with practitioners and academics for methodological advice. For example, the founders of the Open Budget Index wanted from the outset to make the index comparable over time, unlike TI's CPI. Similarly, Publish What You Fund invited feedback from a range of analysts and experts experienced in the construction of indices in the preparation of the 2010 Aid Transparency Index pilot. Overall, new RROs are both learning methodological lessons and drawing upon each other's related expertise when designing and crafting their new rankings and ratings.

Reconfiguring political relations: New transnational networks and domestic changes

Finally, some of our contributors examine how RROs, beyond the material and social pressures they exert, can even reconfigure political relations by changing bureaucratic priorities and relations within states and embedding state policies within broader transnational networks. Just as previous generations of scholarship on international political economy examined the effects of the conditionality of Western

---

[114] Author's interviews with Fund for Peace, Failed States Index representatives. Washington, DC: Fund for Peace, February 2012.

[115] Author's interview with members of the Transparency International Division of Research. Berlin, November 14, 2011.

international financial institutions (IFIs) on the domestic policies of aid recipients, the growing power of certain RROs, especially in the economic sphere, might also serve as an external source of domestic restructuring and transnational linkage. As our authors explore, assessing creditworthiness, measuring corruption, and judging states as failing places RROs within a much broader network of international advisors, bureaucrats, and state agencies working within a particular policy domain and advocating for certain policy prescriptions for which rankings and ratings are invoked.

One recent state response to being ranked is the rise in the practice of "ratings diplomacy" by various ministries and state agencies. States have become more proactive about actually engaging with RROs and now regularly lobby them for improvements in their rankings. The last decade has seen the rise of more intensive ratings diplomacy, much of it attributed by RROs to the MCC adopting external indicators as benchmarks for foreign aid allocation. Organizations such as Freedom House and Heritage that before would receive a handful of curious foreign visitors now typically welcome between thirty and forty country delegations a year. At the World Bank's Ease of Doing Business unit, the demand by ranked states for explanatory meetings became so acute that the research division has now instituted a formal procedure designed to specify, in advance, the particular issue of a state's question of concern and the composition of the visiting delegation.[116] Government officials also seem increasingly willing to comment on these meetings. For example, in April 2013 Kyrgyzstan's Deputy Prime Minister openly complained that his government failed to secure additional funding from the MCC due to Freedom House issuing a poor ranking on media and human rights.[117]

---

[116] Author's interviews with Ease of Doing Business representatives. Washington DC: World Bank, February 2012.
[117] According to Djoomart Otorbaev, "We didn't get into the program and can't receive additional funding because the non-governmental organization Freedom House put us in a very low ranking in the areas of human rights and freedom of the press. It's remarkable that our rating is worse than under [previous autocratic President] Kurmanbek Bakiyev. Do they want the democratization of society and the freedom of press to be like they were under the previous regime? I told them: If that's what you want, then say it openly. We discussed it, they have their observations and we have our own. They noted the interethnic events in the south, but at the current moment the situation has stabilized. I think that we'll work it out." ("Djoomart Otorbaev Doubts the Objectivity of Freedom House's Information," *Kabar* April 26, 2013. Available at: http://www.kabar.kg/rus/politics/full/54186.)

Reassuring RROs even has become a component of crisis management in states. During the March 2011 crackdown on pro-democracy Shia protestors in the Gulf Kingdom of Bahrain, the Bahraini Minister of Finance, who was visiting Washington, also took time to visit with the Heritage Foundation in a bid to reassure the directors of the Economic Freedom Index that Bahrain's commitment to economic openness would be maintained.[118] And, perhaps surprisingly, while many diplomats from countries ranked near the top of the inaugural Failed States Index in 2005 were enraged at cracking the "top ten," the Ambassador of Somalia, the worst-ranked country, expressed his gratitude to Fund for Peace members for drawing international attention to his country's plight.[119]

Though the conduct of ratings diplomacy at first glance may appear to be strategic and even cynical attempts to sway RROs – RRO officials readily admit that at many of these meetings state officials ask bluntly how to improve their scores – such interactions also facilitate new dialogues, knowledge transfer, and networking that are more akin to norm diffusion within transnational linkages. For example, officials at the Heritage Foundation recount that meetings about rankings with economic representatives of countries ranked by the Economic Freedom Index frequently evolve into networking opportunities, as state delegations are introduced to Washington, DC-based government (Treasury), international (IMF), and private actors (Chamber of Commerce) that share similar commitments to the economic freedom agenda.[120] Similarly, Freedom House officials point out that meetings whose purpose at first may be to complain about a ranking often turn into dialogues about the basis and functioning of issues such as media freedom.[121] Thus, according to RROs, even cynical attempts to pressure for a rankings improvement can turn into opportunities for

---

[118] Public statement made by Dr. Kim Holmes, Director of the Heritage Foundation's Economic Freedom Index. New York: Consulate of Croatia, October 2010.

[119] Author's interviews with Fund for Peace, Failed States Index representatives. Washington, DC: Fund for Peace, February 2012.

[120] Author's interviews with Economic Freedom Index representatives. Washington, DC: Heritage Foundation, February 2012.

[121] Indeed, the author witnessed a roundtable involving a Central Asian government delegation that involved discussion about a particular ranking and score and the criteria that were used to generate the score.

social learning and/or strengthening the configurations of new policy networks.

In more extreme cases, we see that responses to RROs might actually reconfigure political relations and bureaucratic configurations within states themselves, an unintended consequence consistent with Campbell's Law. As Schueth details in his chapter, perhaps no other country has targeted an international ranking as successfully as the Republic of Georgia. Following the so-called Rose Revolution in 2003, an old-guard Soviet elite was replaced with Western-trained young technocrats, led by charismatic President Mikheil Saakashvili, who were well versed in the importance of international rankings. Since, the country has seen spectacular improvements across a number of international ratings and rankings; the most dramatic was moving from below 100th to the top 20 in the World Bank's DBI report in just three years (2006–2008). Further, USAID assisted in this process by making improvements in Georgia's international rankings the actual deliverable products of several of its technical assistance projects to improve the country's investment climate.[122] In this case, the DBI prompted Georgian officials to reassign domestic bureaucratic responsibilities and placed the targeting of the DBI indicators within a greater transnational effort to improve Georgia's business climate.

Taken further, Schueth's observation about Georgia suggests that a variant of Campbell's Law might be operating more broadly among the DBI's most successful reformers. Table 1.1 lists the most dramatic

Table 1.1. *Top five all-time biggest climbers in World Bank's Ease of Doing Business Index*

Country	Year of DBI Report	Places Jumped in Single Year	Change in Ranking
Georgia	2007	85	100th to 15th
Rwanda	2010	76	143rd to 67th
Azerbaijan	2009	64	97th to 33rd
Egypt	2008	39	165th to 126th
Croatia	2008	27	124th to 97th

Source: Compiled and calculated from *DoingBusiness.org*, 2002–2013.

[122] For details, see Schueth 2011.

jumps in the index's history. The top three all-time largest movers exhibited leaps of over sixty places in a single year, earning them the title of "top global reformers" respectively in 2007 (Georgia), 2009 (Azerbaijan), and 2010 (Rwanda). Like the Georgian case, the key to Azerbaijan's and Rwanda's spectacular success appears to have been creating or assigning an agency the role of "superministry," giving it the authority to instruct other economic ministries to implement reforms necessary for improving each selected indicator.

In the Rwandan case, the Rwandan Development Board (RDB) explains that it was "set up by bringing together all the government agencies responsible for the entire investor experience under one roof," reports directly to the President and includes "key agencies responsible for business registration, investment promotion, environmental clearances, privatization and specialist agencies ... as well as SMEs and human capacity development in the private sector."[123] In public presentations the RDB recounts how its success in the 2010 DBI was a result of conducting an internal audit of required reforms, prioritizing them in a "Doing Business 2010 Action Plan," and then establishing an inter-ministerial taskforce reporting to the Cabinet and a related new DBI coordination unit within the RDB that was tasked with monthly evaluation of progress.[124] A later presentation acknowledged that post-2010 the RDB would shift its "focus beyond DB indicators."[125]

A leaked US embassy cable from 2007 in Baku describes a similar organizational restructuring in the Azerbaijan case, but more dramatically identifies the Doing Business Director Simeon Djankov himself as a source of advice recommending that the Ministry of Economic Development be granted the authority to implement reforms within other Ministries.[126] Citing other cases, Djankov reportedly noted that this reform had been "effective when the reform minister/ministry has the authority to compel action from line ministries, not simply

---

[123] Rwandan Development Board, "History." Available at: http://www.rdb.rw/about-rdb/history.html.

[124] Rwandan Development Board, "Business Reforms." Presentation delivered by Clare Akazmanzi, Chief Operating Officer.

[125] Rwandan Development Board, "Doing Business past performance and the next action plan." Available at: http://www.cafrad.org/Workshops/bamako17-18_02_11/pre_Rwanda.pdf.

[126] US Embassy Cable, "Azerbaijan doing business easier; transparency not better." Baku, 07BAKU1239, October 16, 2007. Available at: http://wikileaks.org/cable/2007/10/07BAKU1239.html.

'coordinate' among them" and encouraged the United States to support the "reform Super minister/ministry." The cable further observes that Azerbaijan's dramatic improvement in the DBI was primarily due to a Presidential decree that tasked government ministries and agencies "to develop a plan to improve the business climate, including developing a one-stop-shop for business Registration," and notes that although Azerbaijan showed large improvement in the "starting a business" category, in the other categories it demonstrated "only minor improvement or deterioration."[127]

In sum, three of the World Bank's most improved reformers, as ranked by the DBI, achieved this distinction by creating inter-ministry and agency working groups that identified and targeted the indicators themselves, and had the authority to override normal ministerial functional organization structures and authorities. Moreover, in all three cases, these domestic reforms appear to have been embedded in a broader network of international organizations, technical assistance missions, international advisors, and, in the post-Soviet states, the support of various United States government officials and agencies. Beyond inflicting social pressure or exerting material costs, these selected DBI cases suggest a direct influence of an RRO on restructuring the very organization and line authority of bureaucracies within states.

The plan of this book

Our contributors examine many of the themes outlined in this chapter across a broad range of ratings, actors, and international contexts. In the next chapter, Rawi Abdelal and Mark Blyth examine the role played by the credit rating agencies (CRAs) during the ongoing Eurozone financial crisis. In addition to the roles outlined in the introduction to this chapter, they argue that CRAs themselves establish market conventions and trigger movements in what they are allegedly merely measuring. According to the authors, CRAs are forced to measure and assess risk in situations of deep (and immeasurable) uncertainty. Not surprisingly, they often fail to accurately do so. But because of their embeddedness within the *de facto* financial regulatory apparatus, CRAs' judgments and pronouncements have generated deep,

---

[127] *Ibid.*

unanticipated knock-on effects that have accelerated downward market movements, such as casting doubt on the credibility of the European Financial Stability Fund. Moreover, their ratings have been used for advocacy purposes by other powerful actors, especially in the design of new austerity programs and emergency lending packages proposed by the European Troika comprised of the European Central Bank, the IMF, and the European Commission. Thus, CRAs have been important causal actors in their own right, while their delegated authority from governments to perform these functions, despite professed outrage from certain European regulators, is unlikely to be effectively challenged or substituted.

Chapters three and four examine the relationship between the rise of prominent new rankings and the diffusion of a related international norm. Mlada Bukovansky explores the rise of Transparency International as the leading global authority on the corruption issue. She argues that since 1995 TI's Corruption Perceptions Index has played a critical role in disseminating a new corruption norm, designating corruption as a measurable, immoral, and developmentally antithetical activity that exists solely within states. Such understandings tend to expose certain actors to international scrutiny and opprobrium, particularly in the developing world, while shielding other forms of political influence and economic activity in the West as acceptable practices. Similarly, Nehal Bhuta explores the proliferation of "state failure" indices in the post-9/11 world as both a response to and constitutive of the new norm that views fragile or collapsing states as global security risks. Unpacking the methodology of indices produced by USAID and Fund for Peace, Bhuta finds that their indicators are usually derived from second- and third-order measurements and data, often bundled together across different categories and capriciously adjusted with few analytical justifications. With the rise of the related Responsibility to Protect norm, Bhuta cautions that such conceptually shaky indices may play an even greater role within the institutionalization of early warning and monitoring regimes in the United Nations.

In chapter 5, Seva Gunitsky compares and contrasts the democracy scores of the Polity IV data set, frequently used by academic researchers, with the Freedom House democracy scores and the EIU's Democracy index for the post-Soviet states. He finds significant discrepancies among these three indices in the middling cases, including the important cases of Russia, Ukraine, and Armenia. Polity's focus on formal institutional checks on power often yields different assessments than Freedom House's focus on the state of political rights, while the latter tends to exaggerate both the level of democracy and autocracy on the opposite ends of the spectrum. Gunitsky cautions that these discrepancies should be even more concerning to policymakers, given that it is these middling cases where external democracy assistance is presumed to have the best chance of having an impact or nudging political reforms forward.

Sam Schueth's contribution in chapter 6 recounts how, in post-Soviet Georgia, the coming to power of the Western-oriented government of Mikheil Saakashvili in 2003 initiated a drive to stress the country's reform credentials and openness to Western norms and standards. Schueth explores how moving up the World Bank's influential Doing Business Index became a high priority for the new government and led to the formation of new working groups and expert councils designed to target indicators for improvement. He contrasts Georgia's meteoric rise in the DBI, which was officially targeted, with its relatively more stagnant performance in the World Economic Forum's Global Competitiveness Index. Schueth's account also finds important variation, as the Georgian government was more successful in enacting legislation than it was in changing actual institutional performance and business practices. Beyond just providing a fascinating case study of a country so closely engaging with an RRO, Schueth's chapter points to the more general problems that the DBI faces in its methodology of measuring a range of informal business practices and warns of the dangers of indicators substituting for the phenomena that they are supposedly measuring.

In the concluding chapter Jack Snyder and I summarize the analytical lessons learned from these contributions and explore in greater depth the public knowledge function of international rankings. Given their rapid integration into the fabric of global governance, so much is at stake with international rankings and yet, conceptually, their use as policy tools is often confused, inappropriately deployed, and suffers from validity problems. We use consumer choice ratings as a baseline to explore the normative underpinnings and more complicated value assumptions that surround public policy rankings and ratings. Public policy ratings, we argue, differ in important ways from consumer choice ratings. While consumer ratings serve to inform individual choices, RROs are linked to improving public policy outcomes and interface with a plethora of different actors, agendas, and political priorities. We distinguish among three distinct targets of rating public policy outcomes: rating a result, rating the public policy itself, and rating those who enact a public policy (or holding them accountable). What is needed most of all is not merely better rankings and ratings methods, as is commonly called for, but rather a better theoretical and normative understanding of *how* what is being measured and evaluated will purportedly impact public policy outcomes. Integrating different factors into a single measure tends to mask conditional and interactive relationships, burying those nuances that are critical for good policy formulation and targeting. Accordingly, the field of international relations must itself move beyond using various indices exclusively as data sets and engage with the very core public policy questions and political choices that rankings and ratings embody.

2 | Just who put you in charge? We did

CRAs and the politics of ratings

RAWI ABDELAL AND MARK BLYTH

The editors of this volume identify four critical roles that ranking and rating organizations (RROs) perform. They act as judges, global monitors and regulators, advocates, and as branding exercises to claim ownership over issues. In the case of credit rating agencies (CRAs), we see the first three as primary and the fourth as inapplicable in the rating of sovereign debt and in the performance of CRAs in the 2008 financial crisis that originated in repo and mortgage markets.[1]

The first role identified by the editors is what US-based rating agencies do by their own admission. They judge the creditworthiness of bond issuers, but with a twist. Protected by the first amendment to the US constitution, CRAs (the big three CRAs are all private American corporations) offer "opinions" that are taken by market and government actors to be "expert judgments." As Fitch puts it, "ratings are not themselves facts and therefore cannot be described as 'accurate' or 'inaccurate.'"[2] Whether the opinions offered are, or are not, such a thing is a question we shall investigate below, but they are, oddly, both protected speech and a product for sale.[3]

Their second role, as monitors and regulators, is again central to what they are and do. The threat of being put on CreditWatch by Standard and Poor's (S&P), for example, is a particular monitoring category that most sovereign bond issuers would like to avoid. Yet the extent to which this monitoring and signaling actually works as advertised is again something to be investigated rather than something to be assumed.

---

[1] Generally speaking, rating something does not imply ownership of it.
[2] Fitch website, quoted in Rona-Tas and Hiss 2010: 122.
[3] This may change due to the Dodd–Frank reforms currently underway in the United States, as discussed below.

Third, CRAs are also advocates, but not in the hands of the raters themselves. We usually think of ratings as advocacy tools in the hands of social entrepreneurs and NGOs against governments and firms, as, for example, in the case of corruption indices used by pro-democracy NGOs to promote reform. In the case of the relationship between sovereigns and CRAs, however, a different dynamic unfolds. Governments often use CRA ratings to get other governments with lesser ratings to do what they would otherwise not do. Ratings in this case are instruments of power, not advocacy. In the Eurozone crisis, for example, the downgrading of periphery-state debt gave the German government more leverage to press for reforms that these states did not wish to undertake. Indeed, this dynamic is more common than is appreciated insofar as it also gives incumbent governments more leverage to undertake difficult reforms.

This last example of ratings as advocacy tools also shows us how CRAs go beyond the functions suggested by the editors. We propose a different, fourth function: that of establishing market conventions. Contrary to what one would expect, rather than reveal new information, CRAs oftentimes codify what the market already knows: they become a part of the governance of markets by establishing 'the conventional judgment' regarding a borrower's creditworthiness. Econometric research shows that CRA ratings downgrades follow rather than lead market movements. CRAs thereby authoritatively establish what the conventional opinion on an instrument or a borrower in fact is, especially in the case of sovereigns. Countries X and Y are held to be AA– or BB+ not because the market has already priced in the risk that the CRA is measuring, but because the CRAs say so, and that establishes the common sense of the market of the rating as being true. This in turn raises the question: Why do we behave as though an assessment that describes something that everyone already knows is new?

Fifth, finally, and cutting against their other functions, we argue that CRA ratings as advocacy tools can act as *triggers* that can both accelerate downward market movements and promote upward swings. For example, the much anticipated downgrading of France in January 2012 had a knock-on effect on the rating of the European Financial Stability Fund (EFSF), thereby making it harder for the EU to backstop its banks and halt the Euro-crisis; thereby a downward trigger. Prior to this instance, the rating of collateralized mortgage bonds as AAA in an environment where AAA assets were in short supply helped propel the global real estate boom and bust; in this instance an upward trigger.

In these cases we see how CRAs are not something exogenous to the system they examine, passively recording events like a camera or issuing knowledge of the system without affecting it. They are instead, to use the same analogy Milton Friedman used concerning financial theory (and popularized by Donald Mackenzie), an engine driving events forward.[4] Ratings are not just categories; they are causal in their own right. In what follows we examine CRAs' performance in terms of these five functions. We investigate whether CRAs really do perform these functions, and if they in fact do not do so effectively, we ask why they still exist.

To get us there we first briefly recount the history of the rating agencies, a history that is distinctively American, and describe the process by which authorization and delegation created the market for sovereign ratings in the context of an exploration of the peculiar activities of sovereign lending, borrowing, and rating. Then, building up to a discussion of recent CRA interventions in sovereign debt markets, we explore the role the agencies played in defining the contours of the global financial crisis – circa 2007 to the present day – in terms of these functions. After further discussing each of these functions, we note what we call the 'agency-paradox' of CRAs. That is, governments still have not owned up to the fact that the influence of these agencies is their own creation and responsibility, and so complaints by sovereigns, particularly on the occasions of a rating downgrade, are deeply paradoxical. Put bluntly, until governments are willing to take on the regulatory and informational burdens borne by the rating agencies, sovereigns will continue to live by the rules as interpreted by the very agents they have empowered to do the things that they do not want to do. Their longevity suggests that despite this paradox, if they were not there already, in a world of integrated markets, mobile capital, and cross-border investments, we would have to invent them.

CRAs, sovereigns, and the practice of ratings

The three most important rating agencies – Standard and Poor's, Moody's, and Fitch – exercise great influence over the relationship

---

[4] Mackenzie 2006.

between sovereigns and capital markets. The agencies' judgments affect the borrowing costs governments must pay. At the extreme, credit ratings legally restrict the relationship between putatively untrustworthy sovereigns and particular market participants. Paradoxically, sovereigns should be seen, at least potentially, as the least problematic of borrowers. Their debt has near infinite maturities (in principle they can always roll over their debt since states, unlike people or firms, do not die), they can always draw upon future generations of taxpayers to pay bills accrued, and their bonds are generally placed in investment portfolios as near 'risk-free' assets that allow the taking-on of more risk elsewhere in the portfolio. Indeed, as a Moody's research paper from 2007 noted, although the pool of sovereign debt is much smaller than the pool of corporate debt, when one controls for this "sovereign defaults have on average been lower than those for their corporate counterparts."[5] Unsurprisingly then, "sovereign ratings have proved to be more stable than their corporate counterparts," while "downgrade rates have been lower."[6]

Not all sovereigns are equal, however, and there are some types of risk sovereigns carry that markets find difficult to price, at least without help, and this is where CRAs come into the picture. The first is default risk. If a firm defaults one can pursue its assets in bankruptcy courts. Since states with their own printing presses literally cannot go bankrupt, one cannot go after them in the same way – they can just repay with a devalued currency. Moreover, states that look like very low default risks can rather suddenly appear otherwise, as Iceland and Ireland have shown in recent times. The second problem is the inability to redeem the security before maturity, which creates liquidity risk. This means when bondholders become worried about a sovereign they need to sell the bond in a secondary market at a loss to remove it from their portfolios. This produces the familiar 'price down/yield up' dynamic of sovereign debt markets, but it also creates a collective action problem in such markets. While it is rational for any one investor to offset risk in this way, if they all do it at once the net result is a fire sale of the asset in question. CRAs enter the picture here as institutions that try to evaluate, always in relative terms, both of these risks, default and liquidity, thus giving much-needed transparency and stability to sovereign risk markets.

---

[5] Moody's 2007: 11.   [6] *Ibid.*: 1.

To do this CRAs invented a new language to describe risk, a simplification and compression of all the information and judgments that go into pricing such quasi-unquantifiable risks into a few capital letters: the familiar As, Bs, and Cs in the grade book of ratings. The language, the judgments, and the resulting ratings became critical elements of the international financial architecture. Despite these activities helping the sovereign find buyers at better prices, sovereign borrowers often express indignation at this sometimes humiliating activity. Governments submit themselves to the scrutiny of these private, American, New York-based firms, which in turn pronounce on their relative riskiness.

Given the nature of these risks, however, sovereigns do not – and perhaps cannot – borrow from the markets without the rating agencies' passing judgment on their debt securities first, which leads government officials to wonder both privately and aloud: "Who do these guys think they are?" And, more to the point, "Why are they so influential?" Although we do not know the answer to the first question, the second is more straightforward to resolve. The rating agencies are important primarily because governments, particularly the US government, made them so. The agencies did not explicitly seek out this gatekeeping role, and certainly they are cautious not to articulate their ratings as anything more than mere opinions on creditworthiness. But governments' authorization of, and delegation to, the rating agencies unquestionably increased the size of the market for ratings.

A brief history of CRAs

The practice of rating – and thereby simplifying – creditworthiness was invented in the United States.[7] As American railroads, firms with hitherto unprecedented capital needs, began to issue bonds early in the twentieth century, John Moody adapted the letter rating symbols that had been for a century used by firms that collected data on customer creditworthiness. In 1909, *Moody's Analyses of Railroad Investments* was first published, and Moody's Investors Service incorporated in 1914. In 1916 the Standard Statistics Bureau began assigning letter ratings to bonds as well. Poor's Publishing Company merged with Standard Statistics in 1941, thereby creating Standard and Poor's,

---

[7] See Sylla 2002; Sinclair 2005; and Abdelal 2007.

which was acquired by McGraw-Hill in 1966. Dun & Bradstreet owned Moody's between 1962 and 2000.

After a brisk few years between the 1910s and the end of the 1920s, the chaotic 1930s gave way eventually to the boring 1950s. Boring because there was not much, especially of a speculative nature, to rate. So by the end of the 1960s, the agencies were boring, too: unexceptional firms with modest revenues derived from selling reports that compiled ratings and analyses to subscribers. Even the business model was run-of-the-mill. It was, however, about to change due to the confluence of two factors: the invention of the Xerox machine, which made the old business model obsolete (you can only sell a rating once if it can be copied and distributed); and the reemergence of private capital after the collapse of the Bretton Woods system.[8] The latter was particularly significant both for the corporate bonds of highly internationalized firms and for the debt offerings of sovereigns. Far from being instruments of forced saving pushed upon passive populations deprived of other investment choices, as government bonds had been for much of the post-war period, these securities now had to compete in a beauty pageant with other sovereigns and indeed other debt instruments to win the approval of the markets. Key in doing so was to get a good rating.

In response, both S&P and Moody's transformed the business model of ratings during the early 1970s: they began to charge the issuers of securities, rather than their investors, for the ratings. As governments sought increasingly to access these new deregulated private financial markets, these agencies found – and, literally, founded – a new market for sovereign ratings in which private market participants valued the simplicity and comparability of the letter-rating system.

A decisive regulatory change in 1975 turned a merely promising business model into a virtual guarantee of growth and profitability. The United States first began to incorporate credit ratings into financial regulation in 1931. In 1975, however, the Securities and Exchange Commission (SEC) introduced the designation of "nationally recognized statistical rating organization" (NRSRO) for use in US financial regulation, which had been designed to limit the public's exposure to risk. If you wanted to issue debt instruments, you needed these firms to measure your risk. As such, only ratings issued by NRSROs could be

[8] See Helleiner 1994; Eichengreen 2008.

used in the regulatory architecture. The SEC designated three companies as NRSROs: S&P, Moody's, and Fitch.

The NRSRO designation led to the incorporation of ratings into myriad financial regulations in the United States. A security, to be widely held, would have to come with at least one, and most often two, ratings. Investors came to expect, as a matter of practice, securities to be rated by two NRSROs. The combination of designation and ratings-based regulation created what Frank Partnoy calls "regulatory licenses."[9] Although the executives of the agencies expressed ambivalence about ratings-based regulations and the public scrutiny that inevitably came with the regulatory-induced demand of the SEC's NRSRO designation, they nonetheless grew handsomely with this new business model.[10]

This combination of events, therefore, ensured that the sleepy, modest world of ratings became exciting, big business by the late 1980s and early 1990s. Financial internationalization and disintermediation led to increased private sovereign borrowing and, as well, to capital flows into the United States, all of which needed to be risk-assessed by those on the other side of the trade. These new regulations restricted access to American capital markets to securities issuers that hired, most often, two of the three major rating agencies to assess their creditworthiness, creating what was essentially a dual monopoly for S&P and Moody's. These regulations gave ratings the force of law, prohibiting certain investors from holding securities below particular ratings, often "investment-grade." S&P and Moody's moved from the periphery of the markets to their center. Their downgrades became – and have remained – front-page news.

S&P and Moody's are private firms, but their authority is essentially public. The demand for their rating services is enhanced by regulation. The impact of their ratings is magnified by the same regulation. Government officials are keenly aware that someone has to take responsibility for assessing the public's exposure to risk, and they have simply decided not to do that job themselves. They delegated that responsibility to the rating agencies, and so the result is something that is very far from private governance.[11] How curious it

---

[9] Partnoy 1999. Also Smith and Walter 2002; and White 2002.
[10] Sinclair 1999, 2003, 2005; and Bruner and Abdelal 2005.
[11] See, for example, Ruggie 2004; Bruner and Abdelal 2005.

is, then, that governments so regularly complain about the scrutiny of the rating agencies, for that scrutiny was invited and then required by their law.

CRAs and the global financial crisis

Until the onset of the global financial crisis in 2007 few people outside of finance gave much thought to rating agencies. Some scholars had begun to take notice of how they constituted a part of the private architecture of global governance, but they were hardly front-page news.[12] What put them on the front pages was something that would be uniquely painful for a CRA – the discovery that a huge proportion of their ratings were inaccurate, which was true, and that they would be blamed for much of what went wrong, despite their doing exactly what they were supposed to do. No good deed, as ever, goes unpunished.

The origins of the financial crisis lay deep in the so-called 'sale and repurchase' (Repo) markets of the US, where surplus corporate cash is lent out against collateral for very short periods of time. One way to conceptualize this is payroll payments. It would be both impractical and expensive for large corporations to truck payroll cash around the various parts of their business. So what they do instead is to borrow someone else's extra cash overnight, pay it out, and then redeem the assets in question for cash plus a fee – hence "sale and repurchase." For such markets to work, however, one needs to be sure that the borrower has adequate collateral posted in case it cannot pay back the loan in full, and for that to work the collateral in question must hold its value, which is where the CRAs came in.

The collateral of choice in the Repo markets was of course US Treasuries, long regarded (until the downgrade of the United States) as the risk-free asset. The problem was that T-bills were in short supply by the height of the boom (China and Asia were vacuuming up huge amounts of them) and mortgage-backed securities, especially the now infamous "collateralized debt obligation" (CDO), took their place. So why were a bunch of risky and not-so-risky mortgages able to take the place of US sovereign debt as Repo collateral? Because the CRAs rated both securities AAA, which meant that demand for them soared and supply could rise to match.

[12] Abdelal 2007; and Sinclair 1994, 2001.

As we explain below, many of those CDOs were less than accurately priced, and to their credit the CRAs began to downgrade them in early 2007, which was precisely the problem. As the CRAs downgraded these securities, the amount needed to pledge as collateral rose as their price fell. As a result, firms that were Repo borrowing had to post more and more collateral to get less and less funding.[13] Given how highly levered these firms were, only a small percentage of the securities needed to lose their ratings before the ability of the firm using them to fund itself was called into question, as Bear and then Lehman Brothers found out so abruptly. Ironically, then, although the CRAs were pilloried in 2007 and 2008 for their mispricing of mortgage securities, their real role in bringing about the crisis was to do their job properly – downgrading those securities as they lost value. That this ended up destroying companies, and in turn impairing their sovereigns, was what we might call the 'collateral' damage of the crisis. Given this, in terms of the categories laid out by the editors, CRAs failed as *judges* and then acted as *triggers*: and when they corrected their error they got blamed all the more.

Three reasons are commonly cited as to why CRAs failed in the crisis, each of which further illustrates the dynamics highlighted by the editors. The first complaint was that the CRAs used "bad data and bad models" in their CDO risk estimates, hence the original mispricing as AAA. In brief, mortgages were thought an attractive investment because they were uncorrelated with other assets (equities, for example) and uncorrelated with their class. That is, when Baltimore real estate values went down, this had no effect on house prices in Texas or Maine. So when banks began to pool and tranche mortgages into CDOs, this promised to take what was already uncorrelated and low risk and make it super low risk. And the data seemed to back this up.

The generic model used to price these risks was actually an adapted corporate bond model that was parameterized using data from the worst default on record: Texas in the mid-1980s. This suggested that the worst that could happen would be a fall in value of 40 percent that would be specific to particular markets: correlation would be limited.[14] Apart from the Texas default data set, the other data that were available on mortgage defaults were unusually stable and rather short, thus leading firms to underestimate the tail-risks involved.[15] Unfortunately,

[13] Gorton 2010. [14] Interviews with CRA senior executives in 2008.
[15] Brunnermeier 2009: 95 n. 7.

putting mortgages from all over the country into the same bond while pumping huge amounts of money into the sector created a hidden correlation between these assets that the CRAs could not anticipate until it was revealed in the bust. Would more data and better models have helped? Perhaps, but the point is that the CRAs were seen to have failed in their critical functions of *judging* and *monitoring* in terms of risk pricing.

The second charge against them was that a conflict of interest (COI) lay at the heart of their business model. That is, the CRAs' "pay to rate" business model created incentives for the sell-side brokers in the CRAs to give flattering ratings so that business flowed to them rather than to their competitors. With all three firms playing the same game, the average rating was "bid up" such that it did not reflect the true risk premium, even if it had been calculated correctly, which it had not.

The traditional defense for the CRAs against the COI charge was that they rated so many different securities supplied by so many originators that any single COI, even if true, would not bias ratings overall. By 2006 this claim was less than credible. A mere twelve originators supplied 92 percent of all CDOs at the same time that rating structured products became an increasingly important part of the CRAs' core business.[16] Moody's, for example, rated "113 such products in 1997 but 3,257 in the peak year of 2006."[17] In short, there was a conflict of interest deep in the heart of delegating the production of public knowledge to private actors who can profit from misrepresentation. The CRAs certainly failed then to supply appropriate anchoring *conventions* for the true state of market knowledge, more on which below. They also failed to act as accurate *monitors* and impartial *judges* since the "originator pays" business model does generate a deep COI problem that led to the issuance of erroneous ratings.

However, if ratings are just an "opinion," and not a "fact," as Fitch maintain (as described above), then regulating the CRAs to "do their job better" becomes a rather subjective task. For example, the recent Dodd–Frank Act seeks to limit the First Amendment protections of the CRAs in a variety of ways. The Act proposes to establish an Office of Credit Ratings in the SEC to mitigate such problems by limiting these protections. The tools to be used in this regard are more transparency over ratings, allowing litigation (suit) of CRAs over ratings on the

---

[16] Rona-Tas and Hiss 2010: 125.   [17] *Ibid.*

grounds of expert liability (the same as, for example, applies to firms of auditors), and the establishment of a ratings board that would act as a clearing-house for ratings. This last innovation would assign originators to a CRA for a flat fee such that the COI problem, and the gaming of the CRAs' models (more on this below), would be obviated.[18]

While each of these reforms is well intentioned and justified, they offer no regulatory panacea. More transparency, as we shall see, can mean more gaming. Allowing litigation still has the burden of proof attached to it, which, given the econometric difficulties of assessing ratings accuracy, would be a challenge. Nor would a clearing-house do much for regulatory arbitrage concerns where firms use ratings to, for example, lower their reserve capital. Finally, it is not clear that changing the CRAs' model to that of a public agency, another oft-mentioned solution, would make the situation much better. If the CRAs were not paid to rate, then a public organization must take over the task. To the extent that one did, it would probably be national, with different states offering alternate state-run CRAs. In such a world one must wonder whether different national CRAs would have an incentive to help national firms get better ratings, for example. In this regard the COI problem would be transplanted, but not eliminated.

The third, less well-known criticism was that the CRAs were naïve insofar as they were used by hedge funds as part of a "big short," to use Michael Lewis' term, against major banks. That is, ratings can be gamed. Basically, several hedge funds and other players realized by 2005 that the CRAs were incorrectly pricing mortgage bond risk. As such, they could profit by shorting the banks holding this risk.[19] One particularly clever method used was to get the rating agencies to rate high-explosive mortgage junk as AAA and then detonate it inside a highly levered bank.[20]

Back in the mid-2000s, as a part of the fallout from having previously mispriced Enron and WorldCom, Congress mandated that the CRAs open up their models to scrutiny in the name of transparency via the disclosure of past ratings. This allowed hedge funds to reverse engineer their models, effectively figuring out how to make financial manure smell like roses. Not that they had to try any subterfuge to do so since the CRAs in many instances "made the software their analysts used for

---

[18] See the Altman *et al.* 2012 discussion of these provisions at pp. 454–459.
[19] Lewis 2011.   [20] Interviews with hedge fund principals in 2008 and 2009.

evaluation available to arrangers [CDO designers] who could run their proposed CDOs [through the software] ... and receive advice ... on how to get the best possible rating."[21]

Given these advantages, fund-backed originators in many cases set up special investment vehicles (SIVs) to manufacture such bonds, got them rated AAA by the CRAs, and then sold them on to banks and other financial institutions keen to hold AAA assets. The funds themselves then took short positions against these institutions while buying CDS protection, a form of bond insurance whereby third parties underwrite the risk of failure in exchange for an income stream, against these same institutions failing. The resulting upward pressure on the CDS market caused CRAs to lower their ratings on the institutions that had bought these bonds, thereby acting quite literally as *the trigger* that blew up some highly leveraged financial institutions for great profit in 2007 and 2008.[22]

In sum, the CRAs hardly distinguished themselves in the crisis. Their mispricing of risk drew attention to their weakness as *judges* and *monitors* and *triggered* upward market movements that were not justified by any fundamentals. They also failed to act as the generators of *stabilizing conventions*. Indeed, when they re-priced risk they once again acted as *triggers* that accelerated downward market trends to the point that the ratings themselves were used as powerful weapons by hedge funds in the midst of the crisis.

CRAs and sovereigns since the crisis

Moving away from CRAs in the 2008 crisis, their roles have most recently played out on the rather different stage of the US, and especially the European, sovereign debt crises. The two events are of course linked. The bailing, recapitalizing, and stimulus of the economies most affected in the financial crisis – those most exposed, by and large, to real estate losses or to already high debt levels – transferred the balance sheet liabilities of the financial sector to the public sector *en masse*. In the case of CRAs, despite being causally important in generating the crisis as described above, they continue to act authoritatively in the

---

[21] Rona-Tas and Hiss 2010: 139. See also Altman *et al.* 2012: 448.

[22] Needless to say, funds are not keen to go public about this, even if it was all quite legal.

sovereign bond markets. Why then do we still listen to them? The answer lies, we suggest, more in what ratings in this context allow actors to do – how ratings are *advocacy tools* – than with the information content of the ratings themselves.

Following the debacle of 2008, the CRAs' next big public performance occurred on the occasion of the downgrade of the United States in August 2011. This instance supplies us with a fascinating example of how ratings can be used as advocacy tools, in that the CRAs' outputs became tools for critics, particularly in the United States, of the US macroeconomic policy stance. Republican presidential hopeful Mitt Romney described the downgrade as an indictment of the Obama administration: "America's creditworthiness just became the latest casualty in President Obama's failed record of leadership on the economy. Standard and Poor's rating downgrade is a deeply troubling indicator of our country's decline under President Obama."

Yet the United States borrows in its own currency, and the US dollar remains the world's primary reserve currency. Although the Federal Reserve retains infinite capacity to print dollars, and the ratio of US public debt to national output was well below the levels that prevail among many creditworthy sovereigns, the CRAs nonetheless increased their estimated probability – through the downgrade – of some sort of US default. Notwithstanding the fact that a massive increase in the supply of dollars might trigger its depreciation relative to other countries (and therefore a kind of default, albeit one that the CRAs do not generally purport to assess), an actual US default – that the US Treasury might announce to the world that it was not going to pay its debts in full – remained very nearly unthinkable. Very nearly, that is, since it is possible to buy insurance, a credit default swap, on such an event. That such insurance exists is, a moment's consideration reveals, rather absurd, since the day the US Treasury literally defaults on its obligations would likely come on the occasion of – or perhaps would actually produce – a worldwide financial meltdown, the end of this era of globalization, and, in a word, Armageddon. So we have in this instance CRA ratings acting as advocacy tools for agents based upon an event that is for all intents and purposes impossible. But what they are doing there is not rating the probability of an event. Rather, they are telling the markets what they already know and codifying it as "fact."

The Eurozone experience with credit ratings reveals a similar dynamic. The Greek sovereign's debt crisis was the spark for what became a continent-wide catastrophe. Although the Greek economy accounts for merely 2.5 percent of the Eurozone's total annual output, its borrowing practices nonetheless managed to begin a process that threatened the stability and existence of the common European currency. The Greek sovereign has, as everyone has come to observe, borrowed too much capital from abroad while being less than forthcoming about its structural deficit figures. As a result, its bond yields spiked, prices fell, and everyone holding European sovereign debt began to wonder if the rest of their holdings were equally tarnished. Fear of contagion, where selling off a bond to remove it from a portfolio leads to a general fire sale of such assets, gripped the markets.

Yet it is patently impossible for a nation to over-borrow without the markets playing their part by over-lending. The capital markets lent to the Greek sovereign billions of Euros at an interest rate that was, for an extended period of time, merely fifty basis points above what they charged the German sovereign. This was an all-too-familiar moral hazard trade, wherein the markets presumed that Greece's membership in the Eurozone represented an implicit guarantee of its debts by other Eurozone members and/or the European Central Bank (ECB). Given these implicit guarantees, as yields converged between different Euro-based sovereign bonds, the CRAs' ratings followed the markets and graded these bonds upwards. This over-lending/over-rating occurred despite Greece's legendarily weak macroeconomic fundamentals. The Greek government had, in fact, failed to run a single budget surplus in the fifty years leading up to its early-twenty-first-century debt crisis. The Greek nation had not run a single current account surplus over the same period. Yet capital continued to pour into Greece, and the sovereign's credit rating stood within the A range for all three CRAs during most of the 2000s.

When the credit spreads began to widen toward the end of the decade, so, too, were Greece's sovereign ratings downgraded. By 2011 ratings on Greek sovereign instruments had fallen below investment-grade, that is, to junk status. Partly the downgrades reflect the Greek economy's worsening fundamentals, which were driven by rising borrowing costs and debt-to-output levels that were approaching 160 percent. But they were also telling the markets what they already knew: that the real value of these bonds, all of them, was now uncertain. As such, the downgrades and credit spreads reinforced one another in a vicious spiral; the two processes informed one another, each telling the other what both the CRAs and the markets already knew.

What was most curious then was that very little new information about the creditworthiness of the Greek sovereign was revealed to either party in the downgrade or the prior ratings upgrade. For all of the proclamations of bondholders and ratings analysts about the weaknesses of the Greek government, literally none of the putative culprits – budget deficits, current account deficits, and so on – were new. They all had existed for fifty years. All that had shifted was market sentiment, and that worldview was informed most of all by increased fears that the implicit guarantee of the rest of the Eurozone on which the investors and CRAs had long counted might be less solid than they had once believed.

The repeated downgrades of the Spanish sovereign exhibit similar dynamics. Although Spain had among the lowest public debt to GDP ratios in the OECD going into the crisis, once Greece got into trouble the market had to price in the cost of the gigantic real estate bubble Spain had built up over the previous decade, again a function of over-lending by European banks that played a moral hazard trade against the ECB. The markets did this in short order, with yields spiking in Spanish debt at all maturities. Only then did the CRAs actually down-grade the sovereign, codifying what the markets already knew, and only then did they matter. And they mattered not for the new rating itself but because they handed other sovereigns, particularly the German sovereign, whose banks were all on the hook for over-lending, advocacy tools to beat the Spanish sovereign into austerity and reform and to keep the Greeks in the Euro at all costs. In sum, ratings matter in the Eurozone crisis not for what they signal, since that is already priced in, but for codifying the conventional judgment as to what "average opinion ought to be," as Keynes put it many years ago.[23]

CRAs, conventions, and uncertainty

What then explains the persistence of CRAs, given their recent rather lackluster and conflicted performances? If their ratings are not accurate and they tell the markets what they already know, why then do they persist? We suggest two complementary explanations. The first, as explained above, is that they supply the market with the "conventional

[23] Keynes 1936.

judgment" necessary for markets to operate effectively. Second, in order to do this CRAs do something else essential for markets to function. As Bruce Carruthers puts it, they do something impossible – they turn uncertainty into risk.[24] Or at least they provide the illusion of having achieved such an elusive, but valuable, transmogrification. Because CRAs do this, even if their ratings are consistently wide of the mark, or lag what markets already anticipate, they are essential parts of any complex market order. The process of describing uncertainty as risk may be a fiction, but it is a necessary one.

Two unique features define the practice of sovereign borrowing: the unenforceability of contracts and the sovereign's essential ownership of national assets. No third party – no world government, no international court – can actually enforce a sovereign debt contract, while nations never really run out of assets to cover their obligations if they have a printing press. Sovereigns are, to put it another way, often illiquid, but only rarely are they truly insolvent. Thus when the CRAs assess the creditworthiness of borrowers, a characteristic that is some mix of ability and willingness to repay, willingness to sell national assets or ability to extract tax revenue is really the only relevant criterion. This sounds simple, but given that states do not go out of business but can (and do on occasion) default on their obligations, the CRAs have then taken on a near-impossible analytical task: assessing the ability and willingness to pay off borrowers, borrowers whose ability and willingness are functions of their own internal political and economic dynamics, the worldviews of their creditors, the judgments of their assessors, and the random shocks of the global economy.

Econometric research tends to show that ratings for simple products such as single-issue corporate bonds are highly accurate. But the more complex the product, the more susceptible it is to hidden correlation risks, market risk, liquidity risk, and the like. Sovereign bonds are essentially simple instruments and as such both the bonds and their ratings have proven robust over time. However, when such instruments are embedded in wider mechanisms that can increase their downside risks due to correlation with other sovereigns' risk and so on, exactly as the Eurozone is doing today, the rating becomes less accurate since the behavior of the bond is less predictable.[25]

---

[24] Carruthers 2011.
[25] Another reason it is difficult to assess predictive accuracy is that the set of non-issuers is not included in the sample, so there is acute selection bias in any sample, even for the set of sovereign lenders. See Rona-Tas and Hiss 2010: 126.

The first-order problem is one of endogeneity: each of the inputs of CRA risk assessment affects the other inputs in impossible-to-anticipate ways. Consider the following paradoxical results.[26] First, as noted above, ratings tend to lag rather than lead the markets. That is, the markets generally react to the same economic data that are filtered by S&P's and Moody's theories of the world. Indeed, as much as 90 percent of the variation in sovereign ratings can be explained by a small number of quantitative indicators.[27] The remaining 10 or so percent is critical, however; according to one longtime executive at one of the big two CRAs, at stake with that much variation is "one and a half rating categories."[28] Second, ratings changes still affect the markets, even though the CRAs are telling the markets what they already know.[29]

The combination of these two results is possible for two reasons. If market participants know that others tend to react to unhappy ratings changes, then they should as well even if they already knew that a sovereign's credit situation had already begun to deteriorate. The market's reaction will only ensure its deterioration even if it is already priced in. Also, once ratings approach standard regulatory limits, many market participants are legally obliged to limit their exposure, the assessment of which regulators leave to ratings.

A further complication is that moments of sovereign illiquidity are, in an age of highly internationalized capital markets, endogenous to market beliefs. Capital flows out of nations whose policies markets believe are illegitimate or untrustworthy. Capital markets also charge higher interest rates for sovereigns whose willingness to pay gets called – by the markets themselves – into question. As Ilene Grabel and Jonathan Kirshner have argued, policies that the markets do not trust literally cannot succeed.[30] For the CRAs, then, the task of assigning ratings of creditworthiness to sovereigns is exceptionally difficult. At best, the signals are unclear and the appropriate inferences uncertain. The CRAs must guess what sovereigns want and are willing to do to get it; they must come to a point of view about how the markets are likely to respond. But the problem that they face is, we argue, more

---

[26] See Cantor and Packer 1996; Ferri, Liu, and Stiglitz 1999. Also see Carruthers 2011.

[27] Cantor and Packer 1996.   [28] Quoted in Abdelal 2007: 176.

[29] Larraín, Reisen, and von Maltzan 1997; Ferri, Liu, and Stiglitz 1999; Kaminsky and Schmukler 2002; and Reinhart 2002.

[30] Grabel 2000; and Kirshner 2000.

fundamental still. For many markets to exist CRAs must turn uncertainty into risk; or at least the market participants must all agree to play along with the fiction of CRAs' having done so.[31]

Following the distinction popularized by Frank Knight in the 1920s, we argue that situations of risk typify situations where probabilities to an event can be extrapolated from the analysis of past data.[32] That is, the data conform to a knowable distribution, where the expected mean and higher moments converge to their real equivalents. In such a world prediction is possible. Situations of uncertainty pertain when the analysis of past data cannot produce such distributions since what is encountered is, in the words of Knight, "in a high degree unique."

CRAs live in a world of uncertainty and perform the vital function of turning uncertainties (the future value of a complex derivative, the future membership of the Eurozone, the possibility of a US default) into probabilistic risk. That the probabilities calculated are oftentimes wide of the mark and follow what the market has already priced in is secondary to the fact that they give the market such probabilities, since without them they cannot function. The future price of sovereign assets is, as Keynes put it, "something about which we cannot know," since the analysis of past prices cannot exhaust the possibilities for future price movements. Indeed, given the deep causal endogeneity and uncertainty that defines the world of CRA operations, that they manage any degree of accuracy is truly remarkable. Given this, we argue that the continued existence of CRAs has less to do with their accuracy and more to do with their ability to provide the market with estimates of certainty in an uncertain world.

An episode related by Kenneth Arrow describes this dynamic perfectly. During World War II Arrow was a weather officer, assigned to a team that tried to make long-term weather forecasts. Given the complexities involved in such an uncertain world, Arrow and his colleagues asked to be reassigned, given that their predictions were worthless. They were told to continue nonetheless, since "the commanding general is well aware that the forecasts are no good. However, he needs them for planning purposes."[33] In other words, while the first-order

---

[31] Knight 1921; Blyth 2002; Carruthers 2011   [32] Knight 1921.
[33] Quoted among other sources at http://www.ritholtz.com/blog/2009/11/the-cur rent-state-of-the-economy-and-a-look-to-the-future-with-reference-to-wil liam-%E2%80%98sidestroke%E2%80%99-miles-w-somerset-maugham-don-ameche-and-kenneth-arrow.

purpose of ratings, to estimate default probabilities that attach to a given financial instrument, may be worthless as soon as the complexity goes beyond simple corporate or sovereign bond issues, which it inevitably does, the second-order effect, that of stabilizing expectations, means that right or wrong, ratings will remain a hugely important part of the global financial architecture. As ever, Keynes' beauty contest analogy remains appropriate: "We have reached the third degree where we devote our intelligences to anticipating what average opinion expects the average opinion to be."[34] In a world of globally mobile capital, where agents trade instruments of baffling complexity in nanoseconds, they need to know what something is worth. CRAs price the risks associated with the world's financial instruments. That the prices offered are "off" is secondary to the fact that they are "offered." For without such prices portfolios could not be constructed, risks could not be traded, pensions could not be secured, and assets could not be liquidated. Without such prices and estimates of risk complex markets cannot function.

Why then do governments simultaneously delegate regulatory responsibility to CRAs and lament the transfer of authority that they, the governments themselves, caused? The reason is that we cannot really do without something like ratings – some device for managing, through regulation, the public's exposure to risk and the markets' need for future prices. Someone simply has to perform this task and the US and other governments picked out three someones: Standard and Poor's, Moody's, and Fitch. In doing so the CRAs have reached what Keynes might have called the fourth degree: market sentiments, and therefore the viability of sovereigns' policy stances, are shaped and affected by the ratings, which are themselves demanded by the agents affected by the ratings.

Conclusion: A world without ratings?

In the aftermath of the financial crisis, US politicians and policymakers scrambled to discern what about the CRAs might be changed to improve their roles in the financial system. Some Europeans sought to invent a new European rating agency to rival the dominance of the American firms. The German consulting firm Roland Berger developed

---

[34] Keynes 1936: 155–156.

a plan in cooperation with European Commission officials to create a firm that would issue ratings, which would be paid for by investors, rather than issuers of securities. By 2012 it seemed that the plan would fail, and not just because of the logistical challenges of recasting a business model that evolved for obvious logistical reasons away from investor-purchased ratings. The same regulatory designation and delegation problems would remain, of course. And it is not clear that having a handful of Europeans populate a CRA would improve the ability of any firm to distance itself from its inherently complicated relationship with market sentiment.

If, for example, some European CRA had existed before the continent's sovereign debt crisis, what would have been different if it had refused to downgrade Greece as the nation's credit spreads widened and the American firms observed, rightly, that the widening spreads undermined the creditworthiness of the government? In this alternative scenario, the only change would have been that the European CRA would have failed to observe that the change in market sentiment was in fact driving the deterioration of the Greek sovereign's ability to borrow, which would have made the market more unstable and not less. It is not the Americanness of the firms that creates the key *problematique*. The challenges are more fundamental to the practices of regulatory delegation and producing market conventions.

Thus, when the US Department of Justice filed a fraud suit against S&P for its purported role in triggering the financial crisis, the government merely described yet again the extraordinarily paradoxical role of the CRAs generally. The government chose S&P as a scapegoat: Moody's and Fitch were not named in the fraud suit. S&P's legal team undertook in the spring of 2013 its traditional defense: the firm issues opinions, and investors surely, their lawyers argued, would not take on huge financial risks merely because some relatively underpaid folks who work around the corner from Wall Street express the view that they are not risky relative to some alternatives. Even more problematic, the suit revealed that the US government remains unwilling to acknowledge that if S&P were really guilty of fraud, then the US regulatory architecture would have to be named as its primary accomplice. Justice claimed that S&P's ratings were heeded because S&P is important; but S&P is important primarily because US policy and regulation had made it so. If the US government really does not want S&P to shape market outcomes, then it will have to stop delegating that responsibility to the firm. And then someone else will have to take on that role.

So we seem to be stuck with CRAs since both governments and private investors need their ratings to coordinate their expectations and trade with one another in what is after all an unknowable future. Markets, as the institutional outgrowth of the individuals who constitute them, need benchmarks, signals, and prices. CRAs play a vital role in pricing that which has no definitive price – the riskiness of assets in a future that has yet to be realized and that cannot be reduced to its time-series past. That their risk-prices are wrong may from time to time upset both investors and sovereigns, but given that someone has to do what they do, CRAs, like democracy, may be the worst system of all, apart from all the other alternatives.

3 | Corruption rankings
Constructing and contesting the global anti-corruption agenda

MLADA BUKOVANSKY

Introduction

The presumption behind global corruption rankings is that by bringing public attention to a recognized problem, rankings contribute to anti-corruption advocacy. But rankings do more than just spotlight an issue; rankings work to define and structure that issue. For example, corruption rankings have been primarily applied to states, rather than private companies. This already structures the issue so that the focus is on public servants rather than market players. This chapter focuses on the manner in which corruption has been defined and structured by Transparency International's (TI) Corruption Perceptions Index (CPI), reviewing and building on key substantive (rather than methodological) critiques of the CPI. The guiding question is whether the CPI rankings facilitate anti-corruption advocacy, or whether they are little more than a branding exercise for Transparency International. I argue that although the CPI has helped put corruption on the map as a concern for international institutions, its success has also inspired critiques which have successfully pushed for a move beyond rankings into other forms of analysis and anti-corruption advocacy.

Existing critiques of the CPI, and of the closely related but broader array of governance indicators put out by the World Bank's Governance Indicators project,[1] highlight three possibly perverse or deleterious effects of corruption rankings: such rankings can *distract* from more important facilitating conditions for corrupt activity and anti-corruption advocacy, as well as obscuring important differences in the type of corruption experienced by different countries; they can *reinforce* countries' position on either the high or low end of the scale; and they lend themselves to political *manipulation* which can

[1] See http://info.worldbank.org/governance/wgi/index.aspx#home.

60

undermine anti-corruption efforts of opposition parties and grassroots organizations.

This chapter reviews and discusses the plausibility of these critiques, and concludes by acknowledging new developments in anti-corruption discourse and policy, which appear to have emerged at least partly as a result of a learning process brought on by the ascendancy of the CPI and commentary about it by those critical of TI's approach. Although rankings continue to be highly valued in the marketplace of ideas, as evidenced by the explosion of ranking "products" highlighted in the introductory chapter of this volume, critiques of rankings have pushed scholars and activists to develop alternative, and possibly less techno-cratic, approaches to the problem of corruption. This chapter argues that moving away from the rankings-fueled technocratic approach to corruption is a positive development; anti-corruption advocacy requires human beings to exercise ethical agency, something which rankings and indices can neither capture nor directly promote.

The CPI and anti-corruption advocacy: A tenuous link?

In terms of the functions of RROs discussed in the introduction to this volume, Transparency International can primarily be classified as an advocacy organization. Arguably some of the most important work TI does is to establish country chapters, whose primary purpose is corrup-tion monitoring and anti-corruption advocacy. TI also works with other organizations, public and private, to promote its mission of combating corruption. Its advocacy work has both depth and breadth not captured by considering the Corruption Perceptions Index alone. The CPI is just a small part of TI's work, but it is probably the most visible of TI's "products." It may serve as a resource for anti-corruption advocates by putting a number on what might otherwise be construed as a hopelessly complex and culturally relativistic concept. The CPI also serves as the means by which TI asserts its "brand" as the leading organization devoted to combating corruption. Each year's release of the CPI puts TI into the news, even if the day-to-day work of country chapters, or special focal points such as the promotion of integrity in sport, rarely make major headlines. There may be a price to pay for the branding function provided by the CPI, however, especially in that this particular form of branding may distract from and possibly at times even undermine other, more potent forms of anti-corruption advocacy.

The CPI is designed to measure expert perceptions of primarily administrative and political corruption in a large set of countries (183 in 2011, 176 in 2012, 177 in 2013, 175 in 2014). TI constructs its country rankings on the basis of survey data from a group of expert sources, which includes individuals involved in international business, financial institutions, foundations focusing on development, political risk analysis firms, and other research organizations and international institutions.[2] The index assigns countries both a score and a ranking on the basis of this compiled survey data (it is a "poll of polls"). The results are generated and released annually, but are not comparable across time because rankings are relative and based on data from a given year; the data sources and countries covered or omitted may change from year to year. Despite this, even a cursory perusal of news articles will reveal that this methodological caveat does not stop people from making comparisons from year to year, and each release of the CPI is likely to stimulate editorial discussions of whether a country rose or fell in the rankings from the previous year.[3]

The annual release of the CPI generates a media flurry in many countries, complete with press releases, articles, and editorials in national news media responding to a country's position on the index. Thus the CPI may contribute to TI's advocacy function simply by publicizing the issue of corruption. But the CPI does more than publicize; it helps to structure the issue in terms of its definition and measurement. The process of issue construction has been underway since TI's inception, and has been taken up by the World Bank, OECD, the IMF, and other institutions, including USAID. Economists and political scientists have made extensive use of the CPI, and later of the broader set of World Bank Governance Indicators, because the ability to render this traditionally normative and at least somewhat culturally relative phenomenon – corruption – in quantitative terms provides excellent fodder for empirical, comparative research.

Transparency International, along with the World Bank under the leadership of James Wolfensohn, can be at least partly credited for moving corruption onto the international agenda at a time, in the late 1990s, when it was generally not considered within the purview and

---

[2] TI's annual CPIs can be found at: http://www.transparency.org/research/cpi/overview.

[3] Andersson and Heywood 2009: 760.

authority of international institutions.[4] According to Bo Rothstein, an important key to Wolfensohn's success in putting corruption on the Bank's agenda was that he "simply redefined corruption as an economic problem."[5] Approaching corruption from an economic (or in today's World Bank parlance, "political economy") perspective rendered it amenable to systemic, economic analysis rather than moral condemnation. This constitutes a technocratic turn in anti-corruption discourse.

The process of rendering policy problems amenable to technocratic solutions dovetails with the adoption of economic approaches and quantitative methods of analysis in political science. But as many have argued, the concept of corruption has an irreducible moral component, for which rationalist and economic approaches to the problem cannot adequately account. If controlling corruption requires people to act according to some vision of public good rather than for purely self-serving or particularistic interests, then the use of rankings and quantitative indicators may be only tangentially related to the problem of actually fighting corruption. Giving a country a ranking is not the same as engaging in an anti-corruption campaign, after all, and it takes more than "name and shame" to bring about comprehensive institutional reform. What quantitative indicators can do is aid in the development of hypotheses about causes and consequences of corruption, and such research in turn might suggest ways in which incentive structures could be altered so as to diminish the likelihood of corruption in specific contexts; such is the approach exemplified in Susan Rose-Ackerman's definitive study, *Corruption and Government*.[6] However, the ability to articulate what proper institutional incentives should look like, and the ability to actually create and implement such structures, are not the same thing.

The CPI may thus be a tool in the rhetorical arsenal of anti-corruption advocates, and it certainly has publicized and structured the corruption issue, but at a practical level it does not in itself constitute an anti-corruption movement, nor even a campaign. Rothstein has argued persuasively that controlling corruption requires neither incremental institutional alterations nor the tweaking of incentive structures, but rather large-scale and comprehensive transformation of social values and institutions:[7]

[4] Bukovansky 2006.   [5] Rothstein 2011: 40–41.   [6] Rose-Ackerman 1999.
[7] Rothstein 2011: ch. 5.

[C]orruption and similar practices are rooted in deeply held beliefs about the proper order of exchange in a society: personal-particularistic versus impersonal-universalistic. The implication is that to effectively curb corruption and establish QoG [quality of government], the whole political culture has to move from the "limited access" or "particularistic" equilibrium to the very different equilibrium characterized by "impersonal" or "universal" forms of exchange.[8]

The implication of Rothstein's and other broad historical sociological studies of institutions is that we have yet to produce a "science" of the sort of institutional change required to comprehensively control corruption. Nevertheless, the World Bank and other international organizations concerned with broad questions of "governance" routinely deploy rankings and indicators in attempting to lay out some kind of scientific approach to institutional change, and the CPI is a resource for this technocratic activity.[9] It is by no means obvious, however, that a set of rankings would in and of itself constitute advocacy designed to implement institutional change.

Even as a rhetorical anti-corruption tool or as a data set (rather than as a mechanism to produce institutional change), the CPI is not immune to misuse. CPI rankings may have perverse and unintended consequences which could actually work against anti-corruption advocacy. Three possible perverse effects can be gleaned from recent research on corruption, and will be further discussed below. First, focusing international attention on corruption as a characteristic of developing country governments can obscure the broader permissive context of the international financial architecture, through which activities such as offshore tax havens and money laundering operate to sustain corrupt payment systems, not to mention the facilitation of "state capture" by financial interests.[10] This is one aspect of the "distraction" issue alluded to above. Second, it has been argued that rankings may reinforce whatever position a country has on the published scale; for example, if lenders and donors are inclined to withhold aid and investment to low-ranking countries, they may cut them off from some of the resources necessary to initiate substantial institutional change.[11] Alternatively, their privileged position on the scale may create a self-reinforcing dynamic for "virtuous" countries, immunizing them

[8] Rothstein 2011: 109.   [9] World Bank 2007.   [10] Sharman 2011.
[11] Andersson and Heywood 2009.

against closer scrutiny. Third, globally legitimated anti-corruption norms in general may lend themselves to political manipulation for the purposes of boosting status and advantage of powerful political actors at the expense of their opponents. Although it is at least partly the intention of the CPI to be used as a political resource for corruption fighting, it is hard to see how it alone could be an effective resource for those who lack power and status. However, for those who already have power and status, anti-corruption campaigns may be used strategically in any number of ways. Political actors may engage in "mock compliance" with anti-corruption efforts to boost their status internally and among outside investors and donors, for example.[12] Or, they may strategically use accusations of political corruption as a tool to undermine political opponents without actually doing anything about the overall corrupt political structure. Such strategic manipulation of anti-corruption campaigns is of course not a direct effect of the CPI per se, but arguably the issue visibility provided by the annual release of the CPI helps to make anti-corruption rhetoric a source of political legitimacy.

By helping to put corruption on the international agenda, TI and its CPI have also helped to structure the issue in a specific way, which in turn conditions the types of anti-corruption advocacy that are considered legitimate. The next section discusses definitions of corruption, and in particular the dilemma of cultural relativism in the face of efforts to set universal anti-corruption standards.

Defining corruption

Corruption is an ancient concept, as old as law and government. But the manner in which it is defined sets the agenda for efforts to combat it, so it is worth discussing definitional issues in some detail. Early in his voluminous study *Bribes*, John Noonan remarks that "from the fifteenth century B.C. on, there has been a concept that could be rendered in English as 'bribe,' the concept of a gift that perverts judgment."[13] The term corruption connotes more than bribes, of course, but bribes are certainly a significant and perhaps the most easily identifiable example of corruption. To understand a bribe as a bribe, one must have some notion that the bribe distorts the judgment of someone with

[12] Walter 2008.   [13] Noonan 1984: 13.

power. Defining corruption requires reference to a broader array of societal norms as to what constitutes a just decision on the part of someone who holds power over others. Until TI, the World Bank, and the OECD articulated corruption as a global issue requiring multilateral responses, the societal norms in which the definition of corruption was anchored were largely national or sub-national, not global. International studies of corruption were primarily comparative studies of different systems, not studies anchored by a single standard or scale.[14]

Although the term "corruption" has many meanings, Transparency International has narrowed down this potential multiplicity to a concise "corruption is the abuse of entrusted power for private gain."[15] This definition is now routinely used in a broad array of scholarly work and policy-oriented commentary. The context in which this definition emerged was that of the post-imperial focus on modernization and development of political and economic institutions in formerly colonized territories, amidst intensifying global economic interdependence. Samuel Huntington in his book *Political Order in Changing Societies* saw corruption as an inevitable stepping stone on the path to modernity,[16] but others later came to see it as an obstacle to both political and economic development. It was the latter perspective which infused and inspired the attempt to render corruption a problem deserving the attention of international institutions, and especially the World Bank. The presumption was that corruption could be curbed if proper institutional checks were put in place, and this would then improve conditions for foreign investment, integration into global markets, and economic development more broadly.

Eventually aligning with a neoliberal push to roll back government interference in markets, anti-corruption advice came to focus on constraining the discretionary power of public officials.[17] Even as neoliberalism begins to lose its status as dominant ideology (the timing of this decline is sure to be in dispute), the development discourse has adopted the rhetoric of "good governance" as crucial to development. This too aligns very nicely with a focus on providing proper incentives to public officials so that they are less likely to behave in corrupt ways.

---

[14] Scott 1972; Heidenheimer *et al.* 1989.
[15] See: http://www.transparency.org/whatwedo.   [16] Huntington 1968.
[17] Susan Rose-Ackerman's (1999) text provides a definitive articulation.

So although TI's anti-corruption advocacy and the CPI were born in the age of the Washington Consensus, they appear to have survived the erosion of that consensus. The manner in which TI's mission has been articulated dovetails just as well with the concept of "good governance" and the focus on improving institutions as it did with the notion that the discretion of public officials should be curtailed.

From the beginning, an explicitly stated objective of the economic approaches to corruption was to avoid moralizing.[18] As Joseph Nye and others have argued, if analysts could present scientific, empirically compelling arguments laying out the deleterious effects of corruption on political and economic development, and suggest policies and institutional changes on the basis of empirical evidence and dispassionate scientific methodology, this would be preferable and presumably more effective than decrying the moral failings of corrupt leaders. This approach is technocratic in the sense that it does not require us to engage in debate about public goods, moral ends, and virtue; everyone can presumably agree that economic development is a good thing. If an empirical link can be found between lower levels of corruption and better development results, then policy prescriptions can take on the appearance of value-free technical advice on achieving a goal whose value is given and thus need not be subject to debate. Just as everyone can agree that a well-constructed bridge is preferable to a poorly constructed one, a less corrupt government obviously performs its function (development) more effectively than a more corrupt one.

This avoidance of moralizing continues to be the case today, perhaps best illustrated by the World Bank's articulation of governance and anti-corruption as a "systemic" issue:

> Governance is multi-dimensional. A governance system comprises a wide variety of processes, systems, organizations, and rules (that is, institutions) on the public bureaucracy "supply" side and on the "demand" side through which non-executive oversight institutions and citizens hold the bureaucracy accountable for performance.[19]

The technocratic approach tries to deal with the problem of cultural and moral relativism by avoiding morality entirely, or discussing cultural relativism as a side issue distinct from the formal framework of analysis.[20]

---

[18] Nye 1967.   [19] World Bank 2007, Annex A, p. 19.
[20] See Rose-Ackerman 1999: ch. 6.

But this sidelining of moral issues has not been entirely successful, because the problem of cultural relativism still has to be faced, bringing the moral issues in through the back door. When confronting practices deemed corrupt, analysts and policymakers have always faced the problem that practices which appear acceptable in some societies are seen as corrupt in others. Gift-giving and patronage are obvious examples of how difficult it can be to draw the line between unacceptably corrupt and culturally accepted and legitimate practices. Does this mean that corruption is an entirely relativistic concept with no universal content? If so, then how can citizens of one country condemn the practices of those of another country as corrupt? If what counts as corruption can only be determined by the people living within a specific society, then ranking countries according to a single standard is either meaningless or imperialistic, and international institutions should apply the standards of whatever country they are operating in. Indeed, this was the attitude that seems to have prevailed until the emergence of a global anti-corruption effort in the 1990s, as evidenced by the common practice in many countries of allowing corporate tax deductions for bribes paid to foreign public officials, even when such bribes were illegal in the home country. The US Foreign Corrupt Practices Act of 1977, which applied a universal standard and marked the first time a country made it illegal for its citizens to bribe the public officials of a foreign country, was an outlier and an anomaly until the 1990s.[21]

It is very hard, however, to fully accept the claim that corruption is entirely relative and in the eyes of the beholder, or subject only to the unique standards of a specific society. As John Noonan's study has shown, the notion of corrupt dealings can be found in just about every society and culture in human civilization (although Noonan is careful to show that for a bribe to be seen as bad requires the bending of what he sees as the most fundamental norm of social life: reciprocity).[22] If every culture has some concept of corruption, some notion that certain activities – particularly those pertaining to the exercise of political authority – should not be subject to reciprocal exchange, then is there not some universal or near-universal aspect to the concept?

More recently, Oskar Kurer has articulated the problem of definition, and the tension between the universal and relativistic aspects of corruption, in a fruitful manner:

---

[21] See Noonan 1984: ch. 20.   [22] Noonan 1984: ch. 1.

Whereas the concept of corruption is one that is well-nigh universal and thus hardly suffering from cultural specificity, its content – the specific non-discrimination norms – is not; what in practice will count as corrupt will depend on prevailing norms and conventions. This explains the paradox that although the term 'corruption' is readily understood and readily applied everywhere, there is hardly any agreement on where precisely the boundary between a corrupt and a non-corrupt act should be drawn.[23]

The key principle on which Kurer bases his *general* definition of corruption is that of impartiality. Bo Rothstein in his recent book, *The Quality of Government*, follows up on Kurer's analysis and also makes the concept of impartiality central to his conception of quality of government:

The norm that is violated when corruption occurs is the impartiality principle governing the exercise of public power, whose core component is the notion of nondiscrimination, whether for money, race, religion, or sex/gender. The advantage of this definition of QoG is that impartiality rules out not only all forms of corruption but also practices such as clientelism, patronage, nepotism, political favoritism, discrimination, and other "particularisms."[24]

If we accept (as I think we should) the argument that corruption at its core involves the violation of the impartiality principle, we are left with enough flexibility in the definition of corruption to account for a great deal of variation in specific cultural and political contexts. We are also left with plenty of room to vary the context in which impartiality is deemed an appropriate behavior, since there are many conceivable contexts, such as the distribution of certain types of benefits or punishments, or the implementation of affirmative action-type policies, in which public authority should be *partial* rather than impartial.[25]

Evoking corruption as a problem leads directly into discussing quality of government issues, as Rothstein has argued, and different societies may face different sorts of corruption problems, as Johnston's excellent book charting out distinct "syndromes" of corruption so clearly illustrates.[26] However much one wishes to avoid "moralizing," the corruption concept inevitably necessitates moral judgment, because corruption is generally considered a bad thing. That moral judgment is part of the definition regardless of how much economists and rational

[23] Kurer 2005: 236.   [24] Rothstein 2011: 15.
[25] See the discussion in Rothstein 2011: ch. 1.
[26] Rothstein 2011; Johnston 2005.

choice theorists might enjoy pointing out the functionality of corruption in certain situations, that is, corruption can be "good" from
an economic perspective if it facilitates the by-passing of "bad" – i.e.
rent-seeking – laws. Just because a bad action might yield a good result
does not mean that we should re-define that action in ethically neutral
terms. The idea that those who hold authority over others ought to
exercise that authority impartially is at its core an ethical one.

The potential power of the corruption concept further lies in its ability
to evoke deep reflection on the institutional and normative underpinnings of a particular society. As political theorist J. Peter Euben
has argued, one can productively think of corruption in a very broad
sense as "the debasement of the foundations or origins of a political
community,"[27] and following this strand find a classical articulation of
the problem in Thucydides' Melian Dialogue, and his account of
the civil war in Corcyra. Political philosophers from Aristotle to
Machiavelli to Thomas Jefferson have probed the problem of corruption in their reflections on the difficulty of sustaining political institutions in time.

However, our contemporary economic and technocratic definitions
seem to preclude such reflection, either because they take the ends of
political life as given (something on the order of developing or growing
the economy), or because they accept the relativistic view that each
culture has its own standards and that it is therefore inappropriate to
judge others by our own standards. At the same time, the construction
of global rankings gives the impression that there is actually a global
standard to which all governments are expected to adhere. The technocratic evasion of moral issues is ironically accompanied by an assertion
of global standards. But as I have argued elsewhere, this "hollowing
out" of the moral content of corruption precludes reasoned discourse
about the appropriate ends of government and public authority.[28] At
its worst such a rhetorical move entails an exercise of power without
the consent and participation of the "governed" – this was a core
problem of the neoliberal discourse, which has received plenty of
critiques we need not re-hash here. A further practical effect of this
technocratic reticence about the deep moral content of anti-corruption
discourse, when coupled with the fact that in the international
context corruption tends to get discussed as primarily a "developing

[27] Euben 1989: 103.   [28] Bukovansky 2006.

country" problem, may be to close off scrutiny and debate about the quality of institutions in the wealthier, "developed" countries. But as J. C. Sharman has shown, when it comes to playing by the rules of financial transparency (surely a key issue for sustained anti-corruption advocacy), it is the richest and most powerful countries who are the greatest violators of the principles they would have others follow.[29]

The assertion of corruption as a global issue thus came along with a specific definition of corruption (abuse of public power for private gain), and in the context of a certain approach to political and economic development, which went through many permutations, the latest being neoliberalism and then the "post-Washington Consensus" on the importance of "governance." The practice of global corruption rankings has been a central part of the construction of the corruption issue as a global, rather than comparative, country-specific, issue. The process has favored a technocratic over a moral conception of corruption, and as I have already suggested, this manner of structuring the issue has had practical consequences in how the anti-corruption agenda has developed. It has also evoked important critiques. I first flesh out the process of issue structuring and issue linkage in a bit more detail, and then turn to the critiques.

Transparency International and the global anti-corruption agenda

Since its inception in 1993, Transparency International has been pivotal in casting corruption as a global issue. The scholarly and policy discourse in the period following the 1995 launch of the CPI shifted from silence or tacit and sometimes even explicit acceptance of corruption as an inevitable aspect of doing business abroad to widespread condemnation.[30] In a section of his 1968 book *Political Order in Changing Societies* that was subsequently reprinted in Heidenheimer and Johnston's comprehensive edited volume on political corruption, Samuel Huntington famously noted that corruption was to be taken as an indicator of modernization in a society.[31] In the 1970s and 1980s, economists and rational choice theorists had suggested that corruption could in fact be seen as a rational response to inefficient, rent-seeking

---

[29] Sharman 2011.   [30] Bukovansky 2006.
[31] Huntington 1989; Heidenheimer and Johnston 2001.

regulations – a sort of covert assertion of the market mechanism in what would otherwise be a hostile environment for market rationality.[32] But in the 1990s things began to turn around, and policymakers and scholars began to argue not only that corruption was a bad thing, but also that it was the business of international institutions and governments to fight it in a comprehensive way.

It was in the mid-to-late 1990s that the World Bank (and to a lesser extent the IMF) began to put corruption and "governance" more generally at the forefront of its agenda. This shift coincided with the rise of Transparency International; TI's founder Peter Eigen worked for the World Bank prior to founding the organization, and TI has had close ties to the Bank since its founding (and the Bank is now one of its donors). A number of anti-corruption treaties and conventions were passed since the inception of TI, most notably the 1997 OECD Convention on Combating Bribery of Foreign Public Officials in International Business Transactions.[33]

TI and especially its CPI can probably claim a good deal of credit for helping to shift attitudes about corruption among academics and policymakers away from toleration and toward condemnation. It is surely no accident that once a quantitative index of corruption was made available not only to the public but to scholars, we began to see studies correlating corruption to all sorts of development ills, and in particular to lower growth and less foreign investment. The CPI has fed into the quantitative, empirical, data-oriented, behavioralist, and institutionalist turns in the study of politics.[34] It gives number-crunchers some new numbers to crunch, whatever the limitations of those numbers. So, since CPI's inception, scholars have produced numerous studies showing relationships between a country's position on the CPI and other sorts of measurable variables, from foreign direct investment to press freedom, to place on the human development index, to human rights. Overall, indices like the CPI have done much to help extend the tools of economic analysis into the study of international relations. Meeting analysts' demands for numbers to crunch is not the same thing as advocacy. However, the studies which appear to systematically link corruption to other social ills, and in general a failure to "develop," can certainly be used to fuel the arguments of anti-corruption advocates.

---

[32] A classic statement of this position can be found in Becker and Stigler 1974.
[33] For a review see Bukovansky 2006.   [34] For a review see Bukovansky 2006.

But such studies inevitably structure the arguments in a specific, technocratic, amoral manner.

It would be unfair to deny TI's important achievements in putting corruption on the global policy and scholarly agenda, and in mobilizing people to work to curb corrupt practices as well as to engage in empirical studies linking corruption to various other social ills. At the same time, however, the CPI rankings, given that they are important to "branding" TI as an organization, and given their use in a broader array of empirical studies of corruption as a global phenomenon harmful to development, have helped to shape and limit the anti-corruption agenda and channel its focus toward government officials taking bribes, rather than toward business people offering bribes, and toward "developing" countries rather than "developed" countries. The most influential core insight that emerged from TI's campaigns and the scholarship that has emerged using the CPI has been to associate high levels of corruption with low levels of economic development. The idea that corruption hurts economic development has taken on the status of conventional wisdom. That has been probably the most powerful association, the one that has propelled the CPI and the anti-corruption agenda into the realm of international institutions and government policy.[35] From this linkage, the discourse has fanned out to link corruption to such highly visible and popular global issues as environmental degradation, poverty, and poor performance on human rights.

Other issue linkages articulated in TI's strategic framework prior to its reformulation in 2011 (of which more below) were that corruption hurts democracy and rule of law, distorts national and international trade, jeopardizes government and private sector ethics, undermines security of natural resources, reinforces gender discrimination, and compounds political exclusion.[36] Despite this extensive list of issue linkages, and despite TI's claims that its understanding of corruption encompasses more than bribery, bribery has long remained the central focus by virtue of how TI defines corruption: the CPI reinforces the association of corruption with bribery, and sustains a spotlight on those who receive bribes. TI has recognized this and has developed a "Bribe Payers Index" (BPI), which surveys business executives and ranks the world's leading economies according to how likely companies from these wealthy countries are to offer bribes to foreign public

---

[35] For example see USAID 2009.   [36] Transparency International 2007a.

officials and, more recently, to other private sector executives. The focus of the BPI remains on bribery, but attempts to put a spotlight on the private sector as a source of the "supply side" of the bribery equation. But the BPI has less resonance than the CPI; it has only been published five times since its inception in 1999, the latest survey being released in 2011.

As Andersson and Heywood have astutely noted, "[n]otwithstanding the caveats required in any overarching definition, it could be objected that the TI definition explicitly refers to the payment of bribes."[37] It is precisely on the issue of bribery that there has been the most official legal progress: the 1997 OECD Convention on Combating Bribery of Foreign Public Officials in International Business Transactions, and its progressive (though far from perfect) incorporation into the domestic laws of its ratifying states. By association and timing, TI's CPI certainly deserves some credit for pushing along the OECD Convention (and thus enhancing TI's advocacy function), though credit also has to go to pressure from US businesses who have lobbied against the competitive disadvantages imposed upon them by the US Foreign Corrupt Practices Act. The pressure for the OECD convention is surely also a product of such business pressure (though it cannot be reducible to US business lobbying alone, since the time lag strikes me as too long – FCPA is in place by 1977 and the OECD convention comes into force twenty years later).

Over a decade after its inception, however, the anti-bribery framework has proven itself quite limited in its capacity to combat corruption, in ways that go beyond problems in its implementation. Transparency International itself has been vocal in criticizing OECD countries for failing to implement anti-bribery rules, publishing eight annual reports to date reviewing the implementation of the Convention, with gloomy results.[38] The lack of success in implementing the OECD Convention suggests that the wealthier OECD countries are not particularly susceptible to the type of public pressure exerted by Transparency International, even with the support of an international legal framework; without more active participation by those responsible for the "supply side" of the global bribery and kickback network, progress is likely to remain limited. The 2011 BPI notes no real progress

---

[37] Andersson and Heywood 2009: 748.
[38] Heimann and Dell 2012 is the latest.

in curbing the supply side of bribery.[39] But lack of proper implementation is not the only problem of the technocratic approach to corruption facilitated by corruption rankings. There may be deeper consequences, as sketched out in the next section.

Perverse effects of corruption rankings?

As introduced above, I focus here on three possibly perverse effects facilitated by global anti-corruption rankings: distraction, reinforcement, and vulnerability to manipulation.

Distraction

One important line of critique that has emerged following the consolidation of the anti-corruption/anti-bribery consensus is its neglect of the related issues of tax havens, tax evasion, capital flight, and the offshore world. Why has TI's anti-corruption discourse not developed more in the direction of focusing on tax evasion, tax havens, and capital flight? Nowhere in TI's strategic framework for 2008–2010 was there a mention of tax havens, tax evasion, capital flight, or the offshore financial world. Tax havens do not appear in TI's publications subject list, although recently the topic of "financial markets" has been added, and money laundering does make an appearance. There have been some changes in the wake of the global financial crisis of 2008, and the anti-corruption movement does seem to be shifting its focus to include the global financial architecture. But that it neglected it for so long is certainly a problem, and possibly a puzzle demanding further explanation. One possible explanation is that the manner in which the corruption issue has been structured in the CPI-focused discourse puts the onus on governments (they are the ones being ranked, after all), rather than the private sector. This dovetails with the neoliberal context in which the anti-corruption agenda evolved, emphasizing the need to curtail the state and restrain public officials.

However, private sector activities, for example those centered on tax evasion and capital flight, in addition to the offering of bribes for evasion of costly regulations, are surely important lubricants for corrupt activities, and are also implicated in undermining the "good

---

[39] Transparency International 2011a.

governance" that is the underlying objective of anti-corruption efforts. In a paper entitled "New Estimates of Capital Flight from Sub-Saharan African Countries" economists Ndikumana and Boyce argue that:

The analysis of capital flows to and from Africa presents a stunning paradox. On the one hand, African countries are heavily indebted and must make difficult decisions with regard to the allocation of national resources between debt payments and provision of vital social services to their populations. Over the past decades, African countries have been forced by external debt burdens to undertake painful economic adjustments while devoting scarce foreign exchange to debt-service payments. On the other hand, African countries have experienced massive outflows of private capital towards Western financial centers. Indeed, these private assets surpass the continent's foreign liabilities, ironically making sub-Saharan Africa a "net creditor" to the rest of the world.[40]

Dev Car (formerly of the IMF) and Devon Cartwright-Smith, two economists working with a project called Global Financial Integrity, a program of the Center for International Policy in DC, estimate that over the thirty-nine-year period 1970–2008, Africa lost US$854 billion in cumulative capital flight, "enough to not only wipe out the region's total external debt outstanding of around US$250 billion [as of 2008] ... but potentially leave US$600 billion for poverty alleviation and economic growth." Moreover, "cumulative illicit flows from the continent increased from about US$57 billion in the decade of the 1970s to US$437 billion over the nine years 2000–2008."[41]

Nicholas Shaxon, who has written on the oil and the resource curse in Nigeria and elsewhere, argues that "we need to investigate the role of tax havens and the international infrastructure that provides an enabling environment for corruption or, in other words, a supply side furnishing the international corruption services."[42] The existence of tax havens and the whole "pinstripe infrastructure" (that term comes from John Christensen of Tax Justice Network[43]), infrastructure which facilitates the offshore world, is not just a problem for developing countries; it is a problem for all governments struggling to balance their books in the present era of global financial instability. Tax dodging corrupts by undermining public confidence and trust in the

[40] Ndikumana and Boyce 2008: 1.   [41] Car and Cartwright-Smith 2010.
[42] Shaxon 2007.   [43] Christensen 2007.

fairness and legitimacy of the tax system. Shaxon has made the further point that tax systems are a fundamental mechanism for holding public officials accountable to their populations. Yet by systematically deregulating global financial flows in the 1980s,[44] the OECD countries have helped to create the infrastructure for corruption. Surely the CPI overlooks something significant, and that something has to do with not just the supply side of international bribery, but with the financial infrastructure which facilitates all the activities that undermine public trust in governments' ability to deliver public services.

The criticism that the CPI approach has helped to deflect focus away from the financial infrastructure facilitating corruption is reinforced by some further observations. First, the CPI has developed alongside or just after the deregulation and liberalization of global financial flows; timing of its "take-off" in the 1990s comes right on the heels of the liberalization of capital markets. Second, aside from timing, we can see something of a norm convergence, an affinity between two sets of norm complexes: between private corporate interests in profit maximization via often perfectly legal financial innovation and tax evasion on the one hand (an interest that was facilitated by liberalization and loosening financial regulations in the OECD), and on the other hand a norm-entrepreneur TI-driven social movement to combat corruption (which consolidated into the OECD anti-bribery convention). The latter movement may constrain the flexibility of firms in trying to curtail their ability to pay bribes with impunity (though the success of this is questionable), but it still directs our focus to the problem of public officials engaging in individual transactions with private firms – that is, on a certain act of exchange, the bribe – rather than on the overall system which facilitates these exchanges.

Moreover, to the extent US pressure to create the OECD convention was propelled by firms worrying about effects of FCPA on their competitiveness abroad, this helped to cement the focus on public officials taking bribes as the core problem in the global anti-corruption agenda and also suggests that the interests of at least some multinational businesses were an important driver of the anti-corruption discourse. Transparency International itself cultivates relationships with the business community, including private risk-rating agencies and accounting firms, and so it is no surprise that the construction of the global anti-

---

[44] Abdelal 2007.

corruption agenda is business-friendly in many respects. Much of the information that goes into the CPI comes directly from the multinational business and financial community.

Finally, innovative experimental research done by J. C. Sharman has shown that the worst offenders permitting the sort of corporate secrecy (i.e. lack of transparency) which fuels the financial infrastructure and supply side of corrupt practices and money laundering are the United States and EU countries. By contrast, the relatively smaller, weaker countries which tend to get branded as tax havens, such as the Bahamas or the Seychelles, do much more to comply with financial transparency standards than do the powerful rich countries which push these standards upon others but do not follow them themselves.[45]

All of this suggests that the structuring of the corruption issue around the CPI, in a context of global financial deregulation and initial ideological dominance of neoliberalism (since replaced by a focus on "governance"), was overall quite favorable to multinational business, while facilitating a highly suspicious attitude towards politics, politicians, and public authority. No matter how well-founded such suspicions were, they may have distracted attention from the broader issue of the businesses actually offering bribes, and of a financial infrastructure highly permissive of other sorts of practices that could be construed as being just as corrupt as bribery, namely tax evasion, money laundering, and dubious financial innovations which generated the sorts of systemic risks that brought on the global financial crisis of 2008. Further, it may be that the narrow focus on limiting the discretion of bribe-taking public officials inhibits our capacity to reflect more deeply and critically on the role of money in public life. Finally, rankings like the CPI do nothing to ameliorate the role of power and the hypocrisy of the countries such as the US and the EU member states who display a "do as I say, not as I do" attitude toward financial transparency rules; indeed, by making wealthy countries appear more virtuous than their developing country counterparts, the rankings might distract from the role of power in the world political economy.

Reinforcement

Another line of critique of the CPI rankings approach to corruption has focused on the issue of whether the rankings help to reinforce the

---

[45] Sharman 2011.

existing positions of countries on the scale, thereby enacting something of a self-fulfilling prophecy. Although this argument has a certain logical plausibility, it is difficult to find concrete evidence to either support or undercut it. Andersson and Heywood have suggested that the CPI has helped to create a "corruption trap" for poor countries, which reinforces their inferior position on the scale, as they are viewed over time as bad investments and are thus unable to muster the resources to make the governance changes needed to alter their ranking. This is a plausible argument if governments must now demonstrate some sort of anti-corruption efforts in order to qualify for foreign aid and loans from multilateral agencies and major donor governments.[46]

In terms of the institutional rhetoric of aid and development leaders like the World Bank and USAID, it is certainly the case that aid, loans, and investment are increasingly being made conditional on improvements in anti-corruption and governance more broadly. USAID has embraced the anti-corruption movement as structured by TI's CPI, including the issues linkages discussed above, and includes anti-corruption and governance issues in its programming.[47] The World Bank has also incorporated anti-corruption in its overall development strategy.[48] Preliminary evaluations of the Bank's strategy provide some, but not unambiguous, evidence for the contention that poor scoring on governance indicators makes a country less likely to receive Bank resources.[49]

These observations should be balanced by an awareness that implementation of governance and anti-corruption conditionality on the ground is difficult and probably highly inconsistent. While some countries may indeed experience a corruption trap in that their CPI position seems to reinforce donors' and investors' unwillingness to commit resources to them, others which score at the bottom of the ranking, such as Afghanistan, nevertheless remain money magnets for reasons having nothing to do with governance and anti-corruption criteria.

Another angle on the reinforcement issue is the question of whether, by focusing on corruption as a problem primarily faced by developing or transitioning countries, the CPI and related indices serve to reinforce the apparently "virtuous" reputation of countries such as Switzerland and Canada, for example. As already suggested above, countries on the

---

[46] Andersson and Heywood 2009.   [47] USAID 2005c.
[48] Independent Evaluation Group 2011.   [49] *Ibid.*

upper end of the CPI certainly tend to be richer, and there may be a self-reinforcing cycle in that. But one way in which global publicity about corruption may have seeped into rich-country discourse is to sully the reputation of politics and politicians in general, even in countries not perceived as particularly corrupt. Michael Atkinson, for example, finds that Canadians view corruption as a much bigger problem in their country than Canada's high (i.e. good) ranking on the CPI would suggest.[50] He argues that this discrepancy is not due to there being more corruption in Canada than the CPI can capture, but rather that Canadians have developed a very dim view of politics, and have come to associate politics *in general* with corruption. I would venture to guess that one might find something similar were one to study the opinions of the US electorate. The construction of corruption as abuse of *public* power, and the accompanying privileging of market mechanisms and economic analysis in studying corruption, may reinforce public attitudes about politics as being in essence a dirty game, even in societies with strong institutions and good quality of government.

Strategic manipulation

Perhaps the most readily identifiable perverse effect of global anti-corruption advocacy, and more generally of the stamp of legitimacy that may come from pursuing an anti-corruption/good governance agenda, is its vulnerability to manipulation by political actors. Anecdotal evidence abounds for the strategic manipulation of anti-corruption campaigns by political actors seeking to shore up their positions and eliminate rivals. In the highly unstable state of Pakistani politics, for example, corruption charges are a routine part of efforts to discredit political rivals.[51] In a power struggle within the African National Congress, South Africa's ruling party, Jacob Zuma faced a leadership challenge in which one of the central contentions of several of his rivals is that he is too weak on corruption.[52] While it is difficult for outsiders to get the full story, the fall of Bo Xilai on

---

[50] Atkinson 2011.
[51] Rahul Jacob and Farhan Bokhari, "Ex-minister elected Pakistani PM," *Financial Times* June 22, 2012.
[52] Andrew England, "South Africa's ANC losing its way," *Financial Times* June 21, 2012.

corruption charges in China was surely not simply about virtuous party officials ferreting out a corrupt player in their midst. A 2011 editorial in India's *Economic and Political Weekly* argued astutely that anti-corruption campaigns facilitated the rise of dangerous populist politics:

> What this caution and call for introspection does is to alert us to the possibility that anti-corruption struggles, under their apparent progressive exterior may be a Trojan Horse for another, more dangerous form of politics, one which has contempt for the vote, mass politics, and democratic institutions.[53]

In Azerbaijan, an opposition journalist decried an anti-corruption campaign as a show designed to please international organizations.[54]

The list of stories is potentially endless, and surely there is an opportunity here for a scholarly study of the political dynamics and consequences, not of corruption per se, but of corruption charges and anti-corruption campaigns, perhaps along the lines suggested by the *Economic and Political Weekly* editorial cited above. By inciting a global "movement" to contain corruption, and by making anti-corruption credentials a ticket to political legitimacy in the eyes of the World Bank and USAID, has TI inadvertently placed a new tool into the arsenal of partisan politics, a tool which might be dangerous, particularly in countries with highly unstable and unconsolidated democratic systems? I think this is a line of thought worth exploring, though it would be entirely unfair to blame the CPI itself for facilitating such manipulation.

Conclusion

The initial launch of the CPI, and the globalization of an anti-corruption discourse, coincided with the rise of a neoliberal agenda of shrinking government interference in the operation of markets. Even with neoliberalism on the wane, replaced by a more robust "governance" agenda spearheaded by the World Bank, the CPI continues to facilitate the structuring of the corruption issue as one primarily affecting developing countries, and requiring the monitoring and constraining of public officials. Combined with the practice of ranking according

---

[53] "The Anti-Corruption Crusade: there is reason to be despondent and not optimistic about the current anti-corruption campaign," August 20, 2011.

[54] "Outspoken journalist chides anti-corruption 'show' of Azeri government," BBC Monitoring Trans Caucasus Unit May 22, 2011.

to CPI, the neoliberal agenda served to narrow the scope of anti-corruption discourse, rendering it on balance hostile to politics (or at least hostile to the discretion of politicians) and favorable to the notion that market forces could be counted on to efficiently allocate resources, and that market competition could reduce corruption.

The 1997 Asian Financial Crisis was an important turning point because in its aftermath some scholars, as well as a few analysts within the IFIs themselves, began to question the wisdom of neoliberal pre-scriptions, especially the notion that too much regulation provided more opportunities for corruption and thus undermined financial sta-bility and hindered development. The mutually reinforcing relationship between neoliberalism and anti-corruption was most deeply under-mined by the global financial crisis of 2008. It was then that the "state capture" argument which had been a part of the analysis of developing country corruption began to be redirected at the wealthy countries of the capitalist core, most notably in a popular *Atlantic* article by former IMF economist Simon Johnson, who argued that regulatory agencies in the advanced democracies had themselves experienced "state capture" – which is really another term for corruption.

The 2008 financial crisis, as well as the European sovereign debt crisis that has followed on its heels, have shaken up some of the unex-amined assumptions and explicit hypotheses that have long been used to keep the beam of anti-corruption scrutiny focused primarily on the "developing world." These assumptions and hypotheses include: the tendency to define corruption primarily as bribery of public officials; the idea that limiting the discretion of government officials by shrink-ing the scope of government regulation reduces corruption; the notion that privatization and the unleashing of market forces produces competition, which reduces corruption; the belief that democratic competition reduces corruption; and the hypothesis that regulatory harmonization reduces opportunities for corruption.[55] In short, anti-corruption efforts can no longer be comfortably subsumed within a neoliberal agenda.

This is especially evident if one takes into account the major differ-ences regarding how corruption was "read" as a contributing cause of the East Asian crisis of 1997. While the East Asian crisis reinforced,

---

[55] Warner 2007; Johnston 2005.

however wrongly, the notion in the West that the most problematic and destabilizing types of corruption primarily occurred in non-Western states – especially the vilification of Asian "crony capitalism"[56] – the aftermath of the crisis, which included clear evidence of the failure of neoliberal prescriptions and, alternatively, the possibility that previously frowned-upon measures such as capital controls might be applied successfully by governments, proved a prelude to the much bigger shock of 2008, when the "core" was exposed as being as crisis-prone as the periphery and semi-periphery.

Even if corruption rankings no longer seem to reinforce the "clean" image of the wealthier countries, they still seem to be reinforcing the bad image of the poorer, lower-ranking countries, though the evidence that this makes any difference to levels of investment could be tough to find. Beyond this, the manner in which the corruption issue has been globally structured may continue to perpetuate the view that politics is dirty everywhere, basically by definition. So although we have shaken off the neoliberal agenda to some extent, it is far from clear that the subsequent "governance" agenda has developed a more nuanced view of politics and public life. Politics is still very much in the service of economics. Further, under some conditions anti-corruption campaigns, and corruption charges, become useful political tools in the battle for electoral power, further reinforcing the impression that politics is a dirty game. In the meantime it is still a challenge to sustain a focus on the permissive context of a global financial architecture which provides the dirt – money – that makes politics so dirty.

Although the CPI still gets plenty of attention (there is even a CPI app!) and works well as a branding device for TI, the index no longer enjoys a monopoly as the leading symbol of a global anti-corruption effort; alternative approaches to addressing the problem of corruption have emerged and gained traction both within the TI "family" of products and initiatives, and outside it. To TI's credit, it has worked with other organizations and initiated projects to amplify its advocacy and broaden its approach to corruption. Ranking countries on a single scale of corruption is becoming an increasingly tenuous proposition as cultural differences have reasserted themselves, particularly in Asia but also in Latin America and indeed around the world. The focus on public officials enshrined in CPI's definition of corruption is being

---

[56] Hall 2003.

supplemented by renewed calls to address business practices. Such organizations and campaigns as the Extractive Industries Transparency Initiative (EITI), the Financial Action Task Force, the Global Financial Integrity Project, the Financial Transparency Coalition, the Association for Accountancy and Business Affairs Offshore Watch, Global Integrity, the World Bank's Governance Indicators project, and TI's own Global Corruption Barometer survey and Bribe Payers Index have begun to push global anti-corruption efforts beyond a process focused on ranking states according to a single scale, as engendered by the annual CPI ranking. Thus, anti-corruption advocacy is changing and moving beyond the CPI. What is important is the possibility that corruption issues are being re-defined in such a way as to get at problems which were obscured by the CPI, especially problems having to do with the resource curse, offshore financial centers, capital flight from developing countries, "capture" by financial interests of wealthy-country regulatory agencies, and the continuing complicity of rich-country multinationals in facilitating corruption and lack of transparency, not only in the "developing" world but within their own home political systems and institutions.[57] Re-definition of a problem is not a solution, but it can be construed as progress.

[57] Warner 2007.

4 Measuring stateness, ranking political orders

Indices of state fragility and state failure

NEHAL BHUTA

Introduction

In this chapter, I examine two different indices of state failure or state fragility: one produced annually by the US-based NGO Fund for Peace and published in *Foreign Policy* magazine, and the other produced annually by the United States Agency for International Development (USAID) but made available only to US government agencies.

I begin with some reflections on the emergence of the concepts of state failure and state fragility over the last twenty years, and the deep definitional difficulties inherent in these concepts. I argue that the definitional problems are not resolved but rather amplified by a turn to quantification, which generates highly prescriptive conceptions of state-ness that may bear little or no relationship to the empirical phenomena which the indices purport to measure. Moreover, the definitional problems create further, and irresolvable, problems of specification when attempting to identify proxies to measure unobservable concepts such as "political legitimacy." The result are measures which are in fact standards of a certain kind, predicated on a highly idealized concept of the state which is itself the product of a particular historical trajectory. The state failure and fragility indices take this historical type as the measure of state-ness, perhaps exemplifying the role of RROs as "judges," "regulators," and "sources of governmentality" set out by Cooley in chapter 1.

The exact consequences of these kinds of indices on government decision-making remain to be studied empirically. But I argue below that both their validity (in terms of conceptual specification) and reliability (in terms of aggregation of disparate data sets) are highly tenuous, instantiating almost all of the most serious methodological problems identified by Cooley and Snyder. Yet the question remains why such measures continue to attract attention and are of interest to policymakers and others. I cannot offer a conclusive answer to this question, but suggest that their attractiveness lies in part in their ability to simplify and make possible judgments about social and political reality on vast scales. Even if the rankings themselves are of dubious validity, there seems to be an increasing demand for such synoptic and panoramic judgments and numerical artifacts, emerging from the post-9/11 understanding of non-state actor security threats as rooted in failures of governance and state effectiveness. "Snapshot" understandings of the kind made possible by rankings and ratings seem to fulfill a demand for a certain kind of "distributed cognition" made imperative by the scales and scope of authority and decision-making under conditions of globalization and global governance (see Cooley and Snyder, this volume).

Failed, failing, or fragile states: A prototype in search of a definition

The concept of "failed," "failing," or "fragile" states has become ubiquitous. The failing or fragile state is referred to as a source of grave security threats,[1] as a particularly challenging context for development assistance,[2] and as an impediment to the achievement of human development goals. The term "failed state" appears to have emerged in the early 1990s and was used in reference to dramatic cases of state collapse, generally occasioned by severe internal conflict. Indeed, one of the earliest attempts to measure the incidence of state failure – George Mason University's State Failure Task Force – took events such as revolutionary war, regime change, and genocide as instances of state failure. A paradigmatic failed state in this understanding was the former Yugoslavia, Rwanda, Somalia, or Afghanistan (1992–96), where severe conflict meant that no governing authority had effective control over the territory. Obviously, such circumstances are associated with a variety of crises which would be of concern to the international community: forced displacement and refugee flows, violations of humanitarian law and international criminal law, massive destruction of human and physical

---

[1] National Security Council (NSC) 2002: 1; NSC 2006: 37, 44; NSC 2010: 8, 11, 13.

[2] Robert Schuman Centre 2009: 12; UK Department for International Development 2005; United States Agency for International Development (USAID) 2005a; and OECD Development Assistance Committee 2008.

capital, and possible "ungoverned spaces," which might become operational homes to terrorist organizations or conduits for transborder flows of people, drugs, and weapons.

The externalities associated with situations of complete state collapse appear to have triggered an interest in understanding the correlates and preconditions for such situations. It is unclear when notions such as "weak" or "fragile" states emerged as significant concepts, but in September 2002 the United States' National Security Strategy referred to "failing" states as a threat to US security, connoting a set of states which have not yet failed, but are at risk of doing so. In Robert Rotberg's influential article in *Foreign Affairs* in the same year,[3] the author differentiates between "strong," "weak," and "failed" states and argues that there are observable pathways by which states move from one of these conditions to another. Similarly, Krasner and Pascual refer to "weak and failed" states, while the UK's National Security Strategy discusses "failed and fragile" states.[4]

In the context of development assistance, DFID, USAID, and the OECD's Development Assistance Committee (DAC) began referring to "fragile states" from 2004. From 2002, the World Bank labeled certain countries as "low income countries under stress" (LICUS), based on a poor rating in the annual Country Policy and Institutional Assessment (CPIA). The LICUS category has been replaced by "fragile states," which includes a subset of "post-conflict countries." In the development assistance context, the classification of states as "fragile" was directly or indirectly connected with judgments concerning aid allocation. Where allocation was performance-based, certain countries facing severe internal conflict or its immediate aftermath were unlikely to meet performance-based goals for aid eligibility, and yet were in desperate need of development assistance. Thus, in order to accommodate these countries' specific needs for assistance, "fragile states were first identified ... as countries where Performance Based Allocation should not apply ... the answer was then to give [these countries] a specific treatment for effectiveness or security reasons."[5] A state deemed fragile may also be designated for particular kinds of assistance and aid programming, such as access to a special World Bank Trust Fund and the provision of incentives to Bank staff to work in these countries.

[3] Rotberg 2002.   [4] Krasner and Pascual 2005; Cabinet Office 2008: 13, 14.
[5] Guillaumont and Guillaumont Jeanneney 2009: 4.

These two different contexts for the assessment of whether a state is "failing," "failed," or "fragile" have engendered two somewhat distinct imperatives for mechanisms to identify and measure such concepts. One purpose of measurement is to identify that group of countries eligible for special kinds of development assistance, or which should be considered for exceptions to performance-based allocation. The other purpose of measurement is to identify countries at risk of generating security threats, developing zones of ungovernability, or suffering from severe internal conflict – and thus warranting special scrutiny, multilateral diplomatic action, or other responses.

Definitions of state failure and fragility

Despite the ubiquity of the terms "failed," "failing," and "fragile," there is no consensus on the meaning of these concepts, or how to measure the extent to which a state is fragile or failing. Indeed, under these conditions, the process of constructing the measure also becomes an exercise in defining the concept to be measured. There is some degree of convergence, at a high level of generality, concerning what the notion of state failure or state fragility is *believed to be associated with*. That is, most explications of the concepts involve descriptions of the *kinds of symptoms* characteristic of a state which is deemed fragile or failing. Definitions are "prototypical."

In the various definitions, the kinds of symptoms which are said to be characteristic of state failure and state fragility include: illegitimate or ineffective government; the absence of the rule of law; lack of political will or capacity to deliver basic public goods such as border control, crime prevention, and essential services; lack of will or capacity of the government to provide functions needed for development, poverty reduction, and human rights; a "broken social contract" between state and society or a poor "state–society relationship."

The UK's National Security Strategy defines a "failed state" as one whose "government is not effective or legitimate enough to maintain the rule of law, protect itself, its citizens and its borders, or provide the most basic services," and a "fragile state" as "one in which those problems are likely to arise."[6] The *Fragile States Strategy* of USAID describes fragile states as

---

[6] Cabinet Office 2008: 13.

the product of ineffective and illegitimate governance ... Effectiveness refers to the capability of the government to work with society to assure the provision of order and public goods and services. Legitimacy refers to the perception by important segments of society that the government is exercising state power in ways that are reasonably fair and in the interests of the nation as a whole. Where both effectiveness and legitimacy are weak, conflict or state failure is likely to occur.[7]

The OECD DAC defines states as fragile

when state structures lack political will and/or capacity to provide the basic functions needed for poverty reduction, development and to safeguard the security and human rights of their populations.[8]

The Council of the European Union defines fragility as referring to

weak or failing structures and to situations where the social contract is broken due to the state's incapacity or unwillingness to deal with its basic functions, meet its obligations and responsibilities regarding the rule of law, protection of human rights and fundamental freedoms, security and safety of its population, poverty reduction, service delivery, the transparent and equitable management of resources and access to power.[9]

Among academic writers and think tanks, the definition of failed, failing, and fragile states tends to be more expansive, and involves (sometimes quite lengthy) lists of qualities said to correspond to state failure. Rotberg describes failed states in contrast to strong states.[10] Strong states are "places of peace and order," which

control their territories and deliver a high order of political goods to their citizens ... Strong states offer high levels of security from political and criminal violence, ensure political freedom and civil liberties, and create environments conducive to the growth of economic opportunity. Failed [and presumably, fragile] states are tense, conflicted and dangerous. They have some or all of the following characteristics, depending on where they lie on the spectrum between failed and fragile (or failed, weak, and strong):
- A rise in criminal and political violence
- A loss of control over their borders
- Rising ethnic, religious, linguistic, and cultural hostilities
- Civil war
- Use of terror against their own citizens

[7] USAID 2005a: 3.   [8] OECD DAC 2007: 2.
[9] Council of the European Union 2007.   [10] Rotberg 2002.

- Weak institutions
- A deteriorated infrastructure
- Inability to collect taxes without undue coercion
- High levels of corruption
- A collapsed health system
- Rising levels of infant mortality and declining life expectancy
- The end of regular schooling opportunities
- Declining levels of GDP per capita
- Escalating inflation
- Widespread preference for non-national currencies
- Basic food shortages.

RAND describes failed states as those which "typically suffer from cycles of violence, economic breakdown, and unfit governments that render them unable to relieve their people's suffering, much less empower them."[11] Brookings (as a prelude to their attempt to measure state weakness) defines weak states as "countries that lack the essential capacity and/or will to fulfill four sets of critical government responsibilities: fostering an environment conducive to sustainable and equitable growth; establishing and maintaining legitimate, transparent and accountable political institutions; securing their populations from violent conflict and controlling their territory; and meeting the basic human needs of their population."[12] The US Fund for Peace (USFfP) (which authors the Failed States Index [FSI]) describes weak and failing states as having "common attributes. These include loss of physical control over territory, lack of monopoly on the use of force, declining legitimacy to make authoritative decisions for the majority of the community, an inability to provide security or social services to its people, and, frequently, a lack of capacity to act as a full member of the international community."[13]

The limits of symptomatic definitions

A common feature of all of these definitions is that they derive the meaning of state failure and fragility from its symptoms but are vague in the specification of relationships between symptoms and causes (or between symptoms and underlying illness). Does poor governance

---

[11] Haims, Gompert, Treverton, and Stearns 2008: xi.
[12] Rice and Patrick 2006: 3.
[13] Baker 2007: 90. (Baker is President of the US Fund for Peace.)

cause conflict or does conflict cause poor governance? Under most of the above concepts of state weakness, we would answer "both," but as a result the concept of state weakness is not adding much to our understanding of either parameter (conflict or governance). Is a poorly governed state weak even if it is not prone to internal conflict? The above definitions occasionally allude to or mention causal pathways from fragility to failure (such as USAID's definition), but most do not. As such, it is unclear whether the concept of state fragility and failure could ever avoid significant over-determination. It is equally unclear whether the concepts can be analytically useful except as a shorthand for describing a collection of associated phenomena, without being able to assign weight to the relative significance of a given symptom in hastening or restraining failure. If the primary function of the terms is as a categorical shorthand, their utility will be greatest for identifying and labeling members of the set of fragile and failing states (defined stipulatively as exhibiting the symptoms set out above) in need of special attention or development assistance.

But the terms' utility as a means of differentiating between different degrees of weakness (which presupposes some capacity to differentiate the relative role and impact of specific symptoms in driving failure within the set of weak states) seems limited. One related question which arises is whether the concept *over-aggregates* distinct social and political problems, and so obscures our understanding of specific relationships between symptoms and causes (and the possible trade-offs in addressing them). Some scholars make this claim, questioning the utility of the concept for understanding the drivers of conflict and how to address them.[14]

A second important commonality is that each of these definitions includes notions of the legitimacy, effectiveness, and capacity of the state as critical dimensions of the state's strength or weakness/fragility. Several definitions also refer to the "will" of the state to provide certain goods and services to its population. These terms are latent or unobservable concepts. No consensus exists on how to measure them or which proxies reliably capture these phenomena, if any. Similarly, the kinds of legitimacy, effectiveness, and capacity which augment or diminish the fragility of the state are themselves subject to argument.[15] The exact relationship between a particular kind of legitimacy and the

[14] See Newman 2009; Call 2011.   [15] See, for example, OECD 2010.

strength and weakness of a state is not specified in most of the definitions, although some refer to democratic legitimacy.

Among the more foundational critiques of the concept of fragile and failing states is that the concept assimilates many problems of security with problems of development, and too broadly associates security risks with a lack of development.[16] The critique here is twofold. First, there is the claim that the "securitization of development" shifts the focus towards development initiatives which are believed to contain or manage security risks, and thus may skew development funding priorities. There is also the danger that developmental problems within a territory are artificially placed in the framework of "security" in order to attract more funding. Second, the bundling of development, governance, and security under the "metaconcept" of state fragility incentivizes deeper and more intensive forms of intervention in the developing world, and thereby promotes a "civilizing mission" that may be both unrealistic and detrimental in the long term.[17] It also encourages a hierarchy of sovereignty, in which states classified as failing or failed are deemed incapable or unwilling of exercising the prerogatives of sovereign equality and thus are (or should be) less entitled to international legal protections against the use of force and intervention.[18] Other academic writings also contest the extent to which state weakness and so-called "ungoverned spaces" are empirically more likely to foster or become home to terrorist groups.[19]

The concept of the state found in the fragility/failure literature is predicated on a highly particular image of the state, an ideal type of the state form which is sometimes termed "Weberian." In this ideal type, the state is a unified and coherent actor, set apart from other social organizations and sources of social power. Through its officials, the state has its own preferences and can act on those preferences in order to change the behavior of others. The state enacts its domination through a uniform set of rules, backed by a credible threat of violence.[20] At least for some Western European states, this

---

[16] See Adibe 1994; Duffield 2001 and 2008; Ikpe 2007.   [17] See Duffield 2008.
[18] For an example of a recent paper which argues that the challenge of failing and failed states requires the revision of norms of sovereign equality, see Yoo 2010.
[19] See Newman 2007; Call 2008: 29.
[20] Weber in fact never completed a state theory. His concept of the state is scattered throughout his sociology of law and his omnibus work, *Economy and Society.*

ideal type approximates an historical reality – although even among this relatively small group, variation is substantial throughout recent history.[21]

Importantly, for Weber, this ideal type was not to be understood as a normative or normalizing typification of what qualifies as a 'true' or 'proper' state; rather, an ideal type is an exaggerated abstraction from a particular historical reality, used only to better grasp the features of the phenomenon under analysis.[22] This ideal-typical concept of the state – including the much-cited definition of it as an organization which exercises a monopoly of violence over a territory – was an abstraction that sought to identify a common form of political organization that emerged from a specific European experience. As Migdal and Schlichte observe, 'an ideal-type is not itself a hypothesis, but it allows one to build hypotheses on deviations, variations and totally different forms. Once these differences are noticed, the need for a vocabulary of description and explanation becomes obvious.'[23] To the extent that the ideal type of the state is taken as the measure of state-ness, it becomes a norm rather than a heuristic for the development of explanatory or interpretive accounts of how a given political organization works (or does not work). The crypto-normative quality with which the Weberian ideal type of the state has been imbued in the fragility discourse has meant that deviations from the type are taken as evidence of weaknesses or failures.

Efforts at measurement and indices: The Fund for Peace and USAID

In the early 1990s, the CIA established and funded the State Failure Task Force (later renamed the Political Instability Task Force) to explore methods of risk assessment and early warning systems for state failure.[24] The Polity IV data set generated by this project, which spanned more than a decade, would become an important source for current fragility/failure indices, but it is reported that the Task Force also produced classified models and algorithms which are in use by the CIA to identify lists of countries at risk of instability.[25] After 2001,

---

[21] See, for example, Ertman 1997; and Finer 1975.   [22] Weber 1978: 9, 20–21.
[23] Migdal and Schlichte 2005: 3.   [24] Adler 2001.
[25] Interview with USAID official, July 23, 2010.

there was a proliferation of attempts to measure failure and fragility, and to produce ordered lists.[26]

The claim to be able to quantify degrees of state failure or fragility is seductive. It holds out a promise of greater objectivity and transparency in making judgments about risks of conflict and instability in a given state. It also promises comparability across states in terms of the extent of failure or fragility, notionally allowing judgments to be made about which states should be prioritized for policy attention. But as noted above, a key challenge of measurement is definitional. Definitions of failure or fragility are prototypical in the sense that they identify typical instantiations of strength or failure and derive common characteristics.[27] The fundamental difficulty with prototyping is that "the characteristic traits of the phenomenon are collapsed with putative causes and consequences . . . This is a bit like defining cancer as consisting of smoking, uncontrolled growth of cells, and family crisis."[28] Such prototypical definitions do not specify causal pathways between observed characteristics and fragility or strength, and provide no means to understand the relative role of each characteristic or how they interact with each other temporally, and do not propose how each dimension can be logically assembled into a single notion of strength or weakness. But as Munck and Verkuilen point out, specifying the meaning of a concept and its components "affects the entire process" of measurement, from data generation to aggregation, and conceptualization is intimately linked with theoretical claims about the nature of the phenomenon one is seeking to measure.[29]

In this part of the chapter, I examine two significant indices of state failure or fragility. Among the most visible and widely reported indices of state failure is that produced annually by USFfP, and published in *Foreign Policy*. The Index ranks 177 countries based on an aggregate of their scores on twelve indicators. The higher the aggregate, the greater the purported degree of state failure (and thus the higher the rank of the state on the index). In the 2010 version of the FSI, the top five "failed states" were Somalia, Chad, Sudan, Zimbabwe, and the Democratic Republic of the Congo. According to the USFfP, their website (which hosts the FSI) receives hundreds of thousands of page views a month,[30]

---

[26] I have identified ten lists or rankings of state failure/fragility/weakness in the course of this research.
[27] Sanin 2011: 24.   [28] *Ibid*.   [29] Munck and Verkuilen 2002: 7.
[30] Email correspondence with Mark Loucas, USFfP Program Officer, July 8, 2010.

and there is some evidence that the FSI is becoming regularly cited in academic literature as a relevant measure of state failure.[31] Much less known, but potentially more influential, is USAID's "Alert List" for Conflict and Instability, produced annually from 2006, which ranks 160 countries in order of fragility. The USAID index is not public, but is distributed widely within the US Government. In the 2010 version of the USAID Index, the top five fragile states were Chad, Somalia, the Democratic Republic of the Congo, Guinea, and Sudan. It is noteworthy that there is substantial convergence between these two indices at the "top five." It might be taken as evidence of their robustness, but it is equally indicative of the extent to which prototypical concepts "allow the creation of definitions that fit well cases on the margins of the definitional space – that is, the extreme ones – but not necessarily elsewhere. In other words, it can produce an over-fit to a certain set of situations, but the variables that separate well the extreme cases from others do not necessarily fit more moderate examples."[32] In fact, the two indices follow completely different and non-comparable methodologies, suggesting that any convergence in rankings at the extreme ends of the definitional space may well be a consequence of "over-fit" rather than rigorous conceptualization and measurement.

USFfP's Failed States Index

Unlike all of the other indices referred to above, the FSI's twelve indicators are not based on pre-existing measures. Rather, each country is scored between 1 (best) and 10 (worst) for each of the indicators, based on an assessment conducted internally by USFfP. The twelve indicators for which each state receives a score are as follows:
1. Mounting Demographic Pressures
2. Massive Movement of Refugees or Internally Displaced Persons
3. Legacy of Vengeance-Seeking Group Grievance or Group Paranoia
4. Chronic and Sustained Human Flight
5. Uneven Economic Development Along Group Lines
6. Sharp and/or Severe Economic Decline
7. Criminalization and/or Delegitimization of the State
8. Progressive Deterioration of Public Services

[31] Based on preliminary Google Scholar search.   [32] Sanin 2009.

9. Suspension of the Rule of Law and Widespread Violation of Human Rights
10. Security Apparatus Operates as a State within a State
11. Rise of Factionalized Elites
12. Intervention of Other States or External Political Actors.

The meaning of each of these indicators is subjective. The allocation of a score may be subject to high degrees of variation if not carefully controlled. In other indices which rely on a method of intensity scoring (such the Cingranelli and Richards data set and the Polity IV data set), detailed coding manuals (often over 100 pages in length) are created and coders are trained in the assignment of scores based on conformity of the data source with specific formulae and phrases in the code book. Underlying data sources are kept as homogeneous as possible and more than one coder is assigned to the same source in order to ensure consistency and check for divergences or disputable interpretations. Publication of coding manuals ensures both transparency and replicability.

By contrast, the method by which a state is scored between 1 and 10 on each of the FSI indicators is complex. It is not transparent and it is not replicable. No detailed instructions for the interpretation or application of the descriptive terms contained in the indicators are provided publicly.[33] The score is allocated by an incompletely explained combination of qualitative and quantitative methods.

The process as a whole is referred to by USFfP as the "Conflict Assessment System Tool" (CAST), and the software used in the process has been successfully patented.[34] The process begins with the CAST software conducting specified Boolean searches of a mixed data source combining news reports, policy documents, and other materials collected for USFfP. The material is provided to USFfP in English, although USFfP contends that the sources include material "originating from 110 countries in 50 languages."[35] The number and variation of

---

[33] A "ratings guide" and a document entitled "Indicators and their Measures" can be found on the USFfP website, but these do not amount to code books. They provide more detailed descriptions of what is meant by some of the terms in the twelve indicators, but these descriptions add new layers of interpretative uncertainty to how the scores are derived from the underlying data.

[34] January 2, 2003; US 2003/0004954A1.

[35] "The CAST Methodology: Its Use in Producing the Failed State Index." The Fund for Peace, no date.

Boolean searches conducted for each indicator is unclear, although the USFfP explains that for each of the twelve indicators there is a subset of "measures," each of which has a specific search string.[36] The reliability of the sources available for each country in the index is evaluated by the software, through a "computation of the difference in information from the source compared to the same category of information reported from a core of five world sources that include the CIA, NY Times, CNN, BBC and NPR."[37]

The output of the search strings is combined with existing statistical measures which are deemed relevant to the level of the indicator.[38] It is unclear how these numbers are aggregated with numbers of generated hits by the Boolean search process. It appears that the CAST software produces a score from the content analysis and aggregates this with baseline quantitative measures associated with the indicator. The software also produces an estimate of how much this indicator has improved or deteriorated since the previous year.

Parameters of a country's scores are set by taking the number of hits generated through Boolean searches and dividing that number by the sample size (documents per time period per country). The number thus generated is known as the "salience." A "10" for that indicator is set by reference to the worst salience for that country since 1960. For example, in the case of Rwanda, 1994 would be a "10" for the indicator labeled "Legacy of Vengeance-Seeking Group." The intensity of content generated by the relevant Boolean searches for Rwanda for 1994 would thus represent a "10," and all other results could be scaled against this maximum.

The indicator value which is generated in this manner is then reviewed by an analyst, who has formed his own view about whether the indicator has improved or deteriorated for the country in question since the last year. The analyst is an in-house analyst, who is trained in the CAST software.[39] However, it is not clear whether the analysts are substantively country experts. According to USFfP, there are

---

[36] *Ibid.*   [37] Patent Application Publication, p. 3.

[38] By way of example: for Indicator 1, the following quantitative sources are also consulted in forming a view: Proportion of population under 15, Population undernourished (UNDP), Life expectancy at birth, Population annual growth rate, Infant mortality (WHO). Email correspondence with Mark Loucas, July 21, 2010.

[39] Correspondence with Nate Haken, USFfP, July 2010.

fifteen analysts for 177 countries. Initially, outside country experts were used to check country scores, but this practice was discontinued because the experts were not "socialized" into the methods of the index.[40]

Where the analyst's judgment concerning the score and the degree of change of the score is at odds with the software-generated number, there is a process of review and reconciliation. The steps in this process and the criteria for adjusting a score upward or downward are unknown, but seem to rely heavily on the analyst's "feel" for the country situation based on several years of maintaining the index. The results are said to be "peer-reviewed," but it appears that this means that results are reviewed by other in-house analysts, not submitted to academic experts for external review.

A further adjustment in the score may be brought about by an events-sensitive assessment of recent developments. This assessment is supposed to capture "surprises, triggers, idiosyncrasies, national temperaments and spoilers." The software is pre-programmed with incidences that comprise these kinds of events for a particular country, and the events will be allocated a score between 0 and 5 by "country experts" (who also determine which indicators are affected by its occurrence). If the event occurs, the software will adjust the score of the affected indicators.

The indicator score may also be affected by an additional measure of the representativeness, legitimacy, and professionalism of institutions deemed to constitute the "immutable core" of a state, namely:

1. A competent domestic police force and corrections system
2. An efficient and functioning civil service
3. An independent judicial system
4. A professional and disciplined military accountable to civilian authority
5. A capable leadership.

How the evaluation of the legitimacy, representativeness, and professionalism of these five institutions is undertaken is not explained. The evaluation does not have a direct impact on indicator scores, but becomes part of the "country profile," which helps set a baseline for the allocation of scores.

[40] Interview with Nate Haken, USFfP, July 20, 2010.

The final score of a country, and the determinant of its overall rank in the index, is the aggregate of the twelve indicator scores. The higher the number, the more severe the degree of state failure. However, it should be observed that, due to the numerous points in the process at which the basis for aggregation of different kinds of data is not verifiable, it is doubtful whether the indicator levels for each country are truly comparable. Or at least, the basis for comparability is uncertain. Comparability is further complicated by what seems to be an inherently relative scoring standard, in which a "10" for a particular state may be determined by reference to specific historical examples representing a nadir for state failure for that state. As such, the ordinal ranking – which generates so much attention for the index – may be of little or no validity as a measure of *degrees* of state failure.

Another implication is that the number generated by the scoring and ranking is a poor signal for the nature of the problems facing a particular country: without considerable additional context and country-specific knowledge understanding the difference between an "8" and a "6" on a given indicator is impossible. Indeed, in light of the questions arising about the transparency and reliability of the scoring, it is far from clear that anything is actually being "measured."

The producers of the FSI and the CAST software emphasize that of greater interest is the generation of trend lines concerning changes in the level of stability of a state (as measured by the values assigned to the twelve indicators). These trend lines, according to the authors, allow some measure of early warning of states at risk of intensifying conflict and deteriorating stability.[41] USFfP does not claim that the FSI and CAST can predict state failure or state collapse. However, it does claim that they are tools for "diagnosing the risk of violence in weak and failing states."[42]

Apart from the FSI, USFfP generates a variety of knowledge products which it makes available on a commercial basis. It licenses its CAST software and provides training to use it. It provides client-specific country profiles and conflict assessments, but does not disclose its clients. It also provides "real time" updates in the form of alerts and notifications for developments in specific countries. It seems that these are also provided to clients for a price. Country profiles are available for free on their website. These short documents provide an

[41] Baker 2006: v.   [42] *Ibid.*

explanation of the country's FSI score and shed some light on how the
score changed from the previous year.

USAID's Fragility and Risk for Instability rankings

USAID's definition of fragility emphasizes "legitimacy" and "effectiveness" of the government of a state as the essential dimensions of its
strength or fragility. Measuring fragility therefore required creators of
its index to render countable qualities of a political order that are
inherently unobservable and uncountable. Proxies had to be determined for each of these terms, based on theories about how a certain
countable phenomenon (such as infant mortality or economic growth)
was to be understood as representing a dimension of an uncountable
property, such as legitimacy. Indeed, the very definitions of legitimacy
and effectiveness required theoretical foundations, in order to articulate their claimed relationship with another non-observable term,
"state strength" (or state weakness).

In a strategy paper written for USAID as part of the creation of the
Index,[43] the strength or weakness of a state is defined in terms of the
legitimacy and effectiveness of its *institutions*, especially those institutions charged with "the management of conflict." A strong state is one
which successfully creates and maintains "the institutional mechanisms
of 'neutral ground,'" which is composed of "those elements of the social
life of the country that are *non-partisan* in ways relevant to the social
conditions of that country, and which contain a range of *neutral legitimating factors such as legality, erudition and technical or professional
competence.*"[44] The "neutral ground" that characterizes state strength is
thus *composed* of – identified with – the presence of institutions posses-
sing certain qualities of effectiveness and legitimacy, which are in turn
associated with features such as legality and technocratic competence.

These are clearly associative or correlative definitions, and causalities could run in either direction.[45] They are also prototypical

---

[43] Goldstone *et al.* 2004.   [44] Goldstone *et al.* 2004: 5–6 (my emphasis).
[45] *Ibid.*: 8. Additional glosses on the meaning of effectiveness and legitimacy are
provided in the document. Effectiveness is defined as "the degree to which a state
has the administrative capability and resources to carry out the tasks of governance," where governance includes "a disciplined military and bureaucracy"
and "intelligence and administrative capability." Legitimacy is further described
as "rulers being judged – by both elites and popular groups – as being reasonably
fair and just in their exercise of power."

definitions, as noted above. In their attempt to "operationalize" the concepts of "effectiveness" and "legitimacy" in order to render them useful for the assessment of state fragility, the strategy paper authors develop a four row by two column accounting matrix, in which rows represent "four dimensions of state-society relations: political . . .; economic . . .; social . . .; and security," while the columns represent effectiveness and legitimacy for each of these dimensions. An assessment of a state's fragility entails gathering evidence of the effectiveness and legitimacy of the state's political, economic, social, and security functioning and evaluating this evidence against a benchmark of state strength.

The accounting matrix, with its four-by-two enumeration of dimensions of effectiveness and legitimacy, would become a template for developing measures of fragility that would serve as inputs into the Index. A way had to be found to quantify each of eight possible dimensions of effectiveness and legitimacy,[46] rendering them *countable* and so susceptible to aggregation in a one-dimensional rank ordering. Countability requires that data be found or created which successfully measures the phenomena in question. Where the phenomena (however well specified) are unobservable, it is necessary to resort to proxies which can be observed and counted, implying a theory of the relationship between the proxy and the attributes of the underlying concept. Counting is always reasoning.

Analytically, concepts such as political legitimacy or social legitimacy are not well specified in the sense that their stipulated attributes are themselves unobservable. For example, political legitimacy is defined as "political institutions and processes that are transparent, respect societal values, and do not favor particular groups."[47] Each of these terms is non-self-evident, and what might qualify as a measure of each of these attributes is unclear, requiring further disaggregation and conceptualization. Moreover, each of the attributes of political legitimacy is difficult to logically distinguish from attributes of other dimensions of legitimacy, such as social legitimacy or security legitimacy. The former is defined as "tolerance for diversity, including opportunities for groups to practice . . . cultures and beliefs," while the latter is defined as "military and police services that are provided equitably and without violation of civil rights." The problem with logically

---

[46] USAID 2005b.   [47] *Ibid.*: 2.

non-exclusive definitions of attributes of unobservable variables such as political legitimacy is *redundancy* and *conflation*.[48] How do we know that a measure of tolerance is not also a measure of respect for societal values? If we do not know, how can we avoid problems of double counting, or inaccurate differentiation between two measures of the same underlying phenomenon? The analytical difficulties of conceptualization in fact point to the deep difficulty of measurement of multidimensional characteristics such as legitimacy, a difficulty that is at once compounded and made less visible where measures are aggregated into a one-dimensional number, as in an index.

Conceptual problems of this kind are aggravated in the attempt to identify proxies which can be used as observable data representing unobservable phenomena. Given that definitional problems remain severe, it is a puzzle how proxies could be determined: how could one differentiate between good and bad proxies for a concept, when the concept itself is not well specified? The creators of the USAID Index sidestepped this puzzle by *substituting the proxy for the concept*. Instead of identifying measures that successfully capture attributes of the concepts they sought to measure, the creators identified preexisting indicators which they contended measured political, social, economic, and security *outcomes or perceptions*, and maintained that these outcomes or perceptions *amounted to* measurements of the eight dimensions of effectiveness and legitimacy decomposed by the accounting matrix.

Definitions of effectiveness and legitimacy developed by the strategy paper were thus decoupled from the identification of measures, with an emphasis instead on where "good data" could be found that could conceivably be related to the measurement of effectiveness and legitimacy. The result is a bricolage of data sets chosen because of their coverage, frequency of updating, assumed credibility of their source, and some notion of robustness. But the critical question of how and why the outcome or perception data is in fact a measure of the unobservable variable is answered only with the introduction of further, diverse, theoretical and factual claims.

For example, among the proxies chosen to measure "political effectiveness" is the government effectiveness indicator generated by the World Bank's Governance Matters data set, based on an aggregation of

---

[48] See Munck and Verkuilen 2002: 12.

surveys of *perceptions* of the quality of public service. The rationale for choosing this as a component measure of political effectiveness is that "the quality of public service provision is a good, directly observable outcome of effective governments."[49] Yet, the quality of public service provision is not at all directly observable, which is why the Governance Matters data set relies on subjective perception surveys to develop a measure.[50] The relationship between perception and reality is taken as linear and direct by the USAID Index, whereas it has been commonly observed that it is difficult to know what underlying quality is being measured by such surveys: "Are they really making judgments about the quality of governance and particular institutions, or are they implicitly answering the question, 'how do you think things are going today in country X (perhaps compared implicitly to countries in the region)?"[51] Because the concept of "political effectiveness" remains underspecified for the USAID Index, we cannot begin to determine how this indicator *could* be theorized as a component measure of this dimension or what weight to give it.

The USAID Index identified thirty-three outcome indicators claimed to measure effectiveness and legitimacy across political, security, economic, and social dimensions. Each of these indicators suffers from one of the two difficulties described above: it is a subjective perception index, with an erroneous assumption that perception stands in a linear relationship to reality, rather than at best a very "noisy" approximation of complex trends; or, it equates a policy measure with an outcome, or assumes that outcome data reflects effective policy.[52] But in all cases, the relationship between the indicator and higher-order variable of effectiveness or legitimacy is dubious, both because the concepts of effectiveness and legitimacy are poorly specified, and because the arguments made for why the indicator adequately measures these terms are unsubstantiated. The result is a collection of indicators drawn from a large variety of data sets with widely disparate methodologies, which *stand in for* rather than measure concepts of effectiveness and legitimacy. The numbers *become* the concepts rather than represent

---

[49] USAID 2005b: 6.   [50] See Fearon 2010: 27.

[51] *Ibid.*: 28. See also Williams and Siddique 2008; Skaaning 2010.

[52] The latter assumption may be more plausible in the case of infant mortality or literacy, which the Index counts as a measure of "social effectiveness" of a state: see, for discussion, King and Zeng 2001: 652.

or approximate them, creating a misleading impression that analytical problems of specification, commensuration, and aggregation
have been resolved because all inputs now appear as equivalent
quantities.

Of the data sets relied upon by USAID to generate index inputs,
some are regarded as well settled, already widely in use and "hard"
enough to stand in as real measurements of the phenomena they
purport to measure, and not something else. Others remain much
more controversial, and the relationship between measure and refer-
ent is regularly contested. By summarizing data from these data sets in
a one-number-per-country manner, the USAID Index works to absorb
and erase the uncertainty surrounding the data and what it measures.
This is perhaps most clear in the reliance on data sets that purport to
measure the quality of governance, extent of discrimination, human
rights abuse, and regime type. The governance indicators are already
aggregations of a large number of subjective perception surveys, and
as noted above, it is difficult to determine whether each underlying
survey measures institutional quality or some more vague set of
perceptions.[53] The Index also uses indicators derived from the
Minorities at Risk, Polity IV, and Political Terror Scale to measure
discrimination, regime type, and human rights abuses, respectively.
Like the USAID Index into which they are aggregated, each of these
data sets attempts to count inherently uncountable, qualitative phenomena. In order to do so, each relies on elaborate coding processes
whereby a coder allocates a number (0 or 1, 0–2, 0–10, 0–5, depending on the data set) based on his or her interpretation of qualitative
information ("content analysis") about the political and social circumstances in the relevant state, or based on whether a given event
has taken place (e.g. a military coup) in a given year. Vast swathes of
history and politics across numerous, heterogeneous political orders
are thus made commensurate and transformed into a number *rating*
of the country situation.

Reliability, in the sense of complete identity between information
and ratings across different coders, is never achieved. But even where
very high levels of consistency (above 90 percent) are achieved, fundamental uncertainties remain as to what a given rating actually represents in terms of a state's political and social reality. One obstacle is

[53] Fearon 2010: 28.

endogeneity, as described by Fearon in relation to data sets coding discrimination:

these measures of political exclusion and discrimination are based on the subjective judgments of diverse coders, trying to code somewhat impressionistic things. Countries where there has been no ethnic conflict and where ethnic relations have been calm are for that reason judged to have [little] exclusion ... one can reasonably worry that a coder's knowledge that there was an ethnic conflict in a country increases the probability that he or she judges that ... groups were discriminated against or politically excluded.[54]

McCormick and Mitchell note that even where a good level of reliability is achieved in coding human rights violations, there is a basic problem of the *meaning* of a given rating:

human rights violations differ in type not just amount, such that they cannot be clearly represented on a single scale. Imprisonment and torture are different types of government activity [involving] differing uses of governmental resources and capabilities, and differing costs for the government ... Regimes use different mixes of methods of political control, a variation missed by a one-dimensional scale.[55]

Cingranelli, one of the authors of a major human rights scale, concludes that, due to inadequacies in the consistency of underlying data quality and availability, a human rights scale is not reliable beyond three or four categories, and ought not be used to derive an ordinal ranking.[56]

The key point here is not that these various attempts to develop cross-national data sets of political qualia are necessarily meaningless; rather it is that we cannot readily reach conclusions about what they mean, or what a higher or lower number within a data set represents in terms of the "effectiveness and legitimacy" of a state. Yet global scale indices such as the USAID Index perform a further *aggregation of*

---

[54] *Ibid.*: 16.

[55] McCormick and Mitchell 1997: 513–514. In relation to the Polity IV data set, Gleditsch and Ward note, "Categorical data encompass a small number of subdimensions that interact in non-obvious ways ... Data are multipath – there is a wide variety of ways in which polities can receive a single scale value. Vastly different temporal, spatial and social contexts support the same democracy and autocracy scale values" (Gleditsch and Ward 1997: 380).

[56] Cingranelli and Richards 2010: 406, 408. The Political Terror Scale, used by the USAID Index, has five categories and purports to measure human rights "conditions" rather than the narrower "practices."

aggregations: the interpretive ambiguity, noisiness, uncertainty, and measurement error which are an inherent part of each of these data sets are simply erased through addition into a single score. Espeland and Stevens note March and Simon's description of the way in which uncertainty is absorbed as information travels upward within an organization:

"Raw" information typically is collected and compiled by workers near the bottom of organizational hierarchies; but as it is manipulated, parsed and moved upward, it is transformed so as to make it accessible and amenable for those near the top, who make the big decisions. This "editing" removes assumptions, discretion and ambiguity, a process that results in "uncertainty absorption": information appears more robust than it actually is. As March and Simon put it: "Uncertainty absorption takes place when inferences are drawn from a body of evidence, and the inferences instead of the evidence itself, are then communicated."[57]

This insight has particular application to the new generation of global scale indices. What is moved upward to a higher level of abstraction and aggregation is not "raw" information, but already highly artifactual composites and aggregates, the result of laborious construction, parsing, concept-making, judgment-calling, and contestation. Transmitted upwards are sets of inferences and claims bundled into a one-dimensional figure, which the higher-level index then bundles further.

USAID's Index ranking for each country is obtained by averaging the "effectiveness score" and "legitimacy score" for each country into a "fragility score." The effectiveness and legitimacy scores are the aggregations of component indicators selected as proxies for each of the four dimensions of effectiveness and legitimacy. The step of aggregation is indispensable for deriving a single score for each state, allowing a seemingly transitive rank ordering to be obtained. Rank ordering is one of the most seductive features of unidimensional indices: it creates an impression of precise differentiation between objects (in this case, states) in respect of a complex property (stateness) that seems to have been successfully reduced to a unidimensional measure. As Davis, Kingsbury, and Merry note, indicators such as the Human Development Index gain authority in part because they become a "shorthand" for a country's circumstances, and rankings imply

---

[57] Espeland and Stevens 2008: 422. Inline reference omitted.

standards to be met or shortcomings made legible (and perhaps actionable).[58]

For rank ordering to fulfill these ambitions of diagnosis and prediction, the differences between country ranks must in fact capture some real distinctions and interactions in the dimension of fragility – and these differences must be amenable to transitive ordering in the sense that if Sierra Leone is ranked above Cambodia, and Cambodia is ranked above Cameroon, it must be true that Sierra Leone is more fragile than Cameroon.[59] For fragility and its underlying dimensions (and the indicators of those dimensions) to be susceptible to this treatment, the problems of conceptual specification and proxy identification pointed out earlier must have been suitably resolved:

First, the analyst must make explicit the theory concerning the relationship between attributes [dimensions]. Second, the analyst must ensure that there is a correspondence between this theory and the selected aggregation rule, that is, that the aggregation rule is actually the equivalent formal expression of the posited relationship. For example, if the aggregation of two attributes is at issue and one's theory indicates that they both have the same weight, one would simply add the scores of both attributes. If one's theory indicates that both attributes are necessary features, one could multiply both scores, and if one's theory indicates that both attributes are sufficient features, one could take the score of the highest attribute. In this regard, then, it is crucial that researchers be sensitive to the multitude of ways in which attributes might be linked and avoid the tendency to limit themselves by adherence to defaults, such as additivity.[60]

To put it another way, an aggregation function for a multidimensional phenomenon like "fragility" requires the solving of two kinds of problem: determining direction of causalities between fragility and its dimensions, and between dimensions,[61] and determining a *numeraire* which allows one to calculate how many units of dimension A

---

[58] See generally Davis, Kingsbury, and Merry 2012b.

[59] A correct aggregation function is a set of rules that attributes to a vector of characteristics a single element in the range and additionally (a) behaves monotonically, and (b) respects boundary conditions: Beliakov, Pradera, and Calvo 2007, cited in Sanin 2011: 32.

[60] Munck and Verkuilen 2002: 24.

[61] Recall that the USAID Index asserts eight dimensions of fragility (four × two). King and Langche note that establishing interactions for a six-dimensional space (assuming, plausibly, linear and non-linear interactions) is "almost incomprehensibly immense" (King and Langche 2001: 639).

substitute one unit of dimension B. Without resolving these two puzzles, rank ordering beyond pair-wise comparison is arbitrary.[62]

USAID's background paper on measuring fragility contains no discussion of the difficulties of aggregation, and the Index states that Principal Component Analysis is used to derive a weighted average for the component indicators for effectiveness and legitimacy. The average is then standardized to make the mean for all countries 0, and a country's deviation from the mean becomes its fragility score; a positive score connotes higher fragility; a negative score reflects lesser fragility. This generates the appearance of unidimensionality, but only by placing the statistical cart before the theoretical horse, sidestepping the validity problems raised by poor specification, doubtful proxies, and no theory of aggregation.[63]

Conclusion

Within the style of reasoning of contemporary statistical method, the numbers generated by USFfP's Failed States Index and USAID's Index do not appear robust or easily defensible. They are not very good numbers. Rather than consider how one might more successfully measure stateness, it seems to me that a pressing puzzle is the existence and growth of demand for rankings based on relatively poor concepts, data, and methods.[64] As Lampland suggests, it may well be a mistake to assume that the effective use of numbers depends upon their *veracity* or some defensible argument for veracity.[65] Quantification is a formalizing practice that can serve a variety of purposes, even if a number's claim to objectivity and scientificity cannot be readily cashed out under the prevailing exchange rate for scientific method: "Numbers are instruments, not simply transparent signs."[66] But what are they instruments for, in this case?

Synoptic, attention-grabbing, provocative: these terms are used to describe the effects of ordinally ranking state strength, even as they acknowledge that the methodological bases for ranking may not be

---

[62] See Sanin 2009: 30–33 for detailed discussion.

[63] Sanin (2009) rightly points out that for indices of state fragility, "the aggregation function is a substantial part of the theory" of the fragility concept itself.

[64] See Hood, Dixon, and Beeston 2008 for similar puzzlement in relation to a range of rankings.

[65] Lampland 2010.   [66] *Ibid.*: 383.

persuasive to many.[67] The reduction of a complex, multidimensional reality (nothing less than the political and social order of a territory) to a single number is admitted by most to be susceptible to criticism. But as argued above, the category of fragility seems to demand a means of classifying and comparing across vast scales of people, space, and history. Closely intertwined with policy demands to globally forecast security risks and target sources of disorder within states, it is a problematic and heuristic which elicits panoramic techniques – a tendency evidenced by the numerous other attempts to quantify and index state fragility. Panoramas, as Latour argues, are artifacts that aspire to see the whole and *show* it in an ordered and coherent way: "What is so powerful in those contraptions is that they nicely solve the question of staging the totality, of ordering the ups and downs, of nesting 'micro,' 'meso' and 'macro' into one another ... They collect, they frame, they rank, they order, they organize."[68]

A panorama of stateness, such as that presented by the FSI and the USAID Index, integrates a theory of political order (founded in institutions, achieved through technical efficiency and legitimate conflict resolution) with a raft of measures and numbers to generate a macro-level snapshot of degrees of effectiveness and legitimacy of 161 states across the world. Rendering degrees of political order calculable in this manner also changes the way in which it can be made visible and represented: unlike an expert opinion, a human intelligence report, or a historical monograph, the judgments and narratives embedded in a unidimensional number are easy to transpose into two-dimensional space, whether tabular (a list color-coded by degrees of fragility) or pictorial (a map color-coded by degrees of fragility or instability risk). In the color code used by USAID and USFfP, highly fragile is represented by red or orange, and low fragility by green or blue. The map creates a regionalized picture of fragility, in which there are zones of the world suffering lesser or greater degrees. Unsurprisingly, those zones in which red and orange predominate overlap significantly with under-developed or lesser developed countries. Those zones where green and blue predominate are first world/Northern countries and regions, with some exceptions. The effect of this aesthetic is striking: zones

---

[67] Similar terms were used by officials involved in the production of other indexes of state fragility, to describe the value of an ordinal ranking: Author interviews, Washington, DC, July 20 and 22, 2010.

[68] Latour 2005: 187–189.

associated with poor governance and instability are marked with a color connoting danger/threat/heat (red, orange), and zones associated with good governance and stability are marked with a color connoting safety/ease/calm or cool (green, blue). Indeed, the aesthetics of the fragility map resemble a "heat map," sometimes used to represent risks of contagion and spillover of epidemics or (more recently) systemic financial crises.[69]

Panoramas of this kind, then, affect distributed cognition, by tying together different scales of information and different genre systems (theories of politics, models of political organization, measures of economic growth, ratings of government policy, subjective perception surveys) in order to make "an otherwise amorphous composite . . . into a thing that holds together in the imagination of government officials and the general public."[70] Quantification of inputs eases the way to this knitting together, especially where scales are large, and obscures the nature of the genres being linked together. The (messy, unpersuasive) world-making that lies beneath this discrete numerical knowledge-object is obscured, and its seemingly solid and transparent qualities engender what Sally Merry calls "knowledge-effects": "Numerical measures produce a world knowable without the detailed particulars of context and history."[71] A striking example is the way in which the FSI is presented annually in *Foreign Policy* magazine: the Index is always matched with narrative stories and opinion pieces which make strong claims about the causes of state failure and how to address them – claims which are not in any way tested by the FSI. Thus, in the July 2010 *Foreign Policy* issue publishing the FSI for that year, the Index was published alongside an opinion piece by economist Paul Collier, entitled "Bad Guys Matter," in which Collier rehearses his well-known argument that the quality of governance and natural resource endowments are causally related to the onset of civil war and state failure.

The numbers are associated with global judgments about the quality and nature of political order in the territory. The numbers *stand in* for a judgment about a complex social reality (e.g. the "relationship between government and society") but also *tie in* with beliefs, common-sense

---

[69] My thanks to Bruce Carruthers for bringing this similarity with heat maps to my attention.
[70] Espeland and Stevens 2008: 412. See also Bowker and Star 1999: 136.
[71] Merry 2011: s84.

notions, and normative claims about what characterizes good and bad political orders and outcomes. The normalizing tendency of the concept of fragility and failure is reinforced but also rendered less transparent by the process of quantification; it is hidden behind claims of methodological authority and elaborate numerical artifacts.

5 Lost in the gray zone

Competing measures of democracy in the former Soviet republics

SEVA GUNITSKY

Introduction

Recent decades have seen the spread of regimes that claim the mantle of democracy even as their true democratic status remains uncertain.[1] These hybrid regimes reside in the gray zone of democracy indices. They resist easy comparisons, both to each other and across different measures – which has made reliable indicators of their democratic quality all the more important for both academics and policymakers.

The story of two post-Soviet states can illustrate the difficulty. One country saw the rise of crony capitalism, growing restrictions on media freedom, and the increasing centralization of power by the president. The other cut down on corruption, established strong partnerships with the West, and developed a parliament that successfully stood up to the president's unpopular choice of a prime minister. By the turn of the century, as Figure 5.1 shows, their trajectories had irrevocably diverged.

At first glance, these cases seem to be just another example of the diversity in post-Soviet institutional development. The only problem is that the two are in fact *the same country*. What the above figure actually shows is the assessment of Russian democracy by Freedom House (dashed line), compared to a rather more optimistic assessment by Polity IV (solid line).[2] Both are commonly used indices that claim to measure the same phenomenon. So how did they come away with such vastly different portrayals of Russian democracy? In both cases, plausible narratives could be constructed to fit the statistical outcome, but

---

[1] Replication data and supplementary materials for this chapter are available at individual.utoronto.ca/seva/measures.html.

[2] Freedom House measures are reversed so that higher scores mean better democratic quality for both indices.

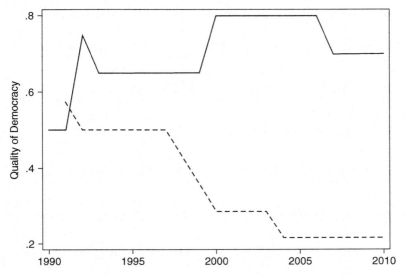

Figure 5.1 Divergent political trajectories in the post-Soviet space

which one is closer to reality? And what are the implications of such broad disagreement for how scholars examine the causes of democratization, and for how policymakers evaluate the effectiveness of democracy assistance?

This chapter examines the sources of these disagreements by looking at how various measures assess democracy in the former Soviet republics. I begin with some general drawbacks of commonly used indices, and the implications of these drawbacks for public policy and academic research. I find that indices often disagree about particular countries, and occasionally draw contradictory conclusions from observing the same event. Measures of hybrid regimes are particularly unreliable, and regional comparisons of democratic quality are also highly sensitive to measure choice.

The methodological weaknesses of popular measures have been extensively discussed elsewhere,[3] and it is not my goal to rehash these criticisms here. Instead I focus on problems of *definition* as the root source of measure divergence. Disagreements such as the example above, I argue, reflect inherent trade-offs in conceptualizing democratic governance. Though at least some of the measures aspire to objectivity,

---

[3] See, for example, Munck 2009 or Munck and Verkuilen 2002.

Table 5.1. *Competing definitions of "democracy" in common indices*

Measure	Broad conception of democracy
Polity IV	Divided patterns of elite authority
Przeworski *et al.*	Electoral turnover
Vanhanen	Party fragmentation and high voter turnout
Freedom House	Individual freedom and equality

they ultimately represent rival notions of the concept of democracy. For example, the Polity IV measure takes democracy to mean "divided patterns of authority," the Przeworski *et al.* measure takes it to mean "electoral turnover," the Freedom House measure takes the view of democracy as "freedom," while the Vanhanen measure takes it to mean "party fragmentation and high voter turnout."[4] To say that one measure is more accurate than another misses the point, since they represent overlapping but non-identical conceptions of a highly complex phenomenon (see Table 5.1).

At the same time, these disputes are not simply a case of reasonable people disagreeing about a complicated concept. Ideological or political motivations can also shape definitional preferences. Democracy, after all, is undoubtedly a politically loaded term: "It is almost universally felt that when we call a country democratic we are praising it," wrote George Orwell in 1946. Thus "the defenders of every kind of regime claim that it is a democracy, and fear that they might have to stop using that word if it were tied down to any one meaning."[5] During the Cold War, for example, both the Soviet Union and the United States proclaimed themselves to be democratic societies but emphasized different conceptions of democracy – individual liberty in the case of the United States and social justice in the case of the USSR.[6]

---

[4] These measures are discussed in more detail below.

[5] Orwell 1946: 132–133.

[6] These conceptions were partly self-serving and partly hypocritical for both states, but also had a profound effect on Cold War politics. As Capoccia (2005: 241) argues, the protection of human rights as enshrined in a number of international treaties had been impossible during the Cold War precisely because the two superpowers could not agree on a common definition of democracy. "However, after the collapse of international Communism," he writes, "a sufficiently general agreement on at least a minimal 'procedural' conception of democracy has become more possible, and international documents providing for democratic rights have suddenly become enforceable, at least in principle."

More recently, Freedom House has been criticized for espousing a pro-American (and anti-Russian) ideology in its rankings. This charge is particularly problematic because Freedom House acts as both an expert on measuring democracy and an advocate for US-led democracy promotion.

The consequences of definitional disputes extend far beyond scholars excavating through footnotes in regression analyses. As the case of Freedom House demonstrates, democracy measures can shape advocacy efforts by non-governmental organizations, and influence popular perceptions of global and regional trends in democratization. Measurements can also have a direct impact on government policies; USAID, for example, chooses its assistance projects based in part on assessments of where they can be most effective, which includes measuring democratic development and judging the potential for further progress. Good measures are particularly important for evaluating mixed regimes, where foreign assistance can make the biggest difference for democratization, and where policymakers need accurate assessments of the impact of aid. As I show below, democracy indices are particularly unreliable for judging mixed regimes, creating the potential for misguided policies and advocacy efforts.

After examining general problems of defining democracy, the second part of the chapter turns to specific measurement problems as they apply to the former Soviet republics. I find that redundant sub-scores can underestimate the level of democracy and exaggerate regime variation across the region. In addition, current measures don't appear to be particularly sensitive to the quality of elections. Fortunately, these problems stem from poor operationalization and can be treated with the careful application of statistics.

More serious problems, however, appear to be intractable. I find that indices often disagree about particular countries, and occasionally draw distinct or even contradictory conclusions (and ratings) from observing the same event. I find that measures of hybrid regimes are particularly capricious. Regional comparisons of democratic quality (in this case, former Soviet republics compared to Eastern Europe) are also highly sensitive to the choice of measure. These problems appear to stem from the way the creators of the measures define and conceptualize democracy.

Since the choice of definition shapes both the choice of variables and how these variables are aggregated, the lack of consensus about measurement is both fundamental and intractable. This conclusion has two implications: first, the inherent limitations of any measure should be made explicit when evaluating democracy's relationship with other often-studied national attributes like economic development or propensity for war. Second, since different indices capture different elements of democracy, the choice of measure should be shaped by whichever element is most salient for the specific research puzzle or policy proposal at hand.[7]

Evaluating indices through a regional lens can serve two purposes. First, it provides a guide for area specialists who wish to know how well a particular region is served by these measures. Bogaards (2007), for example, argues that indices focusing on election outcomes perform poorly at measuring the quality of democracy in Africa.[8] As a result, measures that rely on election outcomes may be particularly inappropriate for judging democratic quality in that region. Second, focusing on a region can expose the hidden assumptions and potential pitfalls of the measures themselves. For Bogaards, looking at the measures using African cases reveals not only which approaches are more suitable for the region, but also some general limitations in how they measure electoral contestation around the world. As I aim to show in this chapter, the former Soviet republics can serve the same useful purpose.

Evaluating statistical measures of democracy

The concept of democracy lacks a consensus definition beyond a core notion of "self-governance."[9] Some approaches adopt a minimalist,

---

[7] A recent step in this direction has been the effort by Coppedge and Gerring (2011) to produce a data set that disaggregates the concept of democracy along its various dimensions. They argue for six separate conceptions of democracy: electoral, liberal, majoritarian, participatory, deliberative, and egalitarian. Many of the conceptual trade-offs involved in emphasizing a particular interpretation of democracy are discussed below.

[8] He concludes that these measures make strong assumptions about the relationship between regime type and the size of electoral victory, "are frequently in disagreement, correspond poorly with Freedom House and Polity classifications and scores, evidently misclassify numerous regimes, and fail to reflect continuity and change" (Bogaards 2007: 1233).

[9] The literature on defining democracy and classifying political regimes is vast. See, for example, Schmitter and Karl 1991; Lawson 1993; O'Donnell 1993; Collier and Levitsky 1997; Mainwaring, Brinks, and Perez-Linan 2001; Altman and Perez-Linan 2002; Reich 2002; Daly 2003; Bennett 2006; and Whitehead 2011.

procedural view while others aggregate a variety of attributes.[10] The Freedom House index, perhaps the most widely known measure,[11] takes a very broad view of the concept.[12] Its civil liberties score, for example, includes measures of media self-censorship, industrial production quotas, government control over sermons, nepotism in university admissions, and socio-economic inequality, among many others (Freedom House 2010). It is thus open to the charge of conflating processes with outcomes. If democracy is measured by positive outcomes like lack of corruption or economic equality, it becomes impossible to measure democracy's causal impact on these outcomes. Countries that promote economic equality become democratic by fiat, and the impact of regime type on economic equality becomes not a subject of study but a tautology. At the same time, economic equality may be necessary for equal political representation if personal wealth determines the extent of political influence. Depending on the electoral rules (such as limits on campaign contributions) and the extent of inequality, socio-economic equality could be seen as either a prerequisite or an outcome of democratic government. A persuasive case can be made for either position, each with its own merits and drawbacks.

A minimalist conception of democracy faces a different set of problems. It may exclude what some might consider crucial elements of democracy. Polity IV, for example, focuses on procedural aspects of democracy at the elite level but ignores mass participation.[13] Thus the

[10] This discussion excludes a number of less common indices, most of which are inapplicable to the former Soviet republics because they either do not cover the region or do not extend beyond 1991. For an overview of other indices, see Munck and Verkuilen 2002.

[11] Relative popularity can be (unscientifically) gauged by search results in Google Scholar: between 2005 and 2010, Freedom House has approximately 6,700 mentions in academic books and articles, Polity IV has 2,400 mentions, and Vanhanen comes in with approximately a thousand (restricted to searches in social sciences, arts, and humanities).

[12] Freedom House has rated every country in the world since 1972 on a scale of 1 (most democratic) to 7 (least democratic). The measure consists of two subcomponents, Political Rights and Civil Liberties, which are themselves aggregates of ten and thirteen subcomponents, respectively, and capture a wide variety of national attributes related to personal freedom. See http://www.freedom house.org for country scores and detailed descriptions of the methodology.

[13] Polity IV is a measure commonly used in the academic literature. It rates most countries in the world (excluding some small states) since 1800, using a scale of −10 to 10, with the latter being the most democratic. Polity measures democracy as a weighted sum of five components – the competitiveness and

United States rates as a perfect democracy after 1871 despite the sub-sequent expansion of suffrage to women, African-Americans, and citizens over eighteen years of age. If mass participation is a key component of democracy, then Polity IV does not adequately capture the concept.

The problem of definition is further compounded by some inherent trade-offs in democratic governance. Not all aspects of democracy are positively correlated. Majority rule, for example, frequently comes into conflict with individual liberties. If democracy is defined as the will of the majority, then the Bill of Rights and the Supreme Court are inherently undemocratic institutions. This tension between mass participation and individual liberty carries through to modern measures of democracy. Thus, the index of democracy produced by the Economist Intelligence Unit (EIU) regards mandatory voting as decreasing democratic quality because it infringes upon individual liberty.[14] At the same time, mandatory voting clearly increases voter turnout, particularly by the poor, who have few alternative venues for exerting political influence and exhibit lower rates of participation when voting is optional. Mandatory voting therefore improves the quality of mass participation at the expense of individual liberty. The index of democracy produced by Tatu Vanhanen, for example, is based in part on measuring the percentage of the national population that votes in elections.[15] Countries with mandatory voting thus receive a higher score on the Vanhanen index and a lower score on the EIU index. In this case, mandatory voting is punished or rewarded based

openness of executive recruitment, the regulation and competitiveness of participation, and constraints on the chief executive (with the latter weighed most heavily). See Marshall, Gurr, and Jaggers 2010.

[14] The Economist Intelligence Unit (EIU) index of democracy has rated most countries in the world (165 states) every two years from 2006 to 2010, and annually since then. The latest index, as of this writing, was released in 2012; this chapter examines the measure up to 2010, although the methodology has remained the same in the latest iterations. The EIU score, which ranges from 0 to 10, is based on sixty indicators combined into five sub-components – free and fair elections, civil liberties, functioning of government, political participation, and political culture. See Kekic 2007.

[15] Vanhanen uses a measure that rates most countries in the world between 1810 and 2004. His score is a product of two sub-components: the percentage of votes not cast for the largest party, and the percentage of the population that voted in elections. The two scores are multiplied and divided by a hundred, yielding a scale that could theoretically range between 0 and 100 (although in practice the highest score is 49, achieved by Italy in 1993). See Vanhanen 2000 and 2003.

on whether the measure emphasizes mass participation or individual liberty. The divergence between the two measures reflects a fundamental disagreement about the essential nature of democracy – a normative choice rather than a methodological one.

In addition to these inherent tensions, the way scholars and policy-makers view the "appropriate" definition of democracy may be shaped by the historical context of the times and even unrecognized ideological biases. As Ido Oren (2002) has argued, over the twentieth century the definition of democracy by American political scientists has been shaped by the context of America's international rivalries. Conflict with other major powers has caused political scientists to view them as less democratic. Before 1914, for example, prominent contemporaries like John Burgess and Woodrow Wilson portrayed Germany as a progressive state with a liberal constitution and an incorruptible bureaucracy. But conflict with Germany in two world wars caused American scholars to re-label the country as a militaristic and semi-feudal monarchy.[16] The fact that Polity scores for pre-World War I Germany are significantly lower than those of England, France, and the US reflects this ideological shift, according to Oren. The Polity measures illustrate "the role played by data sets in objectifying concepts that were originally rooted in a particular *interpretation* of political development," he argues, "an interpretation that happens to associate the trappings of democracy with America's enemies and the substance of democracy with America's allies."[17]

Freedom House has likewise attracted its share of critics for allegedly espousing a pro-American bias (like Polity, Freedom House has assigned the US a perfect score ever since its inception in 1972). The majority of its funding comes from the US government (its 2007 financial statement puts the share at 66 percent; *The Economist* estimates the average figure at 80 percent).[18] It has formally stated that its diverse

---

[16] For example, Bismarck's introduction of unemployment insurance, old age pensions, and national healthcare in the 1880s set the precedent for the modern European welfare state.

[17] Oren 2002: 25. As Martin Walker notes in his history of the Cold War, American descriptions of the Soviet regime often hinged on its status as an ally. When *Collier's* magazine ran a special issue in December 1943 titled "What Kind of Country is Russia Anyway?", they concluded that it was neither socialist nor communist but "a modified capitalist set-up [moving] toward something resembling our own and Great Britain's democracy." Quoted in Walker (1994: 30).

[18] Freedom House 2008; "Measuring liberty: When freedom stumbles," *The Economist* January 19, 2008.

trustees are "united in the view that American leadership in international affairs is essential to the cause of human rights and freedom."[19] Freedom House has strongly denied charges of partisanship, pointing to its willingness to criticize America's strategic partners like Egypt, Pakistan, and Saudi Arabia.

Beyond ideology, the political zeitgeist can also shape what scholars and policymakers consider to be "essential" elements of democracy. Athens was considered a democracy by contemporaries despite widespread slavery and the exclusion of women and metics from political participation. More recently, foreign visitors to the United States in the early nineteenth century called it a democracy despite slavery and the political exclusion of women. But by the 1970s, notes Markoff, "although South Africa had multiparty competition, very few would have called that country a democracy because only its white minority could vote. A great change in the meaning of democracy had occurred."[20] Nor do such shifts require a long time span: attempting to define democracy in 1944, Raymond Aron concluded that "the idea of popular sovereignty is not essential: It can lead as easily to despotism as to liberty. And after all, to a large extent it has been popular majorities that have abused their power."[21] Writing scarcely a decade after Hitler's democratic ascent to power, Aron could not conceive of mass participation as a key component of democracy. Today, however, elections are considered a crucial part of democratic governance. Their importance is revealed in the significance assigned to elections as democratic milestones in countries like Iraq or during the Arab Spring, as well as in the efforts devoted to international election monitoring. To take another example, during the Great Depression prominent political scientists defined democracy in economic and substantive terms as much as in the political and procedural terms prevalent today. Thus Merle Fainsod argued in 1934 that the eradication of poverty and unemployment was as significant to democracy as universal suffrage, while Charles Merriam saw economic equality as a key measure of democracy. It was only after World War II that procedural, Schumpeterian conceptions replaced substantive definitions.[22]

Conceptions of democracy vary across regions and cultural contexts as well as over time. Arab Barometer surveys from the summer of 2011,

---

[19] Freedom House, www.freedomhouse.org, 'About Us' (accessed 2011).
[20] Markoff 1996: 60.   [21] Aron 1944: 175.   [22] Oren 2002: 12.

for example, show that 79 percent of Egyptians see democracy as the best form of government, but they perceive it in terms of social justice and economic equality. Sixty-five percent of the survey respondents listed low levels of inequality or government provision of basic services for all citizens as the most essential feature of democracy. Only 6 percent defined its most essential feature as the ability to change governments through elections, and only 4 percent defined it as the right to criticize the government.[23] This definition is much more consistent with substantive rather than procedural conceptions of democracy.

In sum, measures of democracy face inherent trade-offs in emphasizing different aspects of democratic rule, and choosing among these trade-offs can be shaped by both ideological and methodological preferences. Whatever the predispositions of their makers, definitions vary because the meaning of democracy encompasses competing normative elements. The choice of measurement, to which I now turn, is shaped by these definitional considerations.

Problems of measurement

Growing self-consciousness about measure choice has produced a number of debates about transforming vague concepts into precise measures. For example, should democracy be considered a dichotomous or a continuous variable? Przeworski, Alvarez, Cheibub, and Limongi ("PACL" in this chapter) offer a spirited defense of a dichotomous measure, going so far as to call intermediate measures "ludicrous."[24] They argue that democracy is a type rather than a degree, a notion perhaps best summarized in the words of writer

---

[23] Michael Robbins and Mark Tessler, "What Egyptians mean by democracy," Foreign Policy Middle East Channel, September 20, 2011. Available at: http://atfp.co/1qkpoAH.

[24] Alvarez *et al.* 1996: 21. Their measure tracks most countries in the world (maximum of 149 states) from 1950 to 2008 using a dichotomous measure. Przeworski *et al.* (2000) originally scored countries for the years 1950–1990; Cheibub *et al.* (2010) extended the measures to 2008. A country is considered a democracy if it fulfills all four of the following criteria: the chief executive and the legislature must be elected, more than one party must compete in the elections, and an alternation of power under identical election rules must take place. If any of those components are missing, the country is rated a dictatorship. See also Przeworski *et al.* 1996 and Przeworski and Limongi 1997: 178–179. Samuel Huntington (1991: 11–12) and Juan Linz (1975: 184–185) likewise adopt dichotomous measures.

Amiri Baraka: "A man is either free or not. There cannot be any apprenticeship for freedom."[25] They also claim that dichotomous measures contain less measurement error because they are more transparent and easier to replicate. Thus dichotomous measures are, as Elkins (2000) puts it, theoretically more valid and more reliable.[26] But in testing these claims, he finds that graded measures have "superior validity and reliability" and that dichotomous measures seem insensitive "to the incremental, and sometimes partial, process that characterizes many democratic transitions."[27] Indeed, although PACL aims to be strict in its criteria, the imprecision of the measure means that countries like Venezuela and Sierra Leone are judged to be as democratic as (say) Norway.

Ultimately, as Collier and Adcock (1999) argue, the choice between binary and continuous measures should depend on the specific goals of the research. Donnelly (2006: 88) suggests a three-point checklist for when a dichotomous variable may be preferable to a continuous one: when the dividing line is sharp and clear, when the gray area between the two cases is small, and when few important cases fall into that gray area. By these criteria, a continuous measure is preferable for most kinds of research.[28] Because binary measures are very sensitive to where one makes the cut, they would not work well in examining regimes in the middle of the spectrum, such as competitive autocracies. At the same time, dichotomous measures may be more appropriate for studying major political transformations or tracking the duration of democratic regimes.

Beyond the choice of scale sensitivity, commonly used measures suffer from a number of coding problems.[29] For example, Coppedge

---

[25] Baraka 1962.

[26] The claim of reliability is methodological while the claim of validity is theoretical; Elkins is thus incorrect in criticizing the proponents of the dichotomous approach for neglecting "advances in data collection and analysis" (2000: 293) that allow more precise measures of regime change. Their insistence on binary measures stems not from the paucity of data but the theoretical conception of democracy as a non-continuous concept.

[27] Elkins 2000: 293.

[28] Epstein *et al.* (2006) adopt a trichotomous measure of democracy on similar grounds, and Kellstedt and Whitten (2009: 96) likewise argue that continuous variables are more appropriate for measuring democratization.

[29] For an overview, see Munck and Verkuilen 2002 or Munck 2009. Earlier writing on problems of democracy measurement includes Inkeles 1991 and Beetham 1994.

and Gerring (2011: 250) point out that when human judgments are required for coding, indicators with subjective criteria may produce different results from one expert to another. Bollen and Paxton argue that this subjectivity pervades democracy indices: examining measures between 1972 and 1988, they find "unambiguous evidence of judge-specific measurement errors."[30] It's not surprising, therefore, that regional experts frequently see a disconnect between the measures and their understanding of the region. For example, Bowman, Lehoucq, and Mahoney (2005) find that large-n measures of Central American states are plagued by errors stemming from inaccurate, partial, or misleading data sources. Comparing scores of some African states with qualitative observations, McHenry (2000) finds discrepancies both within and across data sets: measures do not reflect the observed facts on the ground, and measures of the same state do not reflect the same phenomena.

These problems extend to specific measures. Vanhanen, for example, measures turnout as a percentage of the national population, in effect punishing countries that have a relatively large number of people below voting age. Since fertility rates correlate negatively with income, this has the effect of penalizing poorer states and introducing a systemic measurement bias. His measure of competition also favors highly fragmented legislatures, and may thus be capturing the nature of electoral systems rather than democratic quality.[31] Other measures fare no better: Gleditsch and Ward argue that the recruitment and participation dimensions of Polity IV are "empirically extraneous despite their centrality in political theory."[32] They suggest that Polity ought to be treated as categorical rather than continuous: it clusters at the +10 category, for instance, suggesting insensitivity to gradations at higher levels of democracy (see Figure 5.2). Treier and Jackman demonstrate "considerable error in the latent levels of democracy underlying the Polity scores."[33] And Munck points out that while the methods used to compute the Freedom House index have changed over time, scores from previous years have not been adjusted to reflect the new methodology. Freedom House scores thus suffer from the additional problem of internal inconsistency, so that the same score reflects different judgments of democratic quality in different years.[34]

---

[30] Bollen and Paxton 2000: 58.   [31] Berg-Schlosser 2004: 252.
[32] Gleditsch and Ward 1997: 361.   [33] Treier and Jackman 2008: 213.
[34] Munck 2009: 10. Polity IV also appears to re-evaluate its criteria, but recodes the scores retroactively. See footnote 57.

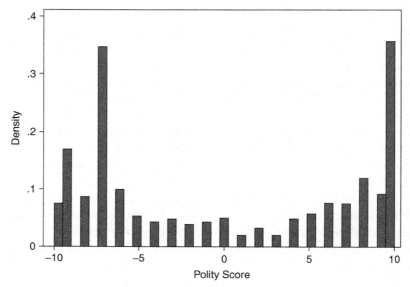

Figure 5.2 The uneven distribution of Polity scores suggests the measure may be categorical rather than continuous

The fact that many indices are highly correlated may suggest that they are measuring roughly the same phenomenon. Polity IV and Freedom House, for example, have a Pearson's R of 0.88. But as Casper and Tufis (2003) point out, highly correlated measures can produce very different regression results. Using three measures of democracy (Polyarchy, Freedom House, and Polity IV), they show that regressions of these highly correlated measures on variables like education and economic development often produce inconsistent results.[35] Moreover, the correlation among measures is highest for clear-cut cases. The correlation between Polity and Freedom House drops to 0.64 when democracies are excluded from the analysis.[36] And when both clear-cut autocracies and democracies are excluded, the correlation drops further to 0.50.[37] This is especially problematic

---

[35] On this point see also Munck and Verkuilen 2002: 29.

[36] Freedom House defines a country as "free" if their score is 2.5 or lower; Polity defines coherent democracies as those that score 7 or higher.

[37] Coppedge and Gerring (2011: 252) note similar trends in correlations of Polity IV and the political rights component of Freedom House. For detailed correlation tests across regime types, see Hadenius and Teorell 2005.

since democracy promotion and foreign aid is often directed at countries in the middle of the range. In these cases, the substantive results of any analysis may be greatly affected by the choice of measure. As I discuss below, this uncertainty remains a problem when comparing measures of democracy in the former Soviet republics.

Problems of aggregation

Aggregation involves combining sub-scores to produce a single measure of democratic quality. It faces two common problems: the choice of sub-scores (which is related to the problem of definition), and how to combine these sub-scores into a single measure. Aggregation can conceal differences among sub-components; Armstrong argues, for example, that the disaggregation of Freedom House scores reveals that many countries receiving the same overall score are "interestingly different from each other" while some countries with different overall scores appear fundamentally the same.[38] As Coppedge and Gerring point out, multicollinearity among sub-components suggests that measures are not independent of each other.[39] They note that the seven sub-components used to create measures of political rights in the Freedom House index have a Pearson's R of 0.86 or higher. While it's possible that all these components move together, their high correlation and ambiguous coding procedures suggest that "country coders have a general idea of how democratic each country is, and ... this idea is reflected in consistent scores across the multiple indicators." As I show below, high sub-score correlations can push the measure distribution toward the tails, making relatively high-scoring countries appear even more democratic and relatively low-scoring countries even more autocratic than they are. The choice of appropriate sub-components is therefore a consequential one.

The choice of the aggregation procedure itself is also crucial, since different methods contain distinct assumptions and produce divergent measures.[40] As a simple example, consider the aggregation of two sub-scores that measure two aspects of democratization. Using factor analysis, Coppedge, Alvarez, and Maldonado have created two such

[38] Armstrong 2011: 653.   [39] Coppedge and Gerring 2011: 251.
[40] Sanin, Buitrago, and Gonzales (2013), for example, argue that the use of weighted averages is based on "untenable" assumptions like strict monotonicity.

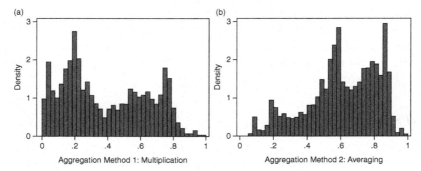

Figure 5.3 Two methods of aggregating contestation and inclusiveness into a single measure (multiplication or averaging) produce dramatically different results.

sub-scores based on what they find to be "two persistent dimensions of democracy" – democratic contestation and inclusiveness.[41] In order to derive a single measure and compare their results to other indices, we can aggregate the two scores in two ways – by averaging them (which, in terms of measure distribution, is equivalent to adding them) or by multiplying them together. Indices have employed both methods – while Freedom House averages scores and Polity uses a weighted addition scheme, Vanhanen and PACL use multiplicative aggregation.[42]

Figure 5.3 compares the measure distributions that result from two different methods of aggregation of their sub-scores. The chart on the left shows the measure distribution when the sub-scores are multiplied, while the chart on the right shows the measure distribution when the same two sub-scores are averaged. The two methods produce clearly different outcomes – the world of sub-component averaging is far more democratic than the world of sub-component multiplication.[43]

Despite the dramatic effects of aggregation choice, Munck points out that "with a few notable exceptions, existing democracy indices have displayed a fairly low level of sophistication concerning the process of

---

[41] Coppedge, Alvarez, and Maldonado 2008. More precisely, each is a principal component factor index of a number of indicators associated with contestation and participation.

[42] PACL is generally not considered to be an aggregated measure, but as I discuss shortly, this is incorrect.

[43] Coppedge *et al.* (2008: 633) state that "the truth of one [dimension] does not imply the truth of the other" and argue that the two dimensions are independent of each other.

aggregation."[44] He and Verkuilen argue that the aggregation method must be explicitly justified and linked to the measure's theoretical conception of democracy rather than constructed *ad hoc*.[45] The weighing of sub-components, for example, reflects choices about which elements of democracy are more important, which is tied to how democracy is defined in the first place. Moreover, the aggregation procedure contains certain assumptions about the nature of democracy. PACL, for example, examines the presence or absence of four factors: the election of an executive and of a legislature, party competition, and electoral turnover. If any of those components are missing, the country is rated a dictatorship. In effect, this scheme uses a multiplicative aggregation method with four dichotomous variables. It follows the logic of individually necessary and jointly sufficient conditions – each component is required for a country to be considered a democracy, and the presence of all four is enough to label a country democratic. Vanhanen also uses a multiplicative aggregation method, deriving his measure from the product of two scores: the percentage of votes not cast for the larger party, and the percentage of the population that voted in the elections. Thus a high turnout in which no other parties competed for office (as in the case of the Soviet Union, for instance) would result in a score of zero. Generally, the use of multiplicative aggregation with sub-components that could in theory equal zero imply strict criteria for inclusion – if any of the elements is zero, the entire score collapses to zero as well.[46] The same is true *a fortiori* if the subcomponents are dichotomous, as in the case of PACL. In effect, multiplicative aggregation in which sub-scores can equal zero takes the view that no country can be considered a democracy if it lacks particular elements or institutions, regardless of other factors. That is, no single factor is enough to label a country democratic.

In short, because the aggregation method contains inherent theoretical assumptions, it should be explicitly linked to the particular conceptualization of democracy. As Goertz (2006) points out, the disconnect between theory and aggregation is a common problem for democracy measures: while most theories of democracy imply necessary and sufficient conditions, most measures of these theories (such as Polity IV) use the "family resemblance" strategy typified by addition or averaging.

---

[44] Munck 2009: 35.   [45] Munck and Verkuilen 2002: 22–27.
[46] In Vanhanen's measure, roughly 35 percent of all cases receive a score of zero.

Evaluating democracy in the former Soviet republics

This section examines how specific measurement problems can distort the evaluation of democracy in the former Soviet republics. I focus on five mini "case studies" that examine redundant sub-scores, the relationship between election outcomes and election quality, measurements of hybrid regimes, regional comparisons, and major disagreements among measures (using Russia and Armenia as two examples). In each instance, analysis reveals potentially serious shortcomings in how various measures evaluate democracy in the region. While some of these problems can be minimized with the careful use of statistics, most are fundamental to the measures themselves.

Sub-score choice and the EIU index

The choice of sub-scores reflects how the measure conceptualizes distinct elements of democracy. As mentioned above, high correlation among sub-scores (as in the case of Freedom House, for example) suggests that these measures are not independent of each other. The EIU index, for example, includes sub-scores that measure the government's ability to function (i.e. the rule of law) and the extent of civil liberties, but also sub-scores that measure the extent of free elections and public participation. It could be argued, however, that free and fair elections and high levels of public participation *imply* and in fact *require* rule of law and civil liberties, so that the latter two measures are redundant, and including all four can produce multicollinearity in regression models. In fact, government functioning is highly correlated with both free elections ($r = 0.85$) and participation (0.84). Likewise, the measure of civil liberties is also highly correlated with free elections (0.93) and participation (0.89).

The statistical effect of these high correlations is to increase measure variance by pulling the distribution of scores toward the tails – the level of democracy in relatively democratic countries will be exaggerated, as will the level of autocracy in relatively autocratic countries. Is this effect indeed present in the EIU scores? Figure 5.4 compares the original EIU score with an adjusted score in which the sub-components of government functioning and civil liberties have been removed. The results show that the difference between the modified and the original score is indeed negatively correlated with the level of democracy. In the revised measure, autocratic countries like Uzbekistan, Turkmenistan, and Tajikistan

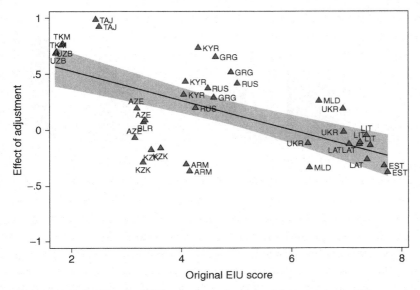

Figure 5.4 Adjusting the EIU score for redundant sub-components. The y-axis represents the effect of the adjustment on a country's score while the x-axis represents the level of democracy in the original score (countries are more democratic as one moves toward the right end of the spectrum).

receive a higher score while countries toward the more democratic end of the spectrum like Latvia and Estonia receive a lower score.[47]

Adjustment has the overall effect of increasing democracy scores in autocratic countries and decreasing democracy scores in democratic countries. The effect on hybrid regimes is mixed. These results suggest that the EIU measure appears to exaggerate regime type at the tails of the distribution, particularly for low-ranked countries (after adjustment, the regional average increases from 4.6 to 4.75). Figure 5.5 compares the distribution of the original and the modified scores for the region. For modified scores, the low end of the spectrum has been "pulled in" (this does not affect relative country rankings, since the omitted measures are highly correlated with the included measures).

---

[47] The standard deviation of the scores decreases from 1.99 to 1.82, as expected. Note also the distinct clustering of measurement effects for three categories of countries – the obvious autocracies (Uzbekistan, Turkmenistan, Tajikistan), the hybrid regimes (Azerbaijan, Belarus, Kazakhstan, Kyrgyzstan, Russia, Georgia, Armenia) and the regional democracies (Moldova, Ukraine, Latvia, Lithuania, Estonia).

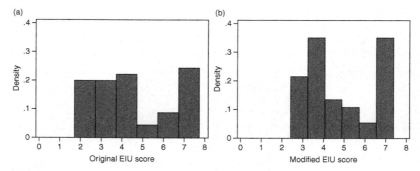

Figure 5.5 Distribution of original (a) and modified (b) EIU scores

In short, the presence of redundant sub-scores in the EIU index introduces two potential errors. First, it exaggerates the range of regime types in the region as a whole. Second, it inflates measures at the tails of the distribution, particularly among autocracies, making them appear even worse than they actually are; the overall effect is to underestimate the regional level of democracy. These problems demonstrate that the choice of sub-components (and their aggregation) requires careful theoretical justification.

Measuring election quality

Traditional measures of electoral participation such as voter turnout may be unreliable indicators of democratic quality, because they ignore differences in the quality of elections. As the playwright Tom Stoppard put it, "it's not the voting that's democracy, it's the counting." This problem is especially acute for competitive autocracies in which incumbents allow popular elections but "routinely abuse state resources, deny the opposition adequate media coverage, harass opposition candidates and their supporters, and in some cases manipulate electoral results."[48] As mentioned in the introduction, Bogaards (2007) has criticized democracy measures in Africa for ignoring election quality, showing that election outcomes in the region are not consistently related to levels of democracy.

I use Judith Kelley's (2012) data set of election quality to see if existing measures of democracy adequately capture the quality of

[48] Levitsky and Way 2002: 53. See also Levitsky and Way 2010.

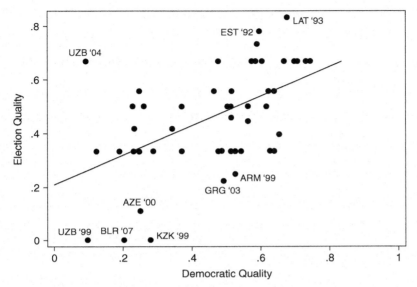

Figure 5.6 Relationship between election quality and overall democratic quality (taken as the average of other measures rescaled from zero to one). Each data point represents an election; selected outliers are labeled with country and year information. The two measures have an overall correlation coefficient of 0.57.

elections in the region. In general, the relationship between election quality and overall democratic quality (measured as the average of other indices) is present though not particularly strong, with a correlation coefficient of 0.57 (see Figure 5.6).

Individual measures do not fare particularly well when compared with a measure of election quality. The correlations between election quality and other measures of democracy are lower than correlations among the measures themselves, and election quality has the lowest overall correlation with other measures (see Table 5.2).

The Vanhanen measure has the lowest correlation with election quality (0.58). This is especially problematic since this measure takes care to incorporate election outcomes (in the form of turnout) into its score.

Comparing election turnout with election quality reveals no relationship between the two, as shown in Figure 5.7. Turnout is in fact a very poor predictor of election quality. Overall, the results are mixed. There is indeed some relationship between existing measures of democracy

Table 5.2. *Correlations among measures of democracy and election*
quality in the former Soviet republics (n = 40)

	FH	POL	VAN	UDS	CAM	OVERALL
Polity IV (POL)	0.83					0.80
Vanhanen (VAN)	0.73	0.71				0.75
Universal Democracy Score (UDS)[a]	0.94	0.90	0.86			0.86
Coppedge *et al.* (CAM)	0.91	0.89	0.89	0.93		0.87
Election Quality	0.72	0.68	0.58	0.68	0.72	0.68

[a]UDS, or Universal Democracy Score, is a measure developed by Pemstein, Meserve, and Melton 2010. It is synthesized using a Bayesian latent variable approach from ten other measures. According to the authors, this approach allows the simultaneous leveraging of a number of indices.

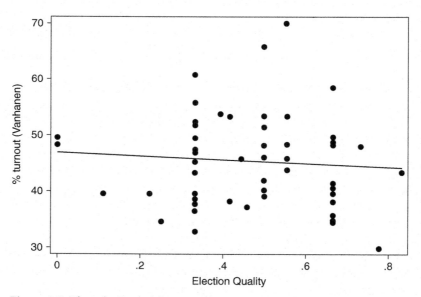

Figure 5.7 The relationship between election quality (from Kelley 2012) and percentage turnout (from Vanhanen 2000). Each dot represents a national election.

and election quality (it would be surprising if there was not), but measures of democratic participation appear insufficiently sensitive to election quality. Research or policy that focuses on the quality of elections should keep this limitation of current measures in mind.

Measure disagreement and regime type

How do the different measures compare in evaluating particular countries? Do certain indices consistently rank countries higher than others? And if there are disagreements among indices, are there any patterns to that disagreement? In line with previous findings, the overall correlations among different measures for the former Soviet republics are relatively high (although the Vanhanen and PACL measures have consistently lower correlation rates; see Table 5.3 below).

As mentioned above, high correlations do not necessarily mean the measures are interchangeable in regression analysis, and could conceal disagreement about hybrid regimes. To gauge their consistency, we need to compare the measures directly. To do so, I rescaled the scores of seven indices – Freedom House; Polity IV; EIU; Coppedge, Alvarez, and Maldonado 2008 (henceforth CAM); Vanhanen; PACL; and UDS – on a scale of zero to one, with higher numbers representing greater levels of democracy.[49] The summary statistics for the modified measures are presented in Table 5.4.

Table 5.3. *Correlations among measures of democracy in the former Soviet republics*

	POL	FH	UDS	VAN	CAM
Freedom House (FH)	0.86				
Universal Democracy Score (UDS)	0.93	0.94			
Vanhanen (VAN)	0.79	0.77	0.84		
Coppedge *et al.* (CAM)	0.92	0.95	0.95	0.87	
Przeworski *et al.* (PACL)	0.75	0.73	0.77	0.65	0.73

[49] This required rescaling the indices so that all measures were non-negative, then dividing them by the highest possible global measure for that index. The latter operation provides a sense of where each index places the country compared to the rest of the world (the global maxima for each rescaled measure are as

Table 5.4. *Summary statistics for the rescaled measures of democracy in the former Soviet republics*

Measure	N	Years	Minimum	Maximum	Mean
Freedom House	300	1991–2010	0	0.86	0.38
Polity IV	300	1991–2010	0.05	1	0.55
EIU	45	2006, 2008, 2010	0.17	0.78	0.47
UDS	270	1991–2008	0.15	0.83	0.49
CAM	149	1991–2000	0.13	0.78	0.44
Vanhanen	209	1991–2004	0	0.86	0.30
PACL	270	1991–2008	0	1	0.43

Before exploring the differences among the measures, we can compare their overall sensitivity to shifts in the levels of democracy. That is, how often do these indices change, and when they do, what is the average size of that change? Figure 5.8 charts the relationship between the proportion of years in which a measure indicates a change and the average magnitude of that change for each measure.

The analysis reveals some fundamental differences in how measures track changes. For example, Freedom House records more than twice as many changes in scores as Polity IV for the same time period. The two most sensitive measures are UDS and CAM, which change every country-year (in the case of UDS, this is not surprising, since it's derived from a number of other measures). At the same time, there is a strong linear relationship between the number of changes and the magnitude of the change. Stable indices are more likely to record large changes; the most extreme case is PACL, which switches classifications only twice (Georgia and Kyrgyzstan are both reclassified as democracies after their color revolutions) but the magnitude of change is great. As we will see later, measure sensitivity may affect the plausibility of regional comparisons – to a non-area specialist, judging the region solely by the PACL measure would suggest that democracy is on the rise.

follows: Polity IV – 20; Freedom House – 14; EIU – 9.88; UDS – 4.22; CAM – 17.35; Vanhanen – 49; PACL – 1). The CAM measure was obtained by multiplying the two sub-scores (the formula for the FH ratio was one minus the ratio to make higher numbers represent more democracy). Since PACL was already scored as 0 or 1, it did not need to be modified.

Table 5.5. *Average differences between measures*

	FH	POL	UDS	VAN	CAM	PACL
FH	–	-0.177	-0.111	0.072	-0.063	-0.055
POL	0.177	–	0.063	0.246	0.107	0.120
UDS	0.111	-0.063	–	0.181	0.039	0.057
VAN	-0.072	-0.246	-0.181	–	-0.146	-0.103
CAM	0.063	-0.107	-0.039	0.146	–	0.040
PACL	0.055	-0.120	-0.057	0.103	-0.040	–

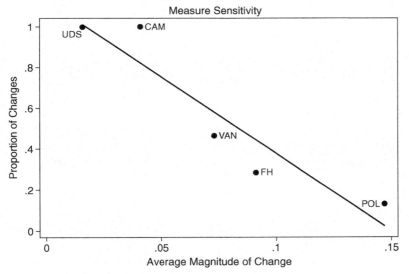

Figure 5.8 Measure sensitivity. The x-axis shows the average magnitude of annual changes in scores for each measure, compared to the proportion of country-years in which a change was recorded (y-axis).

To go deeper into disagreements among measures, Table 5.5 reveals the average difference between each pair of measures.

The number in each cell represents the average difference between the row measure and the column measure. For example, the average difference between Polity IV and Freedom House measures for the same country-years is 0.177, which suggests that Polity scores are on average 17 percent higher than Freedom House scores. On average,

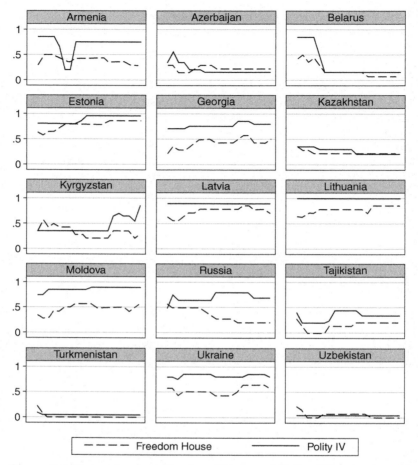

Figure 5.9 Comparisons of Freedom House and Polity IV evaluations of democracy in the former Soviet republics, 1991–2010

Polity IV appears to score countries higher than other measures, while Vanhanen scores them lower.

Of course, such averages may conceal significant variation across countries. Do measures disagree significantly about particular countries? Figure 5.9 compares Freedom House and Polity IV scores for each of the fifteen post-Soviet states from 1991 to 2010.

As the graphs show, there are a number of countries where the measures are basically in agreement. These tend to be clear-cut cases such as Turkmenistan on the autocratic end of the spectrum or Estonia on the democratic end (although even in the latter case there are some minor variations in trends). In other countries, the overall assessment is similar but there are noticeable differences in trends. In Tajikistan, for example, Polity records a decrease in democratic quality in the early 2000s while Freedom House records an *increase* during approximately the same period. Azerbaijan is coded by Polity as becoming less democratic in its early history, while Freedom House records a slight increase during the same period.

For a few countries, the two indices paint very different pictures. Armenia experiences a large but temporary dip in its Polity score in the mid-1990s, while the corresponding decrease in the Freedom House rating is much less noticeable. Georgia, Armenia, Moldova, and Ukraine are consistently ranked lower by Freedom House. The levels might not matter if the two measures had different global distributions – it might be the case, for example, that Freedom House ranks countries lower in general, which would mean that the relative rankings for these countries are the same for both indices. This is not the case, however. In 2008, for example, Moldova received a 4 from Freedom House and an 18 from Polity IV. By comparison, the average Polity score of countries that received a 4 from Freedom House in that year was less than 13. Freedom House ranked Moldova on par with Kuwait and Bangladesh, while Polity ranked it on par with Belgium and South Korea. In short, the two indices do rank Moldova differently. Such discrepancy is greatest in Russia, where the two scores diverge widely. Starting in the mid-1990s, Freedom House records a steep decline in democratic quality, while the Polity index records a slight rise followed by a leveling off.

Below, I will examine the sources of disagreement between Polity and Freedom House more closely, focusing on the cases of Armenia and Russia. But such discrepancies are not limited to those two measures. Figure 5.10 shows how seven different measures assess the quality of democracy in Kazakhstan.

In the case of Kazakhstan, Polity IV and Freedom House are basically in agreement for the past ten years, although the decline in Polity scores is much more gradual (Freedom House sees the country as stabilizing its regime by 1994, whereas for Polity the process takes a decade longer). Vanhanen, on the other hand, records a gradual improvement in democracy during the late 1990s. Depending on which measure is

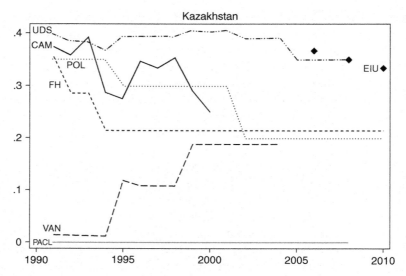

Figure 5.10 Comparing assessments of democracy in Kazakhstan

used, Kazakhstan can be judged as becoming less democratic (CAM, Polity, Freedom House), remaining a stable autocracy (UDS, PACL) or undergoing partial democratization (Vanhanen). At the same time, the measures do converge over time, which may indicate either better assessment as time goes on or the rise of conventional wisdom among some coders about Kazakhstan's rough position on the democracy continuum.

Nor is Kazakhstan particularly exceptional in the level of variation among measures – Appendix 2 includes similar charts for each of the fifteen countries, which reveal that disagreement among measures is common though not universal. The measures do seem to be in rough agreement about clear-cut autocracies and democracies, which brings us back to the question of greater disagreement about hybrid regimes. To find out, I compared the average measure variance for each country-year with its level of democracy (measured as the average of the indices rescaled from zero to one).[50] Figure 5.11 shows the results of this comparison, revealing a clear curvilinear relationship between the

---

[50] The following calculations were performed without PACL due to its dichotomous distribution.

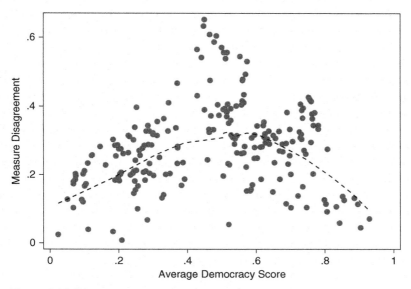

Figure 5.11 Disagreement among measures by regime type

degree of democracy and measure variance. Countries in the middle (0.4 to 0.6 range) have consistently higher measure disagreement. A lowess plot (locally weighted scatterplot smoothing, designed to look for non-linear relationships) shows an inverse-U relationship between democracy and measure variance.

To see if measure variance is consistent across countries, Figure 5.12 compares the average disagreement for each country with its overall democracy score. We would expect middle-ranking countries to have higher levels of variance.

Once again, the results show agreement among measures on clear-cut autocracies like Turkmenistan and clear-cut democracies like the Baltic states. Disagreement increases for more democratic countries and peaks for countries in the middle of the range before declining once more. There is a significant disagreement among measures about hybrid regimes such as Moldova, Armenia, Georgia, and Russia. Overall, these results suggest that measures of democracy for these countries may be particularly unreliable, and that conclusions about the causes and effects of democratic development in hybrid regimes are particularly sensitive to the choice of measure.

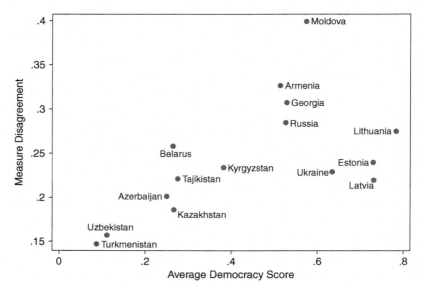

Figure 5.12 Disagreement among measures by country

Measure variance and regional comparisons

How much do the indices agree with each other in terms of capturing overall regional trends? And how do the differences in these measures affect the comparison of the former Soviet republics with other regions in the world? Figure 5.13 shows the regional average between 1991 and 2010 according to five different indices.

Once again, there are significant variations among measures. Polity generally ranks the region as more democratic than other indices, while Vanhanen ranks it as less democratic. Of course, looking at levels alone may not tell us much about how the region compares to other countries in the world. For example, if Vanhanen has a distribution that clusters toward the bottom, a lower regional average would not translate into a lower ranking for the former Soviet republics compared to other regions. To see if this is the case, Figure 5.14 compares the average level of democracy in the former Soviet republics as a proportion of the average level of democracy in Eastern Europe.[51]

---

[51] Eastern Europe is defined as countries in existence between 1991 and 2010 in eastern and southeast Europe: Albania, Bosnia and Herzegovina, Bulgaria, Croatia, Czechoslovakia, Czech Republic, Hungary, Kosovo, Macedonia, Montenegro, Poland, Romania, Slovakia, Slovenia, and Yugoslavia.

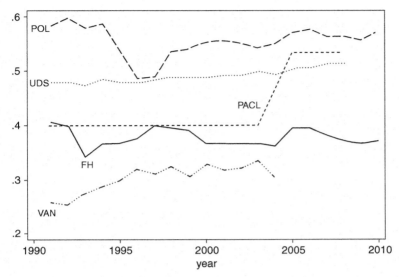

Figure 5.13 Average regional measures of democracy in former Soviet republics for five different indices, 1991–2010

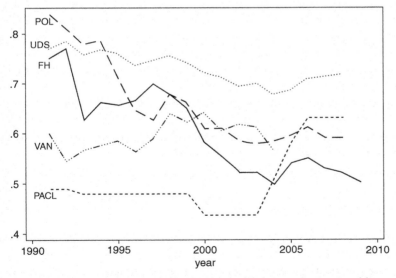

Figure 5.14 Average level of democracy in the former Soviet republics, as a proportion of the average level of democracy in Eastern Europe

There is broad overall agreement among the indices that the former Soviet republics are on average less democratic than countries in Eastern Europe. Yet there are disagreements about the size of that difference, as well as about trends over time. According to Polity, the region has become steadily less democratic compared to Eastern Europe, leveling off in the early 2000s. Freedom House also records a sharp relative decline, albeit one that shows no signs of leveling off. Vanhanen, on the other hand, records no such trend – Eastern Europe is generally more democratic, but this relationship is stable over time. Finally, PACL rates the former Soviet republics as much less democratic, but records a relative improvement after 2004. This change is driven by just two measures, with Georgia and Kyrgyzstan re-coded as democracies following their color revolutions.

A scholar comparing democratic development in the two regions using Polity or (especially) Freedom House would note the steady deterioration of democracy compared to Eastern Europe, and wonder why post-Communist transitions led to such different trajectories in the two regions. A scholar using Vanhanen would note that the region has historically been less democratic than Eastern Europe, but has not become more so since the Soviet collapse. A scholar using PACL would conclude that the former Soviet republics have historically been, on average, not nearly as democratic as Eastern Europe, but recently experienced a large relative gain. Avoiding this spurious conclusion would require some knowledge of the region as well as the coding particularities of that measure.

Given this confusion, it's not surprising that area specialists are critical of large-n measures of democracy. Regional comparisons that use large-n statistics must pay careful attention to both the choice of measure and the state of facts on the ground.

Sources of disagreement: Freedom House and Polity IV in Armenia and Russia

Turning back to disagreements about specific countries: why do measures sometimes present very different pictures of the same event? To explore this in more detail, I examine two examples of disagreement between Freedom House and Polity IV, since these are both very commonly used measures of democratization. First, what causes the

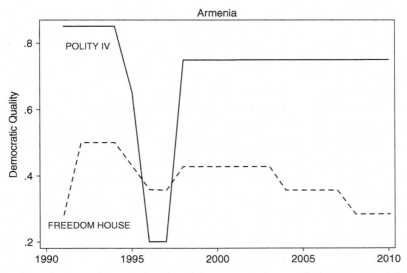

Figure 5.15 Evaluations of democratic quality in Armenia by Freedom House and Polity IV

large dip (and recovery) in Armenia's Polity score in the mid-1990s, a trend not captured or much less pronounced in any other index? Second, why do the Freedom House and Polity measures for Russia diverge so widely in the mid-1990s? Russia is a particularly important case since it forms the background for much analysis of both foreign policy and domestic developments in the post-Soviet region.

In the winter of 1992–1993, the Armenian Revolutionary Federation (ARF) party united with other opposition parties to stage large demonstrations against the government of Levon Ter-Petrossian, who had been elected in a landslide in 1991. ARF is a nationalist party with strong socialist roots that advocates the creation of a Greater Armenia. It enjoys support among segments of the Armenian population and especially among the country's diaspora. In 1994, Ter-Petrossian banned ARF and arrested thirty-one of its leaders. He accused the party of plotting to overthrow the government and of having foreign-based leadership. The move decreased his popularity both with domestic groups and among the diaspora in particular. In the 1996 presidential election, his share of votes fell to 52 percent (compared to 83 percent in the previous election in 1991). The main opposition candidate, a former prime minister, received 42 percent of the vote, in contrast to the 7.2 percent received by the runner-up in the 1991 election. The vote brought accusations of voting irregularities, leading to large public protests, suppressed when Ter-Petrossian sent tanks into the nation's capital.

What happens with Armenia's Polity sub-scores between 1994 and 1996? Openness of executive recruitment remained the same, while the regulation of participation actually improved. The big drops were in measures of executive constraints (5 to 3), competitiveness of executive recruitment (3 to 1), and the competitiveness of participation (4 to 2). Since executive constraint is the most heavily weighted sub-component, a decline in this indicator is particularly influential for the overall score. In Freedom House measures, the civil liberties indicator moves from 3 to 4 in 1993 and stays at that level through the present day. The political rights indicator shows worsening from 3 (1993–1994) to 4 (1995) to 5 (1996–1997) before returning to 4 (1998–2003). The stability of civil liberties during this period is puzzling, because the Freedom House media freedom index for Armenia increases from low to high 50s (a higher number equals less media freedom). In the Freedom House rankings, Armenia declines from 87th place in 1994 to 122nd place in 1996 (out of 191), moving from the 55th to the 69th percentile. The decline is much more precipitous for Polity IV, where Armenia moves from 54th to 119th place (out of 159), or from the 33rd to the 75th percentile. An observer of Armenian democracy who used Polity scores would conclude that the democratic crisis of 1994–1996 was much more severe than would an observer using Freedom House scores.

It is difficult to determine precisely how Freedom House gauges democracy in Armenia during this period, because disaggregated scores are not available until 2006 (this once again demonstrates the need for transparency and disaggregation in democracy measures). A reasonable guess is that while Polity IV focused on elite behavior, Freedom House focused on the democratic situation as a whole. Both measures recorded a decline, but the Polity IV decline was particularly large because the banning of opposition parties signaled a loss of executive constraint, which Polity considers to be the single greatest indicator of democratic quality. Freedom House took the same development as negatively affecting political freedom at the elite level but not the individual rights of Armenia's citizens. In short, the disagreement

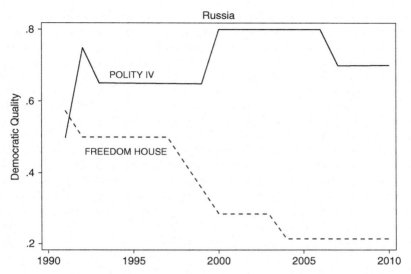

Figure 5.16 Evaluations of democratic quality in Russia by Freedom House and Polity IV

among measures appears to stem from the different ways they conceptualize democracy and the different emphasis they place on the relative importance of elite constraints and individual liberty.

Turning to Russia, the discrepancy between the two measures is striking, as illustrated in the opening of the chapter (see Figure 5.16). The divergence in trends in the late 1990s is particularly puzzling. In this period, Russia's Polity IV measure improves from 13 to 16 (out of 20), while the country's Freedom House score worsens from 3.5 to 5 (out of 7).

Looking at Polity IV sub-scores during this period shows that the increase comes from a change in a single measure – executive constraint, which increases from 3 to 5 between 1999 and 2000 and stays at this level until 2007, when it declines to 4. In fact, changes in the measure of executive constraint accounts for *all* of the variation in Russia's score. For Polity, variation in media freedom or individual liberties was simply insignificant in shaping the measure's assessment of Russian democracy. It seems likely that the increase in executive constraint came from the Duma's unexpected rejection of Yeltsin's nomination of Viktor Chernomyrdin as prime minister in

August of 1998 (the unpopular Chernomyrdin received only 94 votes out of a possible 450). The rejection signaled legislative independence, and since executive constraint forms the most heavily weighted sub-component of Polity, the perceived increase in the power of the Duma led to a significant increase in the country's overall score.

Freedom House records Russia's level of democracy as stable (at 3.5) between 1992 and 1997. In 1998, political rights worsen from 3 to 4; in 1999, civil liberties worsen from 4 to 5; and in 1999, political rights worsen once more from 4 to 5. Both sub-components remain at 5 until 2004. Once again, it's hard to determine what drives the decline in the absence of disaggregated measures. Russia's press freedom index declined during this period, and the financial crisis of 1998 almost certainly undermined socio-economic equality, as did the increasing political clout of the oligarchs and perceptions of corruption among Yeltsin's Kremlin "family" during this period. In short, as Pemstein *et al.* conclude:

> Russia seems to be a case where two measures looked at the same information and came to two different conclusions. Freedom House thought the events from 1996 on indicated a weakening of democracy,[52] while Polity thought these same events led to a strengthening of democracy ... The raters make judgments that are sensible, but incomplete. Both measures cannot be correct but neither have both judges completely missed the mark.[53]

Curiously, the 1996 presidential election, which had been marred by accusations of fraud and American interference, does not lead to a decrease in Freedom House scores. And if the rise of the oligarchs caused a decline in Freedom House scores, their decline under Putin has not brought a corresponding increase. The measure provides ammunition for critics who argue that Freedom House promotes a pro-American agenda. The organization's treatment of Russia has in fact been criticized both by Russian officials and Western academics. Treisman (2011: 341–342) notes that Russian civil liberties are ranked on par with Yemen's, where legislation grants capital punishment for women who commit adultery. Russia's political rights,

---

[52] The authors make a minor mistake here: the decline in Freedom House sub-scores does not begin until 1998.

[53] Pemstein, Meserve, and Melton 2010: 429.

meanwhile, are ranked on par with the United Arab Emirates, a collection of monarchies that did not hold any elections until 2006.[54] According to Freedom House, UAE lacks political parties or an independent judiciary, and severely restricts freedom of expression.[55] In 1998, Polity IV gave Russia a score of 14 (out of 20), while Saudi Arabia and UAE received scores of 0 and 2, respectively. In that year, countries that shared Russia's Freedom House evaluation averaged a score of only 6 in Polity IV. As Treisman concludes:

At a minimum, an acceptable cross-national rating of democracies should be able to distinguish between the kind of system in Russia and government by a federation of dynastic monarchies free from any checks whatsoever, as in the United Arab Emirates. This rules out the Freedom House index.[56]

Turning instead to Polity IV, Treisman finds that by the latter measure Russia's degree of political freedom is unexceptional when compared to countries with similar incomes.[57]

How do other indices measure Russia? As Figure 5.17 shows, most of the other measures fall somewhere between Polity and Freedom House (the exception is PACL, who consistently code Russia as an autocracy). Vanhanen records a sharp spike in 1993, followed by an equally sharp decline after 2002. CAM, UDS, and EIU grade Russia as more democratic than Freedom House but less

---

[54] And even then, the elections were very limited: an electoral college of less than seven thousand people selected by the monarchs was allowed to elect half of the members of the Federal National Council. The other half was directly appointed by the government.

[55] Freedom House 2011 Country Report: United Arab Emirates (http://www.free domhouse.org).

[56] Treisman 2011: 352.

[57] As measured by per capita GDP adjusted for purchasing power parity (Treisman 2011: 352–353). Treisman (2011: 481) notes that even Polity "may not be immune to outside pressure"; in the 2009 update to the index, Russia's score was retroactively lowered by a point for all years after 1992, while Estonia's score was retroactively raised from 16 to 19 during the same period. Since the adjustments were made without substantive justification, Treisman contacted Polity's project director to inquire if the revision was related to the fact that since the late 1990s Polity has been funded by the US government's Political Instability Task Force, which is itself funded by the CIA. The director replied that the perspectives of government supporters were considered as seriously as those of academics and other experts, and that "there has never been any serious arm-twisting from either side."

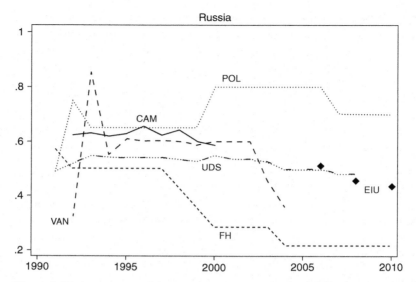

Figure 5.17 Assessment of democracy in Russia using six different measures

democratic than Polity IV, with UDS and EIU recording a slight decline in recent years.

In short, there is wide variation in how the measures view the quality of democracy in Russia. Whether the source is ideological predispositions or the conceptual emphasis on certain elements of democracy over others, this disagreement suggests that the analysis of political and economic development in Russia will be particularly sensitive to the choice of measure.

Conclusion

As this chapter has sought to demonstrate, measures of democracy in the former Soviet republics are fraught with a number of weaknesses. They disagree about particular countries, and about mixed regimes in particular. Because their definitions focus on different aspects of democracy, they sometimes draw different conclusions from the same political outcome. Moreover, since each measure captures different elements of democratic governance, the quest for a "perfect" measure is a futile one. As Munck and Verkuilen conclude, "no single index offers a satisfactory response" to the challenges of definition, measurement, and aggregation, and "even the strongest indices suffer from weaknesses of some importance."[58]

The historical scope of the measure also affects which theories it can test. Arguments about the historical causes and correlates of war may require a longer reach into the past; as Coppedge and Gerring put it, "we suspect that the enduring value of Polity stems partly from its comprehensive historical coverage."[59] The scope of the data can also affect substantive conclusions. The "common restriction of data sets to the post-World War II period," argue Munck and Verkuilen, limits the types of theories they can test.[60] For example, examining the evidence for democratic waves, Przeworski *et al.* criticize Huntington for using a measure based on the percentage of democratic states, and find no evidence for waves when using the criterion of transitions rather than institutional changes.[61] But since two of the three democratic waves of the twentieth century occur before the period in their data set (1950–1990), while the third takes off just as their analysis is truncated, the failure to find evidence of waves is understandable but hardly convincing. Research that examines cross-border diffusion of democracy, particularly before World War II, would thus be better off using Polity IV or Vanhanen for their empirical tests.

The various problems of large-n democracy indices don't mean that statistical measures ought to be abandoned entirely, or even that the application of these measures will inevitably be flawed. However, two crucial caveats are in order. First, once the choice of measure is made, its inherent biases and limitations must be made clear when evaluating the causes and consequences of democratization. This is particularly important for policymakers assessing the impact of external assistance on hybrid regimes, where rankings are especially problematic.

Second, the choice of measure must be justified in relation to what is actually being examined. Since each measure has its own strengths and weaknesses, the nature of the research shapes which strengths are most suitable for the issue being examined, and which weaknesses can most plausibly be overlooked. Binary measures may work well for examining regime duration or when looking at cases of profound political transformations, but less so for examining more modest changes within regimes.[62]

---

[58] Munck and Verkuilen 2002: 28.   [59] Coppedge and Gerring 2011: 249.
[60] Munck and Verkuilen 2002: 6.   [61] Przeworski *et al.* 2000: 40–45.
[62] Collier and Adcock 1999.

Freedom House should not be used to evaluate democracy's relationship with corruption or economic equality, because these substantive elements are already built into the measure itself. Polity IV measures might be appropriate for research that examines constraints on governing elites, but not for studying the expansion of suffrage over the nineteenth century.

Measures of democracy can mislead as much as they clarify, as the first figure in this chapter demonstrates all too clearly. Moreover, the consequences of poor measurement extend beyond scholarly analysis and affect advocacy efforts and policy choices. While a more careful use of these measures is hardly a panacea, self-consciousness about the drawbacks and underlying assumptions of indices can only serve to improve our understanding of democratic development. Highlighting the limitations of a measure can also highlight its strengths.

6 Winning the rankings game

The Republic of Georgia, USAID, and the Doing Business Project

SAM SCHUETH

Although, or perhaps because, there is no consensus about what constitutes place competitiveness (Bristow 2005), recent decades have witnessed a proliferation of regimes of measuring international competitiveness, variously defined, and applied to cities, regions, and states (Malecki 2002; 2004). However, the rise of international rankings appears to have crystallized more specific understandings of competitiveness and judgments of what constitutes a business-friendly state. For many years, the World Economic Forum's annual Global Competitiveness Index (GCI) was the best-known regime of measuring and ranking the economic competitiveness of states (Schwab and Porter 2008). More recently, however, the GCI has been displaced by the World Bank's Ease of Doing Business Index (DBI), which enrolls a global network of analysts to rank state competitiveness using indicators of regulatory quality (World Bank and IFC 2009). Published annually since 2003, DBI is designed to further the World Bank's long-term effort to transform "second" and "third" world countries into "emerging" and "frontier" markets, where economic development is financed by foreign investment (Ó Tuathail 1997; Sidaway and Pryke 2000; Lavelle 2000; Lee 2003).

In terms of its role as an international ranking in this volume's framework, DBI can be viewed as both a source of regulatory power and of expert judgment. More than a schema for measuring competitiveness, DBI is also a tool of what Peck (2002; 2004) calls "neoliberal fast-policy transfer" and "reform at a distance." It works by fostering international competition between policymakers to raise their state's ranking, thereby demonstrating to international investors a commitment to business-friendly policies. Indeed, the considerable authority carried by DBI's institutional sponsor, the World Bank, may explain why the ranking has so quickly become a widely cited assessment of a

151

state's business climate and a tool for rapidly disseminating a particular neoliberal economic reform agenda that calls for the curtailment of specific regulatory practices.

This chapter will show that, during DBI's rapid rise, the ranking appears to be having profound consequences, both in the international arena and within states themselves. In the case of (Caucasus) Georgia, the government carefully targeted its reforms to raise the country's DBI ranking, which vaulted from 100 out of 155 in 2006 into the top 20 by 2008 (World Bank and IFC 2006a; 2007). This rankings ascension, in turn, was used in an investment promotion campaign designed to dispel the country's profile as a post-Soviet failed state and recast it as a new "frontier market." Concurrently, the volume of foreign direct investment (FDI) inflows to Georgia tripled between 2005 and 2007, as a result of which it was the world's ninth-highest-ranked recipient of FDI as a percentage of GDP (UNCTAD 2008).

This chapter details how the Georgia investment promotion strategy targeted higher DBI rankings by using its indicators as a schema for legal reforms. Raised rankings were then used to attract interest from international investors by representing Georgia as an economy with exemplary regulatory institutions. The basis for success of this investment promotion strategy can be analyzed using the concept of "state extraterritoriality" (Phelps 2007). Extraterritoriality here describes how the international ratings and rankings change how the state is "formed out of a nexus of relations and connections, much of which takes its shape from elsewhere" (Allen and Cochrane 2007: 1162). Rather than simply characterizing a particular state, global rankings and ratings are relationally defined, showing relative proximity to an optimal model. Winning the DBI rankings game allowed Georgia to reposition itself vis-à-vis other states, and raise its profile among global investment destinations.

Fitting Georgia to DBI's optimal regulatory model involved combining officials from Georgia's government, USAID contractors, and the Doing Business project, into an assemblage with new capacities for policy transfer and investment promotion. This institutional assemblage – a whole with capacities for strategic action that is greater than the sum of its parts – produced national and global *scale effects*. National-scale effects included new central government capacities to regulate transactions in Georgia's territory. Global-scale effects included new place-characteristics that reshaped the country's extraterritorial relations and elevated its position in the global to-pography of investment locations. A third type of scale effect created gatekeepers that divided global from national access to information about specific investment opportunities in Georgia. In the Georgia case, the state not only strategically responded to the DBI ranking, but, in doing so aggressively, the international ranking helped to reconfigure some fundamental institutions, political relations, and governance structures within the state itself.

The chapter proceeds as follows: I first introduce the concept of state extraterritoriality and the strategic implications of policy credibility for attracting foreign investment. I then move to align the concept of extraterritorial policy credibility with the neoliberal political economy literature, focusing on how competitiveness indices and knowledge networks incentivize the transfer of policy "best practices" from higher- to lower-ranked states. Subsequently, I examine the discrepancy between Georgia's high DBI ranking and its low GCI ranking – the result of DBI-targeted reforms. Following a methodology discussion on relational ethnography, I present data from expert interviews and from participant observation research in USAID's *Georgia Business Climate Reform* (GBCR) project. My analysis traces power geometries within the institutional assemblage that implemented the rankings ascension and investment promotion strategy. I conclude with a discussion of the theoretical implications of the research findings.

State extraterritoriality and establishing policy credibility: The DBI as a tool of neoliberal reform

State extraterritoriality is a useful concept for unraveling the seemingly paradoxical complicity of states in the diminution of their decision-making powers as new, non-state "sites of rulemaking" emerge to govern transnational economic interaction (Phelps 2007: 371). Global rankings and ratings, such as the credit ratings and corruption ratings studied elsewhere in this volume, are part of international regimes that benchmark the economic performance of firms and polities, and further the agendas of international institutions such as the World Bank, IMF, and WTO that support the global diffusion of "best practices" in economic policymaking.

State extraterritoriality and its transnational organization are both prerequisite and consequence of states' pursuit of economic interests beyond their borders. The case of Singapore is illustrative: in the years immediately following its independence, having reached the limits of growth via FDI in labor-intensive manufacturing in the 1980s, Singapore shifted its strategy to promote inward FDI in higher value-added sectors such as research and development, finance, and supply chain coordination and control, while promoting outward FDI in lower value-added manufacturing to Batam and Bintan islands and other regional locations. Singapore's success provides a model case of extraterritorial accumulation for other small developing states.

Indeed, Singapore was an oft-cited model in policymaking circles during my fieldwork in Georgia in 2007–2008. Georgia's immediate goal was indiscriminate FDI attraction and finding buyers for a large-scale privatization program. Hitherto largely overlooked by transnational investors, Georgia lacked any obvious competitive advantage for the pursuit of FDI. Its strategy was to accumulate "reputational capital," i.e. the credibility of a territory as an amenable site for transnational business and investment (Phelps 2007). Among the many sources of reputational capital, policy credibility is undoubtedly important.

Policy credibility can be gained from regulatory undercutting and supply-side interventions that "get the institutions right" in accordance with the neoliberal "competition state" model of economic development (Amin and Thrift 1995; Cerny 1997; Chang 2002; Fougner 2006). Neoliberalism in the periphery rejects state-directed financing to strategic firms and economic sectors, privileging FDI as "the highest form of external finance for development, ahead of portfolio investment, commercial loans, or overseas development aid" (Phelps, Power, and Wanjiru 2007: 84). The basic enabling condition for FDI is the elimination of restrictions on cross-border capital flows – a macroeconomic "Washington Consensus" policy (Williamson 1990) instituted by a global network of government economists trained at select US universities (Chwieroth 2007). Building on capital account liberalization, DBI is a tool for extending the transnational regime of neoliberal policymaking to microeconomic reforms designed to improve local "investment climates": "the laws, regulations, and institutional arrangements that shape daily economic activity" (World Bank and IFC 2008: v).

Minimalist regulation is closely tied to the institutional determinants of territorial competitiveness, as formulated by the ranking methodologies of GCI, and especially DBI. These rankings provide transnational investors and market analysts with ready comparisons of states' institutional and regulatory environments, and policymakers with policy objectives imbued with extraterritorial legitimacy. Rankings and ratings thus narrow the available set of reputable policy options; however, this narrowing also frames a strategic opportunity for gaining extraterritorial policy credibility by ascending in the competitiveness rankings, a feat accomplished via transferring policy "best practices" from higher-ranked states.

Competitiveness indices as tools for policy transfer

Begun in 2003 by the World Bank's research division, the DBI is now widely accepted by states as an authoritative external judgment of their comparative business climate. But more than simply measuring competitiveness or regulatory quality, the World Bank's Doing Business project also is designed to facilitate specific reforms:

Since its start in October 2003 the Doing Business project has inspired or informed 113 reforms around the world. In 2006 Georgia targeted the top 25 list and used Doing Business indicators as benchmarks of its progress. It now ranks 18 on the ease of doing business, and the government has set an even more ambitious goal. Saudi Arabia and Mauritius have targeted the top 10. Both have made tremendous progress: Saudi Arabia now ranks 23, and Mauritius 27. (World Bank and IFC 2007: 7)

Each Doing Business report includes a "user's guide" for finding reform examples from other states, while the Project's website (http:// www.doingbusiness.org) offers a "rankings calculator" and extensive details on the EBDI methodology – useful for determining which reforms will produce the greatest ascension in the rankings. At the center of the DBI knowledge network, the website functions as a type of knowledge clearing-house for policymakers to reference as they work to adopt regulatory "best practices" that DBI identifies.

What I like about *Doing Business* ... is that it creates a forum for exchanging knowledge. It's no exaggeration when I say I checked the top 10 in every indicator and we just asked them, "What did you do?" If there is any advantage to starting late in anything, it's that you can learn from others. (Dr. Mahmoud Mohieldin, Egypt's Minister of Investment, quoted in World Bank and IFC 2008: vii)

The above quote recalls Gerschenkron's (1962) argument that developmentally "backwards" states should "catch up" by adopting technology from more advanced states, and skip over intervening "stages of development." Such evolutionary metaphors – widespread and problematic features of competitiveness discourses (Schoenberger 1998; Sheppard 2000) – are belied by the fundamental incongruity between evolutionary economics and competitiveness indices such as GCI and DBI. An evolutionary approach would examine the historical and relational contexts of competitiveness, as well as stochastic factors such as entrepreneurship through which new developmental trajectories may unexpectedly emerge (Boschma 2004; Grabher 2009). In contrast, competitiveness indices use methodological territorialism and quantification to block out historical and relational contexts. This renders states as clearly bounded and internally coherent territorial economies with competitiveness attributes that are their exclusive possessions (Sheppard 2000; Bristow 2005).

By quantifying competitiveness attributes and benchmarking their relative quality via rankings, an index defines an optimal development model that is approximated by the highest-ranked territories (Malecki 2007). Further, quantification abstracts competitiveness attributes from contexts and renders them fungible – low-growth, low-productivity policies can be replaced with better policies, infrastructure can be upgraded, etc. (Sheppard 2000; Bristow 2005). DBI in particular is an exemplary technology of fast policy since it quantifies business environment quality as "simplified, disembedded, and reproducible administrative routines" (Peck 2002: 349). This implies a "level playing field" for competition, i.e. all territories are presumed to be equally positioned to succeed since the optimal development model can be achieved by adopting the proper mix of "best practice" economic policies. The development "magic bullet" is thus identified as the capacity of policymakers to successfully transfer competitiveness-enhancing attributes from higher-ranked territories.

When competitiveness ratings and rankings are used to evaluate the technocratic prowess of policymakers in different territories, state competiveness is individualized as a competition between different policymakers (Malecki 2004, Bristow 2005). Part of the global proliferation of techniques for performance auditing (Power 1997; Strathern 2000a; Yeung 2002; Dunn 2004; Ward and England 2007; Kipnis 2008), competitiveness indicators are useful for incentivizing the adoption of international "best practices" in economic policy. Clear costs and benefits must however be assigned to rankings and ratings for these to function effectively to regulate behavior, as in "New Public Management" (Lane 2000) competitive regimes for distributing funding (e.g. British academe's Research Assessment Exercise). Hence, IFIs and international donors increasingly attempt to motivate conformity with perceived best practices by making the allocation of development assistance conditional upon a country's scores on indicators of "good governance" (Hermes and Lensink 2001; Hout 2004; Soederberg 2004; Zanotti 2005; Nanda 2006; Mawdsley 2007; Roberts, Wright, and O'Neill 2007; Löwenheim 2008).

Further monetary incentives for policy transfer – less direct but nevertheless salient – are found in multi-country econometric models that show a positive association between higher scores on various indicators of institutional quality, and greater volumes of FDI (Stein and Daude 2001; Globerman and Shapiro 2002; Benassy-Quere, Coupet, and Mayer 2007). Market analysts at firms such as Standard and Poor's use GCI and DBI rankings and various other governance indicators to assess country risk (Hessel and Hall 2007), and to create customized knowledge for investor decision making (Arndt and Oman 2006). Unlike "developed markets," which generally occupy high competitiveness rankings, competitiveness indicators may provide relatively more important data for investor decision-making vis-à-vis "emerging" and "frontier" markets, where information on investment opportunities is often scarce (Sidaway and Bryson 2002; Lai 2006). Policymakers may thus expect greater international aid and/or investment from adopting policies that cause their state's scores to improve on governance indices such as DBI. This set of incentives forms "the basis for a national and international market in transferable policy lessons and strategies, the unpredictable and inescapably slow process of institutional learning having been reduced to a technocratic process of administrative cloning" (Peck 2002: 349).

Playing the rankings game: Comparing Georgia's performance on DBI and GCI

If competing policymakers and organizations expect benefits to follow from ascending in a league table, then they will be likely to "play the rankings game." In the context of state competitiveness, the rankings game similarly involves "trying to 'Best the System' by re-presenting/configuring . . . data in the most favorable way or otherwise attempting to influence the input metrics" (Hazelkorn 2008: 194). As in the case of Georgia, shortcuts to extraterritorial policy credibility were found by exploiting connections between competitiveness indicators, capital markets, and international development assistance. In this way, Georgia's rankings ascension strategy furthered its effort to attract foreign investment. Some input metrics are, however, easier to influence than others, as revealed by comparing Georgia's DBI and GCI rankings.

While Georgia was ranked in the bottom 35th and 32nd percentiles respectively on the 2006 editions of DBI and GCI, by 2009 Georgia occupied DBI's 92nd percentile, while its GCI percentile ranking languished at 32nd.[1] The difference between Georgia's 2009 percentile ranks on the two indices is the single largest of any country – nearly three standard deviations from the mean.[2] Because such discrepancies in country rankings may cast doubt on the validity of DBI's measures of international competitiveness, the authors of *Doing Business 2009* attempt to reassure readers with the claim that "economies that rank among the top 20 are those with high per capita income and productivity and highly developed regulatory systems" (World Bank and IFC 2008: vii). Yet, despite its rank of 15th (see Table 6.1), Georgia's GDP per capita is far below any other country's in the top 20 – only 14 percent of the average.[3] In another attempt to support the claim that DBI measures economic competitiveness despite outliers such as Georgia, *Doing Business* reports a high overall correlation between DBI and GCI rankings (World Bank and IFC 2009: vi). Indeed, the two indices' 2009 rankings are correlated with a Spearman's coefficient

---

[1] Georgia's DBI ranking reported in the yearly editions of *Doing Business* increased from 100/155 in 2006, to 37/175 in 2007, to 18/178 in 2008, to 15/181 in 2009, to 11/183 in 2010 (World Bank and IFC 2006a; 2006b; 2007; 2008; 2009). The country's GCI ranking was 85/125 in 2006, 90/131 in 2007, 90/134 in 2008, and 90/133 in 2009 (Porter, Schwab, Lopez-Claros, and Sala-i-Martin 2006; Porter, Schwab, and Sala-i-Martin 2007; Schwab and Porter 2008; Schwab, Sala-i-Martin, and Blanke 2009).

[2] To be exact, 2.96 is the normalized difference (Z-score) for Georgia's DBI and GCI percentile ranks.

[3] Georgia's 2007 per capita GDP was $4,405.44 measured by purchasing power parity in constant 2005 international dollars. The average figure for DBI's top 20 states in 2009 was $31,423.08. Source: World Bank, World Development Indicators.

Table 6.1. *DBI top-20 ranked states and corresponding GCI rankings*

Country	DBI 2009 Rank	GCI 2008/9 Rank
Singapore	1	5
New Zealand	2	24
United States	3	1
Hong Kong	4	11
Denmark	5	3
United Kingdom	6	12
Ireland	7	22
Canada	8	10
Australia	9	18
Norway	10	15
Iceland	11	20
Japan	12	9
Thailand	13	34
Finland	14	6
Georgia	**15**	**90**
Saudi Arabia	16	27
Sweden	17	4
Bahrain	18	37
Belgium	19	19
Malaysia	20	21

of 0.811.[4] The rankings scattergram depicted in Figure 6.1 sets Georgia's data point far in the top left-hand corner: the furthermost outlier vis-à-vis the close overall correspondence between the indices' rankings.[5] This position reflects strategic planning and concerted effort to use the DBI guide to policy transfer, in order to hit targets for rankings ascension.[6]

[4] I deleted countries not ranked by both of the indices from the data set when I calculated this correlation coefficient (N = 130). The coefficient is significant at the 0.01 level.

[5] Though the non-parametric Spearman's rank correlation coefficient is best suited for evaluating the level of correspondence between the two indices' percentile ranks, there is also a strong linear relationship represented by the solid line in Figure 6.1. The dashed lines represent the 95 percent confidence intervals of the linear R^2 statistic of 0.657.

[6] Though my arguments about Georgia's outlier status are even more relevant to its 2010 DBI rank of 11/183 (6th percentile) than its 2009 rank, I analyze the 2009 rankings for consistency with data analysis presented in the paper's later sections on how the 2009 rankings were targeted.

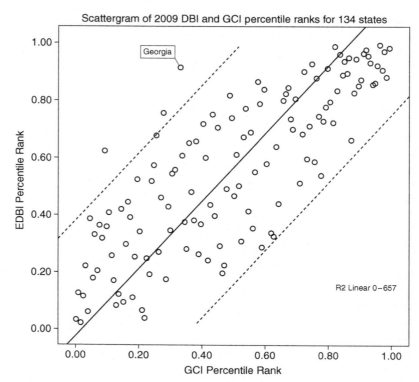

Figure 6.1 Scattergram of 2009 DBI and GCI percentile ranks for 134 states

Methodological differences between the two indices create the structure of opportunity for Georgia's unparalleled ascension on DBI. Whereas GCI seeks a comprehensive model of the "set of institutions, policies, and factors that determine the level of productivity of a country" (Schwab and Porter 2008: 3; authors' italics removed), DBI provides a narrower model of competitiveness focused on regulatory rules. In its 2009 edition DBI included ten indicators of the quality of "regulations for starting a business, dealing with construction permits, employing workers, registering property, getting credit, protecting investors, paying taxes, trading across borders, enforcing contracts and closing a business – as they apply to domestic small and medium-size enterprises" (World Bank and IFC 2008: v).

Minimalism and parsimony are the overriding criteria for quantifying regulatory quality; DBI uses a Taylorist methodology to count the cost in time and money for a "standardized case scenario" – usually a medium-sized limited liability company or local equivalent located in the country's largest city – to comply with regulations. Transactions between firms and state institutions are broken down into separate steps in order to provide time-to-completion estimates. Data are collected from textual analysis of regulations, laws, and fee schedules, as well as surveys of lawyers and business people with first-hand knowledge of regulatory compliance. The highest-scoring states have the lowest official cost of regulatory compliance. For example, the state with the fewest separate taxes and separate payments, lowest tax rates, and fastest (electronic) payment system will score highest on the "paying taxes" indicator. States that score the highest on the "employing workers" indicator have the least regulation of hiring and firing decisions. The measurement focus on legally mandated procedures and fees enables states with the capacity to quickly pass reform legislation to leap upward in the DBI rankings faster, and further, than is feasible with GCI.

The relative "stickiness" of Georgia's GCI ranking results largely from the use of "stages of development" and opinion surveys to compile the index. At Georgia's (low) stage of development, GCI's opinion survey data on institutional quality are heavily weighted determinants of overall competitiveness (Schwab and Porter 2008: 7). *Doing Business*, on the other hand, rejects weighting indicators according to "stages of development," arguing that "one size can fit all" (World Bank and IFC 2004: xvi) – there is one global "best practice" model of minimalist regulation which is equally applicable to all states. Further, opinion surveys are disavowed since sampling and survey design biases are difficult to avoid (cf. Lall 2001), and "perceptions measures are often driven by general sentiment but do not provide useful indicators of specific features of the business environment" (World Bank and IFC 2004: 13).

To be sure, fast-paced reforms such as the 2007 changes to Georgian laws on protecting minority shareholders, which improved Georgia's rank on "protecting investors" from 135/175 in 2007, to 33/178 in 2008, may outpace perceptions of their impacts. Yet, without the use of perceptions data, DBI's indicators cannot capture institutional interdependencies that affect legal norms and the implementation of new legal rules (Davis and Kruse 2007). DBI's methodological myopia makes it possible to game the system of measuring economic competitiveness by legislating dramatic rankings improvements, which may not reflect prevailing relations between firms and the state.

Like other transparency regimes and types of performance auditing, the type of visibility that DBI produces works simultaneously to conceal what is not or cannot be measured through its methodology (Strathern 2000b). In particular, the representation of an exemplary regulatory environment created by Georgia's DBI ranking ascension is strategically valuable for concealing institutional deficiencies revealed by GCI and other sources, such as insecure property rights and the lack of an independent judiciary (Papava 2006; Transparency International 2007b). Using data from opinion surveys of Georgian businesspeople, GCI ranked Georgia 109 on "property rights," 112 on "judicial independence," and 123 on "protection of minority shareholders' interests," out of a total 134 countries (Schwab and Porter 2008: 169).[7] Despite the seemingly fundamental importance of these factors to the quality of a country's business environment, DBI methodologically ignores them.

Nevertheless, outperforming peer countries according to DBI's investment climate benchmarks was an effective extraterritorial strategy for promoting certain types of investment and attracting foreign investors to privatizations of state assets. Figure 6.2 shows the strong

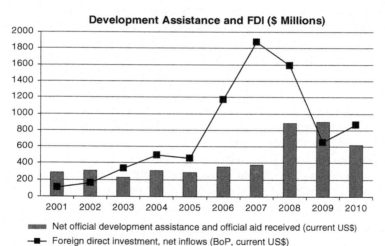

Figure 6.2 Amount of development assistance and FDI received by Georgia annually

---

[7] These indicators are counted by GCI as sources of competitive disadvantage that outweigh Georgia's rank of 6/134 on GCI's "burden of government regulation" indicator.

increase in the volume of inward FDI to Georgia since 2005. By 2007, FDI far exceeded international development assistance as a source of finance, but after Georgia's August 2008 war with Russia, and the onset of the global financial crisis, assistance again rose to a higher level than inward FDI. The policy credibility reflected in Georgia's raised international rankings undoubtedly contributed to the willingness of the World Bank, IMF, and international donors to provide over $2.42 billion in assistance in 2008–2009. This assistance amounted to over 10 percent of Georgia's nominal GDP for the two worst years of the global financial crisis. Few of these funds were spent on repairing war damage, as nearly all of the destruction occurred in the breakaway territory of South Ossetia, which passed to Russian military control as a result of the conflict. Rather, the foreign assistance made up significantly for the shortfall in international investment and allowed Georgia to weather global economic turmoil without a major bank failure or balance of payments crisis.

Relational ethnography

I use a relational methodology to analyze how Georgia won the DBI rankings game by building a set of strategic connections and interdependencies between specific actors and state institutions. The capacity to promote investment did not reside with any particular agency, but rather emerged from the relations composing an institutional assemblage.

My effort to use ethnography to "compose the global from below" (Burawoy 2001: 343) involved becoming enrolled as a participant and observer. I gained access to weekly staff meetings at USAID's Georgia Business Climate Reform (GBCR) project in Georgia's capital city, Tbilisi, observing a total of fourteen meetings between April 2007 and March 2008. These meetings of the project's entire staff usually lasted between one and two hours, with twenty to thirty persons in attendance depending on the presence or absence of short-term consultants working on specific project objectives. I also observed seven meetings between GBCR's top staff and top officials from Georgia's State Ministry for Reform Coordination (SMRC) – the primary Georgian government agency tasked with writing commercial legislation and business regulations. In these latter meetings, as well as several other instances when I observed meetings between GBCR's staff and

Georgian government officials, I attempted to be an unobtrusive observer of the interactions of Georgian officials with project staff. When I was in attendance at GBCR staff meetings, however, I was asked to make a brief weekly report on my research activities outside the project. I also contributed editing work on the website of the Georgian National Investment Agency (http://www.investingeorgia.org).

My presence in the meetings and around the project's offices was quickly accepted by the staff as a normal part of the life of the project, and I was able to wander freely through the offices and informally interview staff. My credentials as an academic researcher facilitated my access to the project, including deliverables and internal documents. Further, my presence in some respects conferred an added level of legitimacy and importance to the project, and Georgia's overall reform effort, as worthy of scholarly attention. This access to GBCR enabled my observation of the power relations surrounding the design and implementation of the strategy of targeting investment climate indicators, building extraterritorial policy credibility, and promoting foreign investment.

In addition to data gathered through participant observation at GBCR, this chapter is informed by data collected from thirty individual interviews conducted over two different periods of fieldwork in 2005 and 2007–2008. The interviewees included foreign experts, local professionals, Georgian government officials, and USAID officials. All of the interviewees exercised various capacities in the design and implementation of Georgia's economic reforms. Their names remain confidential. Depending on the respondent, interview questions focused on the causes of success or failure of particular reform efforts, the politics surrounding reform implementation, relations between the Georgian government and international aid agencies, as well as the departures between the new legal frameworks being created by the government and the actual functioning of regulatory institutions.

Composing the institutional assemblage

USAID's strong support for Georgia is part of a larger context of geopolitical competition between the US and Russia (O'Loughlin, Ó Tuathail, and Kolossov 2005; Ó Tuathail 2008) over control of export routes for hydrocarbons from Central Asia (Ericson 2009). In a display of support for this important ally, USAID designed the five-year, $12.9

million GBCR project not to act on its own assessment of Georgia's needs, but rather to implement the reform priorities of the Georgian government. GBCR described this as "a fundamentally different approach to development," which gives the Georgian government "unprecedented influence over the project's agenda and the allocation of its resources."[8]

GBCR's mandate also signaled USAID's satisfaction with the results of the 2003 regime change it had helped foster in Georgia, i.e. the "Rose Revolution." The revolution consisted of massive street demonstrations against a rigged parliamentary election, and resulted in an election re-run in which the major opposition party gained the parliamentary supermajority necessary to change Georgia's constitution. The leader of the opposition, Mikheil Saakashvili, then won the presidency with 96 percent of the vote. USAID helped set the stage for these events by diverting funding from the government of President Shevardnadze to Georgian civil society groups that organized the revolution (Antaleva 2003). The leaders – mostly youthful, westernized Georgians educated at US universities through federal exchange programs – joined the new Georgian government, and donor funding followed them back to the national budget. In this way, USAID and the Georgian government began to form an institutional assemblage with new capacities for economic reform and investment promotion.

The Saakashvili government's sweeping mandate, reformist zeal, neoliberal economic policies, and expertise at interfacing with foreign aid donors made it a strong counterpart for USAID. Styling itself as a revolutionary vanguard leading the Georgian nation away from its Soviet past to its rightful place in Europe, the lack of any legislative check on the government was coupled with a penchant for radical "heroic action" that placed great onus on reforms that would provide immediate, visible impacts (Bruckner 2009). For example, in 2004 approximately 50,000 public sector workers were dismissed in the effort to build a minimalist, administratively efficient state free of petty corruption (Taylor 2004). The post-Soviet *militsia* was entirely disbanded and a new, Western-style police force was created. Regulatory reforms slashed the number of licenses, permits, and endorsements required to operate a business from over 900 to 160, and various inspectorates, including health and sanitary inspection regimes,

---

[8] GBCR First Quarterly Report (September 20, 2005 – December 19, 2006), p. 3.

were eliminated entirely. Privatization meant that Georgia would sell "everything that can be sold, except its conscience," according to GBCR's main partner, Kakha Bendukidze, the State Minister for Reform Coordination.[9] The success of GBCR as a partner for the government depended on fast results and high-impact, high-profile reforms that would create extraterritorial policy credibility for the Saakashvili government.

Of the many international aid projects ongoing in Georgia, GBCR was the preferred partner of Bendukidze and SMRC because its mandate enabled the flexible allocation of resources in support of the government's changing priorities. By June 2006, continuous consultation and collaboration between SMRC and GBCR led to the convergence of both organizations' priorities on making sure that DBI reflected the progress already being made in regulatory reform. GBCR replicated DBI's methodology with data that it collected independently using business process mapping methods – e.g. GBCR staff counted the number of documents and days necessary to clear goods through Georgian customs terminals, and visited the offices, filled the forms, and paid the fees necessary to register a new business. GBCR compared the results of its independent research with the indicators published for Georgia in the 2006 edition of DBI (World Bank and IFC 2006a).

The World Bank team, led by project manager Simeon Djankov, met with the [GBCR] project twice in June to discuss a comparison table of World Bank 2006 data with data collected by the project over the last three months ... Georgia's standing in the 2007 survey will be even better than it might have been because the World Bank was so impressed with the methodology and baseline results collected by the project that they accepted the more accurate data we collected ... Business Climate Reform will be listed in this year's survey as an official contributor and we anticipate an even closer working relationship with the World Bank in compiling data for the 2008 survey.[10]

In this way, GBCR became part of the DBI global network, with several GBCR staff listed as contributors in the 2007, 2008, and 2009 editions of *Doing Business*.[11] By the time I began participant

[9] Kakha Bendukidze, "A different sort of oligarch," *The Economist* July 29, 2004.
[10] GBCR Third Quarterly Report (March 20, 2006 – June 30, 2006), p. 13.
[11] Perhaps recognizing a potential conflict of interest between writing regulations, measuring their quality, and basing claims to project success on rankings ascension, *Doing Business* no longer lists among contributors GBCR or any other development projects funded by international donors.

observation of GBCR's activities in April 2007, Georgian policymakers were enjoying international publicity from the award of the "Doing Business – 2007 Top Reformer Prize" by the World Bank. GBCR was highlighting its own contribution to Georgia's success story in its reports to USAID, and counting the implementation of its recommendations as "responsible for improving Georgia's performance from 59th to 36th in [rank on the DBI indicator] 'Starting a Business' and 149th to 95th in 'Trading Across Borders'."[12] GBCR staffers were preparing their data contribution to the 2008 edition of DBI. GBCR and SMRC were working closely together to draft legislation that would break Georgia into the top-25-ranked countries, and retain the "Top Reformer" title. Working towards a common, extraterritorial goal produced new interdependencies between GBCR and SMRC – the success of both organizations would be judged in no small part by how far Georgia ascended through the DBI rankings. The assemblage of actors and institutions around DBI targets produced new state capacities to regulate Georgia's economy, as USAID resources were channeled into drafting new legislation, information systems, and training for officials.

Campbell's Law in practice? Targeting the indicators and transferring policies

Pursuing the common goal of achieving a rank in the top 25 created new relationships between members of the Georgian government and GBCR's staff, as well as between Georgia and competitor countries in the DBI rankings. In April 2007 GBCR was closely watching Sweden's seventh-ranked performance on the "registering property" indicator. GBCR sought to replicate Sweden's best practice system, such that property registration would require only one procedure completed with the payment of a standard fee at any bank branch. New information technology purchased out of the GBCR budget, and regulations drafted by GBCR staff, enabled Georgia to ascend to the rank of 2nd out of 181, surpassing Sweden's rank of 7th on the 2009 DBI. Reforming Georgia's national property registry was an area where power relations within the GBCR–SMRC–DBI assemblage were relatively synergetic. Nevertheless, when SMRC wanted to push a law

---

[12] GBCR Year Two Work Plan Update (May 31, 2007), p. 5.

through parliament requiring collateralized property to be repossessed within twenty days of a loan default, GBCR was able to use its analysis of DBI methodology to demonstrate that passing this law would lower Georgia's "registering property" rank. SMRC then shelved the draft law. The emergence of this asymmetrical power relation of GBCR–DBI over SMRC demonstrates how DBI became a site of extraterritorial rule when one of its indicators was adopted as a performance target. In this instance, targeting a top rank on the "registering property" indicator governed Georgian policymaking by not only incentivizing resource outlays on building the capacities of Georgia's National Property Registry, but also by interdicting a reform initiated by the government.

Unlike the successful cooperative effort to improve Georgia's "registering property" rank, targeting the "trading across borders" indicator was an area where the institutional assemblage was less capable of policy transfer. GBCR considered customs reform in F.Y.R. Macedonia to be a model for Georgia in 2007, and flew in consultants to replicate Macedonia's risk management system. The computerized system would only flag for inspection those shipments and customs declarations categorized as carrying a relatively high risk of fraud. Declarations from the "gold list" of the largest, most trustworthy importers would be accepted without inspection, drastically improving Georgia's ranking by speeding the clearance of goods through Georgian customs.

Despite the will of the Saakashvili government to remake Georgia into a Singapore-like entrepôt to Central Asia, Georgia's low capacity to collect taxes complicated the transfer of DBI's "best practices" for customs. Nearly all manufactured goods sold in Georgia were imports, entering the country in small and irregularly packaged lots that were difficult to value for taxation. Final sale usually took place in Georgia's pervasive informal bazaars unobserved by tax officials. Given these conditions, customs terminals were the key sites for capturing tax revenue from merchandise sales. Customs worked under the assumption that every importer worked to evade payment of customs duties, and exhaustive inspections were the norm.[13] This had helped raise tax revenues by more than 300 percent over

---

[13] This perception was a common refrain across several expert interviews that I conducted in Tbilisi in July 2007.

Table 6.2. *Georgia's 2009 Ease of Doing Business rankings,*
all ten indicators

Indicator	Rank
Registering property	2
Starting a business	4
Employing workers (ease of hiring and firing)	5
Dealing with construction permits	10
Getting credit	28
Protecting investors	38
Enforcing contracts	43
Trading across borders	81
Closing a business	92
Paying taxes	110
DBI rank (aggregate)	**15**

2003–2007.[14] Yet, as indicated by Georgia's low 2009 "trading across borders" rank (see Table 6.2), customs clearance under these conditions was a difficult, expensive, and time-consuming ordeal.

While SMRC supported GBCR's risk management initiative, it was unable to clear the way for its implementation, as new power relations emerged to incapacitate the work of the assemblage towards policy transfer and ranking ascension. Opposition arose from some large importers that had histories of customs violations and would therefore be competitively disadvantaged by exclusion from the proposed "gold list" of trusted firms. Most importantly, mid-level bureaucrats in the revenue administration opposed risk management and created the bottleneck where GBCR's policy transfer was interdicted. The revenue administration would take GBCR's latest draft regulations and rewrite them so as to disenable risk management, whereupon GBCR would draft a new set of regulations, and hand them back to the revenue administration to again subvert.

---

[14] Total Georgian tax revenue averaged only 7.6 percent of GDP over 1997–2003. This made the Shevardnadze regime heavily dependent on foreign aid to fund state expenditures, and was considered a symptom of pervasive official corruption by the donor community (OECD 2005). By 2007 tax revenue had grown to 23 percent of GDP. Source: World Bank, World Development Indicators, GEPLAC 2008).

I followed the back-and-forth over customs reform and risk management through GBCR staff meetings in the spring and summer of 2007, noting an ever increasing level of frustration with the lack of progress. When the 2008 edition of *Doing Business* was released at the end of September 2007, GBCR staff learned that President Saakashvili was disappointed by Georgia's low rank of 64th out of 178 on the "trading across borders" indicator. The President ordered the government to "fix customs" by December 1, 2007, and the government set a new target of the 35th rank on "trading across borders" for the 2009 DBI. To hit the target, the Minister of Finance promised to implement 90 percent of GBCR's recommendations. Yet, lack of progress on customs reform made Georgia slip down the rankings to 81st out of 181 in the 2009 DBI, while its competitor, Macedonia, moved up to 64th. "Trading across borders" was thus a case where the work of the assemblage was impeded by the context of Georgia's effort to build the capacity to extract taxes from firms and individuals. With a more sustainable tax system in place by 2009, the institutional assemblage finally succeeded in customs policy transfer, and Georgia ascended to the rank of 30th out of 183 on the 2010 DBI.

The limits to policy transfer are illustrated by the variation in Georgia's 2009 DBI rankings, displayed in Table 6.2. Georgia's rankings on DBI's ten indicators are listed in order from highest to lowest. Rankings ascension was easiest where the measurement focus of the indicators was on legal rules, and where SMRC and GBCR enjoyed the greatest autonomy to co-draft laws and regulations. Saakashvili's parliamentary supermajority ensured the quick passage of SMRC's laissez-faire labor laws, producing a high rank on the "employing workers" indicator. On "dealing with construction permits," SMRC and GBCR hit the target by collaboratively rewriting the relevant regulation more than twenty times. New legislation alone produced Georgia's upward leap on "protecting investors," discussed above. In addition to reform legislation, rankings ascension on the other indicators required the popular uptake of new services such as credit registration and tax e-filing, as well as the development of new institutional capacities for quickly processing service requests. Building new institutional capacity was easiest where bureaucratic offices were relatively autonomous, i.e. where bureaucratic functions did not much depend on the work of other agencies, and where local political interests were not strongly affected by reforms. Good examples include the bureaus responsible for the property and business registries, which were relatively free to act on GBCR's legal recommendations and to reorganize operations around the new information technology procured by GBCR. This produced high rankings on the "starting a business" and "registering property" indicators.

Targeting the indicators that fall at the bottom of Table 6.2 was complicated by political context, and interdependencies among state institutions with varying levels of capacity. While Georgia's ranking on "enforcing contracts" improved as a result of the new legislation co-written by SMRC and GBCR, ascension was impeded by the relatively long period of time that it takes for courts to rule on a dispute in Georgia, in comparison to other states. The assemblage was least capable of policy transfer on "paying taxes" and, at least initially, on "trading across borders." Here the priority of combating widespread local practices of tax evasion sometimes overrode DBI's extraterritorial performance incentives.

Georgia's relatively low 2009 rank on "closing a business" resulted not from impediments to policy transfer, but rather from a failed departure from the policy transfer model of the institutional assemblage. State Minister Bendukidze and the creator and director of the Doing Business Project, Simeon Djankov, co-drafted Georgia's 2007 bankruptcy law without significant involvement from GBCR. According to *Doing Business 2008* (World Bank and IFC 2007: 55), the new law created "bankruptcy procedures that should take less than 1 year in the event of reorganization and just 6 months if the business is slated for liquidation. That would allow Georgia to enter the top 10 list on the speed of resolving bankruptcy." Here, a power asymmetry of DBI–SMRC over GBCR emerged in the effort to use Georgia as a kind of laboratory for establishing a new global benchmark on bankruptcy reform. New legislation set time-to-completion requirements, yet failed to reduce the average time to resolve bankruptcy. Slow resolutions were the result of complicated auction procedures that are theoretically sound but practically dysfunctional in the Georgian context, discouraging potential buyers of distressed assets.[15]

---

[15] The "closing a business" indicator measures whether a typical bankrupt firm's assets do in fact change hands quickly, not whether the law says that they must. Georgia's DBI indicator of time to close a business was unchanged at 3.3 years from the 2008 to 2010 editions of *Doing Business* (World Bank and IFC 2007: 121; 2008: 105; 2009: 122). Cross-country comparison of auction procedures is missing from otherwise extensive background research on "closing a business" (Djankov, Hart, McLiesh, and Shleifer 2008).

Investment promotion and international scale effects

Georgia's improved DBI rankings provided the central focus of an investment promotion campaign designed to "imagineer" (Lai 2006) Georgia as an investment destination. Although *Doing Business 2008* would not be published until September, the data gathering for Georgia's 2008 rankings was completed by mid-June 2007. After vetting its calculation of how the year's reforms would affect Georgia's 2008 rankings with Doing Business Project officials, GBCR was positive that Georgia would meet its objective of moving into the DBI top 25, and be included on the list of the top 10 reformers.[16] The government wanted to maximize the international publicity that Georgia's reform performance would receive when *Doing Business 2008* was published. The international advertising firm M&C Saatchi was contracted to design an advertising campaign to promote investment in Georgia that would run through the second half of 2007.

The Georgian government allocated $7.8 million to the first year of its investment promotion campaign,[17] targeted at "key opinion formers, and businessmen in Western Europe and the United States."[18] The campaign included the production and placement of print advertisements in *The Wall Street Journal*, *The Economist*, and *The Financial Times*, as well as television advertisements aired on CNBC and CNN. It culminated with Georgia's prime minister, other top officials, and favored Georgian businesspeople traveling on a road show of investor relations forums held in Vienna, London, and New York, and hosted respectively by *The Economist*, *The Financial Times*, and Dow Jones.

Using the slogan, "And the winner is: GEORGIA," the advertisements drew directly on DBI rankings to make favorable comparisons between Georgia and other countries. Examples from the advertising

---

[16] Because other states had made larger moves up the rankings from lower starting points, Georgia won fifth place among the world's top reformers, despite having made the most reforms of any state according to Doing Business. Ministers from the top 10 countries attended the "Doing Business Reformers Club" event held at the New York Stock Exchange in June 2008.

[17] "Extra GEL 2.7 million allotted for support to the global advertising campaign for popularization of Georgia," *Black Sea Press* September 18, 2007.

[18] "The Winner is: GEORGIA ad-campaign has been very well received and much commented on in the USA and Western Europe" (interview with Aneil Bedi, representative of M&C Saatchi, UK), *Georgia Today*, *Invest Today monthly supplement*, October 2007.

campaign include, "Georgia vs. Georgia: which Georgia – country in Europe or the state in the US – has the most attractive climate for overseas investors?" "Georgia vs. Germany: where is it easier to start a business?" "Georgia vs. Australia: Which country has lower bureaucracy and more liberal employment laws?" Georgia is declared the winner of each contest, and DBI is cited to support the claim that Georgia outcompetes richer and better-known territories as an attractive site for foreign investment.

By conforming Georgia to DBI's optimal regulatory model, the institutional assemblage disseminated new characteristics for Georgia's territorial economy across the *Doing Business* knowledge network. Advertising the country's competitive performance on DBI in global business news media expanded the circulation of knowledge of the Georgian reform trajectory among transnational investors. Using DBI rankings to contrast Georgia's investment climate with other states constructed new relational proximities between Georgia and other sites of investor opportunity. This shifted the territory's relative position in the global economy by extending and reorganizing Georgia's extraterritorial connections. This shift in positionality – i.e. how the trajectory of economic development in a place depends upon its connectivities with other places (Sheppard 2002) – was a scale effect that emerged from the assemblage of the Georgian government, GBCR, DBI, and finally M&C Saatchi.

I observed the emergence of a related scale effect in mid-2007, when the work of targeting the DBI indicators and using them to fuel Georgia's rebranding effort was largely complete. M&C Saatchi's advertising campaign was directing internet traffic to the website of the Georgian National Investment Agency (GNIA). GNIA was understaffed and undertrained for handling the volume of investor inquiries coming in via the advertisements. The director of GNIA was replaced several times, forcing GBCR to start building investor-servicing capacity anew with each new director. Despite this slow start, GBCR saw the transformation of GNIA into a "world class" investor-servicing agency as the next step in Georgia's investment promotion strategy.

The consultant that GBCR brought to Georgia in June 2007 was critical of the fact that, while Georgia was receiving increased attention from foreign investors, there was as yet no real "product" to offer them. He saw a "time-to-market" advantage for investments in Georgia arising from regulatory streamlining as the key to outcompeting other regional states attempting to attract FDI. Maximizing a time-to-market advantage involved creating a freely accessible online database of investment opportunities pre-packaged for multinational enterprises. Investment sites would be profiled as either an undeveloped "greenfield" or previously developed "brownfield" and mapped with details such as local labor market characteristics and proximity to major cities, ports, and other transportation and communication infrastructures. Particular sectors of the Georgian economy, such as transport and manufacturing, would be targeted for investment promotion. In short, by creating a new information infrastructure and new capacities for the global marketing of investment opportunities in Georgia, GNIA would become a "one-stop shop" for investor servicing.

SMRC, however, disagreed with the notion that particular sectors of the economy should be targeted for investment promotion, in keeping with State Minister Bendukidze's arch-neoliberal view of economic development, and his concomitant opposition to "picking winners" or industrial policy in any form. Other aspects of GBCR's recommendations for GNIA met with resistance from factions within the Georgian government, and little changed at GNIA. A necessary law re-defining GNIA's capacities was not introduced to parliament. Foreign investor relations, including privatization decisions and also the selection of those Georgians who would participate in the "Invest in Georgia" forums, continued to be handled directly, and non-transparently, by SMRC and President Saakashvili's office. By November 2007 GBCR had drawn a line under its unsuccessful efforts to reform GNIA, and refused to provide any more support to the agency unless SMRC and GBCR could agree on a unified approach to investment promotion.

In this way, as the volume of FDI inflows rose dramatically in 2007 and the first half of 2008, the institutional assemblage reached the limit of its capacity for investment promotion. High Georgian officials positioned themselves as "gatekeepers" for investment inflows, and refused to be displaced by investor-servicing via GNIA. This form of emergent power in the institutional assemblage produced a global/national scale effect − GBCR's role in the investment promotion network would be relegated to the global branding of Georgia, as a group of Georgian elites of non-transparent composition formed a national boundary for foreign investors to cross. The gatekeepers to Georgia's inter-territorial "networks and subsequent geographies of information that are embedded in these relationships and networks" (Torrance 2009: 80) kept GBCR outside the national "inward investment regime" (Phelps and Wood 2006). In this way, power asymmetries in the GBCR–DBI–SMRC institutional assemblage interdicted the global–local extension and "deepening" of an investment promotion network that would connect foreign investors directly with local sites and investment opportunities within Georgia. The DBI rankings produced by the assembled agencies thus came to define Georgia's external boundary for inward investment. Manning this boundary, and directing investment inward, are gatekeepers who are well positioned to profit.

Conclusion: Global governance by rankings and ratings

DBI's rankings functioned as an "attractor" around which a set of agencies – the Georgian government, USAID and GBCR, the Doing Business Project, and finally, M&C Saatchi – assembled to reconfigure Georgia's extraterritorial connectivity, and promulgate "brand Georgia" as a frontier market. Attractors are points with respect to which dynamic systems move, but which may never be reached (e.g. limit cycles). The DBI attractor is the shifting "best practice" regulation model, which is defined according to the relative efficiency of different states' business regulations, and which therefore cannot be entirely actualized even by DBI's top-ranked countries. Receding ahead of the territorially dispersed reform trajectories plotted by the Doing Business Project, the optimal model is a *virtual attractor* that reform trajectories may close with indefinitely, but never reach (Delanda 2002: 29).

Though the attractor is virtual, it is nevertheless real, and has definite effects (Delanda 2002: 32). It produces new relational characteristics for territories and adds ruling or organizing capacity to the extraterritorial assemblage, as states pursue strategies for rankings ascension in order to gain credibility with transnational investors. The attractor also draws together "intellectual, policy, and practitioner networks that underpin the global expansion of neoliberal ideas" and, when used as a strategic focus for extraterritorial accumulation, it impels neoliberalism's "manifestation in government policies and programs" (Larner 2003: 510). If capital flows to peripheral states continue increasing in volume after the 2008–2009 global financial crisis, then incentives will grow for grasping the extraterritorial policy credibility that accompanies ascension through DBI, and similar competitiveness and governance rankings. We should thus expect that more policymakers will engage in competitive policy transfer and efforts to play the rankings game. At the extreme, institutional isomorphism towards the receding DBI optimal regulation model could impel a kind of neoliberal "Red Queen's race" – i.e. "it takes all the running *you* can do to keep in the same place," the queen tells Alice in *Through the Looking Glass*.[19]

The case of Georgia serves as an example of the power of international rankings not only to influence state behavior, but to reconfigure institutional relationships both within governments and across broader international policy networks. Relational ethnography enabled tracing the relational geometries and power dynamics that emerged in executing the Georgia investment promotion strategy. Successful ascension through the DBI rankings positioned Georgia as a neoliberal vanguard state able to "catch up" and even "leap ahead" by transferring the regulatory best practices that create an attractive destination for transnational investment. This vanguard positionality means that the World Bank's neoliberal discourse and ideology was not simply imposed "from above." Rather, the policy transfer was used tactically for accumulating extraterritorial policy credibility, while simultaneously masking illiberal aspects of doing business in Georgia not measured by DBI, such as weak property rights and a lack of judicial independence.

In this same vein, one high-level USAID official in Georgia criticized the GBCR project as "teaching to the test," while not doing enough to push the government on reform priorities not highlighted by international rankings.[20] More generally, if such fast and successful results can come from playing the DBI rankings game, then country rankings may reflect little else than relative success at transferring specific policies. This calls into question the significance of DBI's indicators of institutional quality. DBI-impelled reforms that fail in implementation because of a lack of support from other interdependent institutions, such as judiciaries, will reduce or undermine the accuracy of the DBI indicators as reflections of a state's economic competitiveness and developmental capacity. In a similar sense to Bukovansky's account (Chapter 3) of how states respond to corruption ratings and Bhuta's

---

[19] Carroll 1982: 104; Robson 2005. Thanks to Luke Bergmann for pointing out this implication, and to Eric Sheppard for his input on attractors.

[20] Author interview, June 26, 2007.

account (Chapter 4) of how development agencies substitute "state failure" indicators for their own judgment of humanitarian need across targets, defining reform priorities according to rankings targets may divert attention from alternative, and potentially more developmentally beneficial policy choices. Such policies may be more context-specific than allowed by indicators that are commensurable across countries; e.g. technical and financial assistance to promote the growth of indigenous small and medium-sized enterprises is one area of development policy that is lacking, but sorely needed, in Georgia. Perhaps not coincidentally, this area of development policy is not measured by DBI.

This chapter suggests several trajectories for future research on policy transfer processes and how quasi-markets for fast policy are created by various benchmarking techniques, how place contexts limit policy transferability, and on the consequences of extraterritorially driven policy-making for economic development. There is as yet little scholarship that examines sources of extraterritorial policy credibility, and the general importance of this form of reputational capital relative to other influences on a territory's attractiveness for investment. While it is clear from the case study that policymakers perceived a positive relation between rankings ascension and greater FDI inflows, and that these coincided in Georgia, this chapter establishes no quantifiable causal linkage. Further research is necessary to understand how competitiveness indicators are used in investor decision-making, and how investor networks are linked to various technocratic networks that produce and disseminate knowledge about investment environments.

7 | Conclusion

Rating the ratings craze: From consumer choice to public policy outcomes

JACK SNYDER AND ALEXANDER COOLEY

Judging by the recent ubiquity of ratings and rankings of everything from colleges to kleptocrats, it would seem that the world has discovered the magic elixir for consumer choice, public policy evaluation, and social accountability. Systematic ratings purport to offer consistency, transparency, impartiality, scientific authority, and efficiency in support of policy evaluation.[1] Yet the foregoing chapters portray public policy ratings as often incoherently defined, anchored in confused and untested theories, measured idiosyncratically, and subject to manipulation by both the raters and the rated, leading to unintended, unwanted consequences. If our authors are right, what is at stake may be nothing less than global financial disaster due to self-fulfilling prophecy, or poorly grounded decisions to intervene to stop genocide.

What has gone wrong in this enterprise? And if ratings are so fraught, why are they so popular? Can they be done better?

The underlying reason for the public policy ratings boom is the powerful allure of the technocratic model of policy evaluation and performance accountability, which has in recent years been given a boost by changes in information technology and open information policies. Adopting practices of technocratic policy evaluation is in the long run better than not adopting them, despite the fact that sometimes, to borrow James Scott's example in *Seeing Like a State*, the technocratically over-managed forest becomes vulnerable to tree blight. Technocracy is very complicated, so technocrats make mistakes. The proper response to weaknesses in systematic evaluation strategies such as ratings is to improve the ratings, not to abandon them.

Members of the rankings communities and their critics usually point to two important types of shortcomings: methodological problems and

[1] Davis, Kingsbury, and Merry 2012a, 2012b.

178

political bias. They observe, usually correctly, that rankings require better data, more original research, less subjective measures, and better standardization to make comparisons truly meaningful. For example, expert opinions should be integrated within a broader mixed-methods approach, and not be the sole source of measurements, as they were in many of the earlier rankings of the 1990s. In addition, governments and academics accuse rankings organizations of harboring political biases, whether intentionally serving the agendas of hegemonic states or unthinkingly reproducing biases that favor Western approaches and institutional interests. These charges carry considerable weight.

But what emerges from our contributors is perhaps an even more pressing concern: the judgments embedded in rankings may be undermining the clarity of analytical debates about the policy values they purport to serve. As Bhuta puts it in his chapter, rankings and indicators not only pass judgments, but they have started to act as "substitutes" for judgment in the public policy sphere. This is a dangerous turn of affairs, especially as indices garner increasing authority and are deployed for advocacy and governance purposes.

A root problem linking many of the shortcomings that our contributors describe is the raters' failure to conceptualize coherently what is being rated – in our volume, democracy, state failure, corruption, press freedom, and investment quality. Raters commonly identify a mixed bag of attributes and processes that encompass a syndrome of desired (or undesired) elements that seem to go together in emblematic cases of success (or failure). Rather than using theory to sort out which things in the grab bag are causes, which are consequences, and which relationships are variable or conditional, raters assign arbitrary weights to elements that are assumed to be additive, when in fact they are interactive in complex ways. Since the interesting cases for public policy are often ones in which the elements do not fit tidily into coherent syndromes, the result may be an index that obscures the very distinctions that are most important for policy evaluation.

It is on exactly this issue that social scientists – and international relations theorists in particular – should have a significant role to play. Yet, for the most part, social scientists have become relatively passive consumers of ratings, using the research produced by rating organizations mostly as data sets to explore causal relationships across many spheres of global governance: Do authoritarian regimes more effectively control corruption than democracies? Are failing states more likely to militarize their foreign policies? Such findings are potentially important, but risk reproducing many of the unexamined assumptions of these rankings. Exploring public policy ratings' causal assumptions and normative judgments, disaggregating their targets, and understanding their broader role in the policy process should be critical priorities for social scientists. Before reviewing our contributors' critiques, let's first consider what normative standards ratings systems should try to meet.

What is the normative standard for ratings?

At the most general level, the purpose of a rating is to serve as a criterion for informed choice. Let's begin with the simpler case of the normative standard for consumer choice ratings, and then turn to the more complex question of normative standards for rating organizations and public policy ratings, which exhibit some of the same complications as consumer ratings, but in spades.

The analogy of choosing among ranked colleges

The example of college ratings offers a useful analogy to the public policy sphere. Individual consumers want to know the rating of a college, for example, so that they can choose the best one *for themselves* from a menu of options. College ratings typically purport to rank colleges ordinally according to some weighted composite of many criteria. As an aid to an individual's choice, however, the rating of "overall best" is less useful than the rating of each of several component indices, which assess a college on dimensions that may or may not matter to the chooser: selectivity, median SAT score, the size of an endowment, the faculty:student ratio, percentage of students receiving financial aid, proximity to a major city. Ratings of various features can help the chooser to eliminate alternatives that lack necessary features – I can't afford it, I can't get in, they don't have the degree program I want – and to construct their own weighting of the various features that they value – they are highly selective, classes are small, they have a good reputation.

Rated attributes might be valued in themselves, or they might be features that are thought to be means to obtain other valued outcomes. This distinction is critical. A very helpful rating might try to establish whether the rated features really are indeed related to desired subsequent outcomes. For example, does small class size mean I will learn more? Do the supposed reputational advantages or networking opportunities of Harvard College lead to later higher incomes or greater chances of becoming a Supreme Court clerk, compared to similar applicants that attended the University of Illinois? In general, a good rating system will justify the value of the features it rates, *and* it will present the ratings in a way that allows consumers to weight the value of features based on what matters *to them* for specific purposes.

At a more operational level, ratings should also meet some standard of validity and reliability. For an applicant who wants to go to law school after college, a college's law school acceptance rate would probably be a valid measure of value if it is adjusted for the applicants' SAT scores and high school GPA. In contrast, the college's average class size or average financial aid package might be too blunt an instrument to be a valid input for that applicant's choice if pre-law classes are far larger than average or if the student comes from a very poor family. What the student needs is fine-grained class size data and a tailored financial aid calculator, not a summary rating.

Further, for an applicant who wants an intensely intellectual college experience, various indicators might individually be somewhat valid: GPA or SAT scores of the freshman cohort, numbers of Nobel Prizes among the faculty, percentage of graduates continuing for the PhD, or a curriculum based on "the great books." Weighting these, however, would seem quite arbitrary unless done by the actual consumer. Since intellectual environment is as much a subjective phenomenon as a measurable correlate, a reputational ranking might capture this with even more validity. Moreover, reputation arguably solves the weighting problem better than a cookbook formula does. Indeed, for an applicant who simply wants to go to the highest-prestige college, *only* a reputational ranking would be fully valid.

Although all of the above indicators are socially constructed facts, all except the reputational rankings can probably be measured reliably in the sense that any two raters would get the same answer if they used the same set of complete coding rules and had full, accurate information. Reliability is not a substitute for validity, of course.

Ratings should also meet the standard of non-manipulability, also referred to as "reactivity." If the entity being rated can improve its rating without increasing the value of its product, the manipulability of the measure is compromising its validity. For example, colleges look more attractive when a higher proportion of admitted students accepts its offers. Colleges discovered that they could manipulate this rate by accepting a higher proportion of students via "early decision." This also had the effect of forcing students to choose the college without comparing financial aid offers from other colleges. Similarly, the LSAT score, once a part of a broader portfolio required for admissions for prospective law students, has increased in importance as it has become a component in ranking the selectivity of law schools. As a result, most schools now offer merit scholarships solely on the basis of LSAT scores in order to attract students that will raise their performance on this critical overall indicator.[2] These policies, and the manipulable indicator that encouraged them, made these educational institutions a worse deal for the student body, not a better one, and rewarded individual aspiring law students who can take a standardized test.

Many consumers also want an indicator that is parsimonious. One of the reasons to use ratings is that they boil down extensive, complex data into a seemingly understandable summary form. When people do not have much at stake in making a choice, they are likely to place great value in the simplicity of an indicator and their ease in obtaining and using the information it embodies. They might be satisfied simply to know that their favorite charity helps starving children and that it spends only 2 percent of its funds on administrative overhead (never mind that this may not be enough to operate intelligently and efficiently). Even when they do have a lot at stake, people might sometimes be misled by a simple, prominently featured indicator like full-price college tuition, not realizing their eligibility for financial aid.

One task of a good indicator is to get the benefits of parsimony while not sacrificing validity. This will be hardest to accomplish in situations where multiple values are simultaneously in play in a decision, where different users of the indicator might have different purposes or face different constraints, and where the validity of the indicator depends on causal assumptions that are debatable and hard to make transparent. Rating potato peelers will not be much troubled by such problems, but rating colleges or rating public policy outcomes in transitional democracies will.

---

[2] Espeland and Sauder 2007.

The challenges of ranking for the purpose of public policy

The ratings and rankings discussed in this book are mainly evaluations of public policy outcomes (though investment ratings bear on private choices as well as public outcomes). Public policy ratings introduce a greater level of complexity than consumer ratings, which are meant to serve the interests of the private consumer who is making the choice. Producers' interest in ratings is derivative of their concern to satisfy consumers.

Ratings of public policy outcomes, in contrast, might be addressed to diverse kinds of concerned principals: citizens or other individuals who are affected by the policy, people or institutions who are responsible for advancing the public good, and various do-gooders, special-issue activist groups, or other interested audiences. Some of these parties might be in a position to make a choice that is influenced by the rating (allocate resources, vote, speak up authoritatively); others may be constituencies whose interests are to be served by others' choices; still others may be mainly concerned onlookers. Moreover, to effect any change, multiple actors will need to coordinate with each other their responses to whatever information the rating conveys. Accordingly, the act of producing an index of global corruption, aid transparency, or human rights as a tool for advocacy is neither necessary nor sufficient for advancing that particular cause without an accompanying theory of how the concepts in the ranking, or the production of the ranking itself, will be deployed by actual policy actors.

Private consumers care about more than one value in making a choice, including various dimensions of quality and price. This value complexity increases exponentially when a rating is designed to help different kinds of concerned audiences to evaluate, deliberate, and decide on public policies. Useful ratings will either need to state and defend the value position that motivates them, or they will need to be explicit about how holding different value preferences would affect the rankings. The rationale for "weighting" different values for a composite score either needs to be explicitly defended, or component scores must be rated and reported separately so that consumers can decide on their own weighting. And in cases in which different values are in direct conflict, they should not be "weighted," but rather the trade-off between them needs to be analyzed for optimization.

It is here where many of the ratings in public policy fall woefully short: rather than acknowledge the policy trade-offs, embedded values, or assumptions involved in assigning weights, ratings organizations do so with little overt justification. To take the original World Health Organization ranking of healthcare systems, discontinued after its inaugural release in 2000, assigning "equity of access" the same weight as "responsiveness" made little sense given that US and French officials, for very different domestic and historical reasons, have themselves placed different priorities on these components. Rather than spotlight the reasons behind these different priorities, and their accompanying public policy implications, an index made the arbitrary choice of weighing them as equally important, itself a value-laden move. Aggregation, then, not only has the potential methodological cost of missing subtle shifts in any one component indicator, but it papers over the complex political and social relationships between weighted components.

The targets of public policy ratings

In public policy ratings, moreover, a distinction needs to be made between rating outcomes and rating those who are accountable for outcomes. In deciding which college to attend, consumers want to know whether the college will serve their needs, not who is responsible for its shortcomings. In public policy ratings, sometimes the point is to evaluate an outcome (corruption got worse), sometimes to evaluate a public policy (improving police salaries failed to reduce corruption), and sometimes the point is to hold some authority accountable to an audience (the Justice Ministry refused to investigate corruption).

Often, however, public policy ratings conflate these three kinds of objectives. For example, media freedom indices typically combine measures of media independence, media freedom from government interference, non-governmental assaults on media, media professionalism, diversity of voices that can articulate views in media, and the overall availability of information in media. Whereas separate ratings on each of these dimensions might be of some value to audiences concerned with outcomes, policy effectiveness, or accountability of some actor, a summary "media freedom" statistic is nearly meaningless for any diagnostic purpose. A summary measure might, we suppose, be of some use for a risk-averse journalist deciding on whether to take up an assignment in the country, but otherwise simply muddles any implications for choice or policy. The irony here is that many media ratings organizations like the Committee to Protect Journalists or IREX started issuing ratings for the most part as a public service, providing information that would be used to better allocate technical assistance and foreign support for developing media freedoms within target countries.

Designing ratings systems: Normative assumptions and public policy outcomes

In turn, the purpose of public policy ratings typically requires explicit consideration of causal issues in designing the rating system. In choosing a college, the applicant normally cares only that the college is good, not how the college managed to become good. In evaluating public policy processes and outcomes, ratings should have a logical connection to theories of how reforms will improve outcomes or how to allocate resources to different projects.

According to our contributors, prominent public policy ratings fall seriously short of many of these normative criteria.

How well do ratings meet normative standards?

Perhaps the most unsettling finding of our contributors is that many of the ratings they examined were based on no coherent conception of the outcome being rated. Failed states indices, for example, typically define their object as the state's failure to do its job in providing order and other public goods, which is assessed in terms of a long, heterogeneous, arbitrarily weighted list of demerits such as civil violence, weak courts, poor public health services and/or outcomes, and the like. Such lists fail to discriminate between causes and effects, and they fail to distinguish who or what is responsible for this state of affairs. If a country improves its score from one year to the next, the index may not reveal if this is because institutional reforms succeeded or because the world price of its main export went up. Indeed, Bhuta analyzes indices that are comprised of a wide range of components, some of which measure state policies (commitment to economic reforms), others state capacities (quality of transportation), and still others social statistics, such as demographic trends, that are actually divorced from the state, except in their measurement. This kind of index obscures what needs to be done to improve state capacity. Nor can it show which states will benefit the most from foreign help. Nor are the consequences of being on the list clear: some governments hate being on the list of failed states, whereas others think it will bring attention to their plight and send resources their way.

Less egregious, but still eyebrow-raising, is the measurement of complex, composite outcomes such as democracy or media freedom by adding together loosely related components that can vary independently. Thus, does democracy mean strong civil liberties, electoral turnover, high voter turnout, or separation of powers? How such aspects of democracy are weighted, Seva Gunitsky shows, determined whether raters saw Russia as becoming less democratic or more under Putin. Arguably, individual liberty, mass participation, and institutionalized pluralism are simply different values to which democrats may attach different intensities of preference. If so, they should be measured and reported separately, not lumped together.

Alternatively, a rating system might try to justify empirically a formula for integrating these different components in an overall measure of democracy, showing that multiple elements must be present to some degree to produce jointly an outcome that could be called democracy. Although mature democracies have both majoritarian elections and liberal values, Fareed Zakaria has warned that many illiberal electoral regimes achieve none of the beneficial outcomes that we expect from democracy, such as stability, civil peace, prosperity, and fair treatment of citizens.[3] Thus, rating such countries' degree of democracy should be based on an empirically supported theory of how such mixed regimes actually function rather than on mechanically adding up features of the ideal type of democracy.

Media ratings suffer from a similar problem of trying to add together components that are interactive and potentially conflictual. Does a good media freedom rating mean that the government represses less or that more information is available to citizens? These different criteria, each a plausible measure by its own logic, can move in opposite directions when increases in information, say from the internet or satellite TV, motivate leaders to crack down on free expression in response.[4] Indeed, dangers can arise when international donors

---

[3] Zakaria 1997.   [4] Whitten-Woodring 2009.

zealously promote media freedom in mixed ethnic societies undergoing a political transition. In Rwanda or the former Yugoslavia, donors were so hung up on making media openness an overall goal, they ignored the potential for media outlets to be used to spread national myths and inflammatory hate speech, culminating in large-scale clashes along ethnic lines.[5]

Rather than basing ratings on theories that specify conditional or interactive effects, raters often take a short cut. Their approach to measurement implicitly assumes that the outcome of interest constitutes a syndrome in which all good things (or all bad things) go together. They may believe this because all good things do tend to go together in the wealthy, democratic, liberal, capitalist countries. This becomes the model outcome that the index seeks to capture. As Mira Rapp-Hooper put it to us, the liberal "end of history" created a common scale of aspiration that became the basis for many rating schemes.[6] International organizations such as the European Union, the Council of Europe, and NATO have adopted benchmarks and performance along common standards as their main prerequisites for admitting aspirant countries.[7]

But in transitional countries that are only partially liberalized and semi-modernized, outcomes often vary independently along the dimensions that are the components of the index. This problem cannot be solved by "properly weighting" the components, since components like repression of speech and political information are interactive rather than additive. What is needed is not a single metric but a valid theory of how these elements combine to produce the outcomes that the raters are interested in. Ratings that skip over this task mislead rather than inform.

Raters examined in this book generally seem to lack such theories. Sometimes they don't have a theory at all, as in the failed states index. Sometimes they don't try to have a predictive theory, but content themselves with a rating that retroactively models what has already happened. Abdelal and Blyth, for example, show that credit rating agencies make no attempt to research whether a borrower is likely to

---

[5] Snyder and Ballentine 1996.
[6] Columbia University International Politics Seminar presentation, February 28, 2013.
[7] Vachudova 2005.

repay a debt in the future but simply use an algorithm to summarize and track past behavior.

Despite these shortcomings, some of the ratings systems described by the contributors do seem to be converging on the normative model. One potential use for a rating is as a variable in hypotheses than can be used to test the theory that justifies undertaking the rating in the first place. Bukovansky notes, for example, that Transparency International's Corruption Perceptions Index permitted testing of the conjecture that high levels of corruption depress economic development. This had previously been contested by Samuel Huntington's argument that corruption can be a modernizing development in states that hinder market transaction. Having a good indicator helped to settle that debate.

Having a coherent, tested theory is a necessary step in moving from rating an outcome to intervening in the causal process to improve the outcome in the future. Bukovansky also shows how anti-corruption monitors have gone beyond the blunt instrument of the original measure of perceived corruption in the CPI to develop more targeted measures of the resource curse, offshore financing, capital flight, and regulatory capture. These measures correspond to a better-differentiated theory of economic opportunism and market inefficiency, creating the potential for better-targeted policy interventions. At the level of public policy, the Corruption Perception Index has initiated a vigorous debate about the determinants of corruption and what tools can be used to effectively fight it. The mixed effectiveness of the transparency regime suggests that Transparency International and similar advocates still have a long way to go to improve the accountability of public officials, yet in terms of initiating a debate and setting a normative standard that corruption should not be an acceptable behavior *anywhere*, the CPI has played a positive role in the global public policy process.

Not all ratings of economic performance are improving, however. Some are still hindered by the one-rule-measures-all syndrome. For example, according to neoliberal economic orthodoxy, all good economies make it easy to do business through standard types of facilitating legislation and universal "best practices." But pseudo-reformist Georgia, Sam Schueth shows, was able to manipulate the Ease of Doing Business Index by passing laws and promulgating administrative rules that had little or no effect on actual economic transactions. As a result, poor economic competitiveness and continuing corruption coexisted with a stratospheric rise in this ranking. Moreover, the World Bank's inability to adjust for the reflexivity of Georgia's targeting of the indicators, like Azerbaijan and Rwanda after it, risks making Doing Business a tool that rewards a government's proximity to a skilled network of international actors and advisors who understand the components of the index, rather than an actual commitment to improving the business environment or, more importantly, to promoting broad-based economic development.

Ratings as politics

Another reason for the ratings boom is that liberal public advocacy networks have been in a global crusading mode since the end of the Cold War, and these reformers see ratings and rankings as powerful tools for naming and shaming slackers and norm-violators. Ratings also serve reformers well in establishing standards of appropriate behavior and in gatekeeping issue priorities for the reform agenda. However, even the most normatively motivated of organizations cannot exclusively concern themselves with accurately judging the performance of states on the issues they care about, such as compliance with human rights norms, preserving the environment, or promoting gender equality. As in the case of Transparency International, ratings organizations simultaneously play the role of judges, sources of governance, advocates, and self-promoters. Ratings, in other words, are inherently political, subject to multiple agendas.

The shortcomings of prominent rating systems arise both from the substantive difficulty of the rating task *and* from its political character. Devising useful, valid public policy ratings is a complex, daunting enterprise that is inherently in conflict with the need for cognitive and institutional short cuts. Limits of consumers' knowledge, time, attention, memory; the need for standardization and fungible concepts, the value of focal points, and regulation by generic rules – all of these unavoidable mental and organizational limitations work against the kind of complex, nuanced, valid ratings outlined above in the section on normative standards. Some degree of failure is built into the nature of the problem.

But these difficulties are exacerbated by the instrumental nature of ratings. Advocates instrumentalize ratings when they base them on aspirational ideal types that can be used to mobilize activists and brow-beat the non-compliant. Ratings that were based on tested causal relationships rather than on ideal standards would serve these instru-mental purposes less well, while being better tools for policy diagnosis. Likewise, ratings that were more sensitive to different contexts in which policy is chosen and implemented would make shaming harder, while making accountability standards more realistic. Meanwhile, for those being rated and ranked, the diagnostic value of rigor, clarity, and objectivity is likely to be far outweighed by the practical costs of getting a bad rating in terms of access to funds and exposure to sanctions.

A related problem is that ratings serve expressive purposes as well as analytical and diagnostic ones. Ranking countries against an ideal type gratifies the idealism of activists and serves as a way of expressing a sense of vocation and purpose. For those who rank and those who are ranked, the exercise puts in play highly freighted questions of status, recognition, self-presentation, envy, and identity as modern.

Ratings may detract from both their informational and advocacy roles when they assign such disparaging labels that government officials are prompted to challenge the label and the rating organization, rather than engage in a discussion about the policy context of the underlying beha-vior. In the extreme, as in the case of Russia, the social outrage felt by officials as they are compared to similarly poorly rated countries on civil liberties such as North Korea, Iran, or Turkmenistan may shrink the space for a useful policy dialogue about issues like "democracy" or "transpar-ency." As such, there is a potential public policy downside to NGOs and IOs becoming aggressive advocates for their ratings and indices: they are likely to offer convenient targets for recalcitrant governments to blame outside actors for their own failures. Though such engagement might be useful for an organization in its bid to attract the global spotlight, it is also clear that many post-Soviet governments would prefer to pick a fight with a Western-backed organization like Freedom House rather than publicly defend the dismal fate of civil liberties.

The structure of the international media and the rise of new social technologies may actually be exacerbating this problem. Rather than produce better data or more informed ratings, or raise the quality of public policy debate, global informational outlets appear more likely to rapidly reproduce and disseminate indicators and rankings without actually questioning their origins, validity, normative underpinnings, or broader public policy role. With web pages, press releases, and a steady diet of newspaper stories accompanying the public release of each new ranking, and the home state's performance in it, the global media may be amplifying the pathologies of the rankings frenzy rather than providing a much-needed corrective.

Finally, the value of ratings is undermined by the endogeneity of the ratings process. A poor credit rating is likely to be a self-fulfilling prophecy. This is bad enough when the rating is anchored in sound fundamentals, but to the extent that a rating is arbitrarily constructed, self-fulfilling downward spirals become a gratuitous risk caused by the methodology itself. Reporters who solicit and quote the supposedly authoritative judgments of rating organizations when penning a story about corruption or democratic backsliding in a particular state reproduce these pathologies.

The ultimate danger, which several of our authors have flagged in ratings of creditworthiness, failed states, and corruption, is that official agencies and journalists that once carefully analyzed the nuances of public policy decisions will implicitly abdicate this role to the organizations that produce rankings. The more that rankings are incorporated into formal legal regimes and public policy institutions, such as those determining thresholds for foreign aid decisions, the more likely that these delegated roles will become ossified and never re-evaluated.

Despite their shortcomings, ratings and rankings are too useful to abandon. They will continue to be widely employed in all spheres of social life and public policymaking. Although to some degree their imperfections are inevitable, a modicum of methodological self-awareness can improve them at the margins. It is here that social scientists can play a critical role.

How can ratings be improved?

Based on the insights from our contributors' case studies, several recommendations emerge for best practices in designing public policy ratings systems:

> *Be explicit about the purpose that the rating is intended to serve.* Explain the logical connection between the rating and its implications for action.
> *Be explicit about the value preferences that are reflected in the rating.* Where a rating integrates or conflates more than one value, say

what those values are, discuss the implications of the rating system for each value separately, where values are weighted explain how and why, and discuss assumptions about whether there are trade-offs between values.

Be explicit about causal assumptions that are built into the rating system. How are the elements of the rating thought to be causally related to each other? Distinguish purported causes, consequences, intervening processes, reinforcing effects, and feedback effects. State whether these assumptions are based on tested theory or whether they are just conjectures. State whether the value of the rating system is sensitive to the correctness of these causal assumptions.

Be transparent about reporting all component measurements. Make it easy for users of the ratings to use these component ratings to construct their own composite rating that reflects their own preferences or theories.

Be transparent about how the part of the organization producing the rating interacts with the other parts of the organization working on policy. Do the researchers producing a rating work for a separate unit? Is the production of ratings systematically incorporated in the other activities, including advocacy or technical assistance, provided by the organization? Explicitly state which steps, if any, have been taken to minimize conflict of interests.

Consider combining indicators based on "objective" measurements with indicators based on reputational or subjective expert assessments. Objective measures often have advantages in reliability and transparency. Reputational or expert assessments may sometimes be better at integrating multiple components in comparison to arbitrary, mechanical weighting schemes.

Be alert for the possibility that an indicator can be manipulated by those being rated. Distinguish between indicators that are very directly related to the outcome of interest and therefore cannot be gamed, as opposed to indicators that are based on some theory of how some more remote process or practice is supposed to be related to the outcome. The latter indicators might be interesting for hypothesis testing, but they are easier to game and so should not be confused with direct measures of the outcome of interest.

Above all, do not base a rating system on an eclectic list of ideal-typical attributes. Instead, base the rating system on the best available empirically grounded knowledge about how real countries in the transitional portion of the scale succeed in consolidating improvements.

Ratings are here to stay, but we are still unsure just how important they will become to the public policy process and to the exercise of global governance. Yet, their astonishingly rapid rise challenges us as a scholarly community to not only engage with them as consumers of their measures and data sets, but as engaged analysts and critics of their findings, assumptions, and emerging roles in public policy decision-making. We look forward to other scholars in the international relations field advancing this engagement further.

Appendix 1 List of prominent rankings and ratings, categorized according to issue area

Notes: N = 95, through 2014. List is non-exhaustive and data are culled mostly from public information sites of the issuing organizations. Only indices listing states as units of evaluation or comparison are included. Each index is listed only once and must be cited or referred to by name in international news stories in LexisNexis and ProQuest Searches. Non-cited indices as of December 15, 2014 have been excluded.

Business and Economics (N= 17)

Index Name	Organization	Founded in	Frequency
Bertelsmann Transformation Index – Status Index, Economic Transformation	Bertelsmann Stiftung	2003	Annual
CIPA/IDA Resource Allocation Index	World Bank	2005	Annual
Ease of Doing Business	World Bank	2003	Annual
Economic Freedom	Heritage Foundation	1995	Annual
Economic Freedom of the World	Fraser Institute	1996	Annual
Ernst & Young Globalization Index	Economist Intelligence Unit for Ernst & Young Global Limited	2009	Annual
Global Competitiveness Index	World Economic Forum	2004	Annual
Global Dynamism Index	Grant Thornton and Economist Intelligence Unit	2012	Annual
Global Innovation Index	INSEAD, WIPO and Cornell University	2007	Annual
Global Talent Competitiveness Index	INSEAD, HCLI and Adecco	2013	Annual
International Property Rights Index	Americans for Tax Reform	2012	Annual
IT Industry Competitiveness Index	Economist Intelligence Unit	2007	Annual 2007–2011; Discontinued
KOF Globalization Index	KOF Swiss Economics Institute	2002	Annual
Legatum Prosperity Index	Legatum Institute	2008	Annual
Microfinance Business Environment Index	Economist Intelligence Unit	2009	Annual
Tax Misery and Reform Index	Forbes	2006	Annual
Travel and Tourism Competitiveness Index	World Economic Forum	2007	Annual

Country Risk *(Sovereign and Political) (N=11)*

Index Name	Organization	Founded in	Frequency
Country Risk Classification Report	OECD	1999	Annual
DBRS (formerly Dominion Bond Rating Service)	DBRS	1976	Subscriber-based
Egan-Jones Ratings	Egan-Jones Ratings Company	1995	Periodic
Euromoney Country Risk	Euromoney Magazine	1993	Quarterly since 2011 (previously annual, biannual)
Fitch Credit Rating	Fitch Group	1924	Subscriber-based
Global Political Risk Index	Eurasia Group	2007	Monthly
International Country Risk Guide	The PRS Group	1980	Monthly
Japan Credit Rating Agency	Japan Credit Rating Agency	1984	Subscriber-based
Maplecroft Political Risk Atlas	Maplecroft	2010	Annual
Moody's Sovereign Rating	Moody's Investor Services	1909	Subscriber-based
Standard and Poor's Credit Rating	Standard and Poor's	1916	Subscriber-based

Note: Only Credit-rating Agencies that are Nationally Recognized Statistical Ratings Organizations by the US Securities and Exchange Commission and that rate the sovereign debt of multiple states are included. As of 2013, Fitch, Moody's, and Standard and Poor's had about 95% market share.

Democracy and Governance (N=18)

Index Name	Organization	Founded in	Frequency
Arab Democracy Index	Palestinian Center for Policy and Survey Research	2008	2008, 2009, 2011
Bertelsmann Transformation Index – Management Index	Bertelsmann Stiftung	2003	Annual
Bertelsmann Transformation Index – Status Index, Political Transformation	Bertelsmann Stiftung	2003	Annual
CIRI Human Rights Data Project	Cingranelli-Richards	1981	Annual
Civil Society Index	CIVICUS	2001 (pilot)	2001, 2008, 2009
Civil Society Organization Sustainability Index (NGO Sustainability Index)	USAID	1997	Annual
Democracy Improvement Ranking	The Democracy Ranking Association	2008	Annual
Democracy Index	Economist Intelligence Unit	2006	Biennial 2006–2010, Annual 2001–
The Democracy Ranking	The Democracy Ranking Association	2000 (pilot)	2000, Annual 2008–
Failed States Index	Fund for Peace and Foreign Policy	2004	Annual
Freedom in the World	Freedom House	1972	Annual
Ibrahim Index of African Governance	Mo Ibrahim Foundation	2007	Annual

(cont.)

Index Name	Organization	Founded in	Frequency
Index of State Weakness in the Developing World	Brookings Institution	2008	Once, Discontinued
Nations in Transit	Freedom House	1995	Annual
Polity (I, II, III, IV)	Ted Gurr/Political Instability Task Force/Center for Systemic Peace	c. 1974	Annual since Polity III
Rule of Law Index	The World Justice Project	2008 (pilot)	Annual
Transition Indicators	European Bank for Reconstruction and Development	1994	Annual
Worldwide Governance Indicators	Brookings Institution & World Bank	1996	Biennial 1996–2002, Annual

Environment (N=4)

Index Name	Organization	Founded in	Frequency
Energy Sustainability Index	World Energy Council	2012	Annual
Environmental Performance Index	Yale University	2006 (pilot)	Biennial
Environmental Sustainability Index	Yale University, Columbia University, and World Economic Forum	1999	1999–2005; Discontinued
Environmental Vulnerability Index	South Pacific Applied Geoscience Commission and United Nations Environment Programme	1999 (pilot)	1999, 2001, 2004, 2005

Media and Press (N=5)

Index Name	Organization	Founded in	Frequency
Freedom of the Press	Freedom House	1980	Annual
Freedom on the Net	Freedom House	2011	Annual
Impunity Index on the Murder of Journalists	Committee to Protect Journalists	2011	Annual
Media Sustainability Index	IREX	2001	Annual
Press Freedom Index	Reporters without Borders	2002	Annual

Security Issues and Conflict (N=9)

Index Name	Organization	Founded in	Frequency
European Foreign Policy Scorecard	European Council on Foreign Relations	2010	Annual
Global Militarization Index	Bonn International Centre for Conversion	2004 (pilot)	Annual
Global Peace Index	Vision of Humanity	2007	Annual
LGBT Military Index	Hague Centre for Strategic Studies	2014	Annual
Nuclear Materials Security Index	Nuclear Threat Initiative	2012	Annual
Peace and Conflict Instability Ledger	University of Maryland	2001	Biennial
Political Instability Index	Economist Intelligence Unit	2007	2007, 2009, 2011; Discontinued
Political Terror Scale	Individuals	1976	Annual
Terrorism Index	Center for American Progress & Foreign Policy Magazine	2006	Semi-Annual 2006–2008; Discontinued

Social Welfare (N=20)

Index Name	Organization	Founded in	Frequency
Better Life Index	Organization for Economic Cooperation and Development	2011	Annual
Gallup-Healthways Global Well-Being Index	Gallup and Healthways	2013	Annual
Gender Inequality Index	UNDP	2010	Annual
Global Food Security index	Economist Intelligence Unit and DuPont	2012	Annual
Global Gender Gap Index	World Economic Forum	2006	Annual
Global Hunger Index	International Food Policy Research Institute	2006	Annual
Global Slavery Index	Walk Free Foundation	2013	Annual
Global Youth Well Being Index	Center for Strategic and International Studies, International Youth Foundation, Hilton Worldwide	2014	Annual
Happy Planet Index	New Economics Foundation	2006	Every 3 years
Human Development Index	UNDP	1990	Annual
Index of Global Philanthropy and Remittances	Hudson Institute	2005	Annual
Mothers' Index	Save the Children Federation	1999	
Multidimensional Poverty Index	UNDP	2010	Annual
Quality of Life Index	Economist Intelligence Unit	2005	Once, Discontinued

(*cont.*)

Index Name	Organization	Founded in	Frequency
Social Institutions and Gender Index	Organization for Economic Cooperation and Development	2009	Every 3 years
Trafficking in Persons Report	United States State Department	2001	Annual
Where to be Born Index	Economist Intelligence Unit	1988	1988, 2013
Women's Rights in the Middle East and North Africa	Freedom House	2005	Every 5 years
World Giving Index	Charities Aid Foundation	2010	Biennial
World Health Report	World Health Organization	2000	Once, Discontinued

Transparency (N=11)

Index Name	Organization	Founded in	Frequency
Aid Transparency Index	Publish What You Fund	2011 (pilot)	Annual
Basel Anti-Money Laundering Index	International Centre for Asset Recovery	2012	Annual
Bribe Payers Index	Transparency International	1999	Every 3 years
Corruption Perceptions Index	Transparency International	1995	Annual
Defense Companies Anti-Corruption Index	Transparency International UK	2012	Once
Financial Secrecy Index	Tax Justice Network	2009	Biennial
Global Integrity Index	World Bank	2004 (pilot)	Every 3 years
Government Defense Anti-Corruption Index	Transparency International UK	2013	Biennial
Open Budget Index	International Budget Partnership	2006	Biennial
Public Integrity Index	Global Integrity	2006	2006, 2011; Discontinued
Revenue Watch Index	Revenue Watch Institute	2010	Annual

Appendix 2 Comparing democracy measures within the former Soviet republics

In the following charts, measures of the quality of democracy (on the y-axis) are rescaled from 0 to 1 to enable easier comparisons among measures.

Legend:

CAM – Michael Coppedge, Angel Alvarez, and Claudia Maldonado (1991–2004)

EIU – Economist Intelligence Unit (2006, 2008, 2010)

FH – Freedom House (1991–2010)

PACL – Adam Przeworski, Michael Alvarez, Jose Antonio Cheibub, and Fernando Limongi (1991–2008)

POL – Polity IV (1991–2010)

UDS – Universal Democracy Score (Daniel Pemstein, Stephen Meserve, and James Melton) (1991–2008)

VAN – Vanhanen (1991–2004)

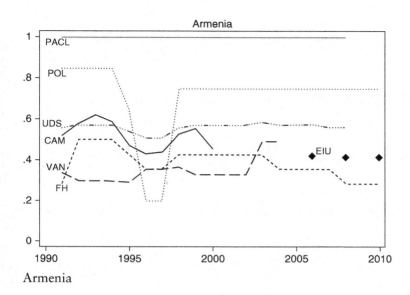

Armenia

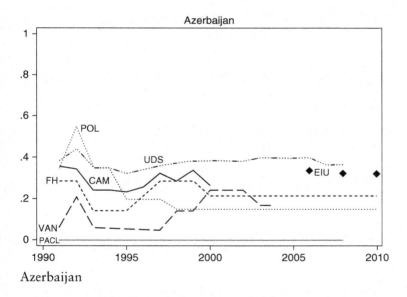

Azerbaijan

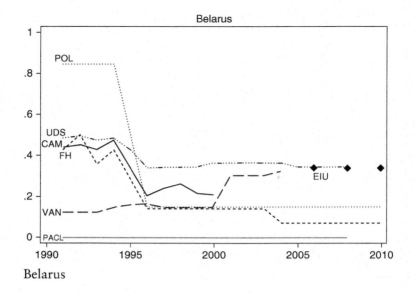

Belarus

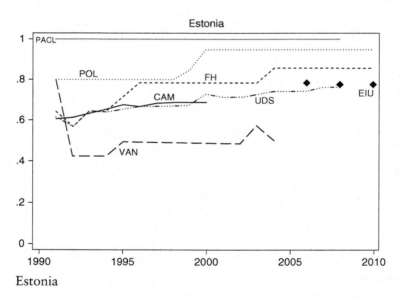

Estonia

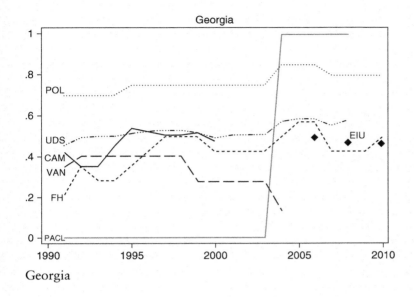

Georgia

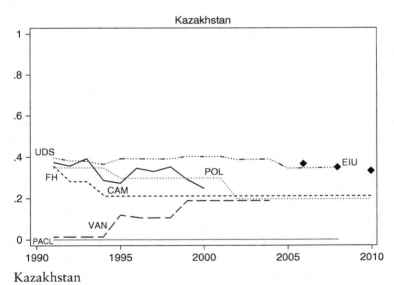

Kazakhstan

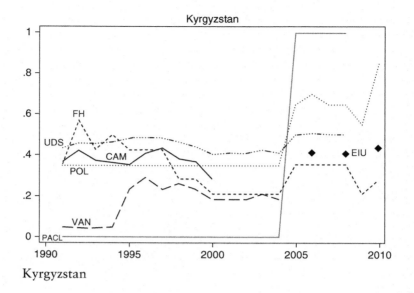

Kyrgyzstan

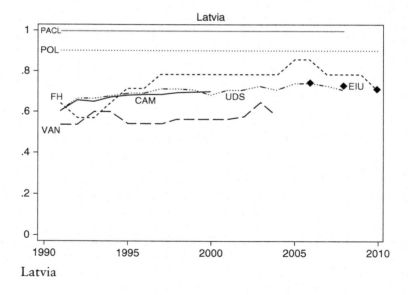

Latvia

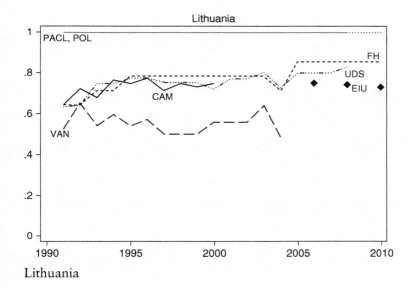

Lithuania

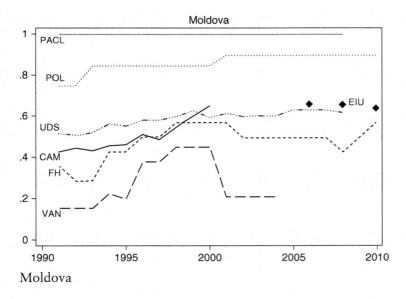

Moldova

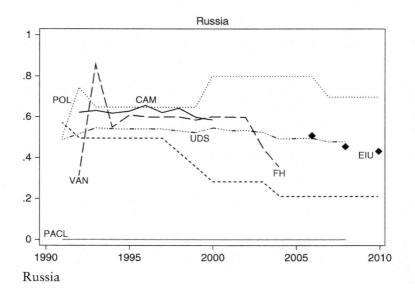

Russia

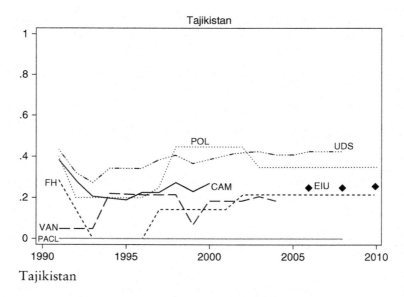

Tajikistan

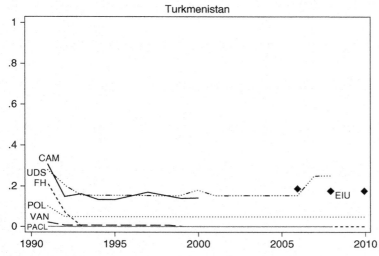

Turkmenistan

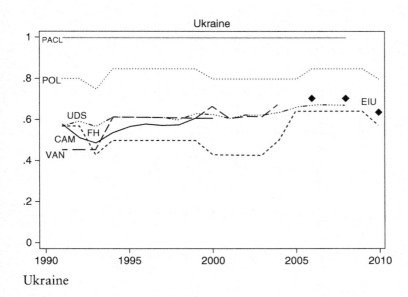

Ukraine

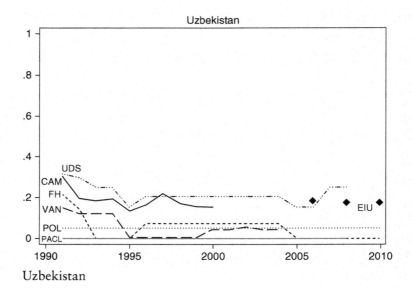

Uzbekistan

References

Abbott, Kenneth W., and Duncan Snidal. 1998. "Why states act through formal international organizations." *Journal of Conflict Resolution* 42: 3–32.

Abdelal, Rawi. 2007. *Capital Rules: The Construction of Global Finance.* Cambridge, MA: Harvard University Press.

Adibe, Clement Eme. 1994. "Weak states and the emerging taxonomy of security in world politics." *Futures* 26: 490–505.

Adler, Robert. 2001. "The crystal ball of chaos." *Nature* 414 (6863): 480–481.

Adler-Nissen, Rebecca. 2014. "Stigma management in international relations: Transgressive identities, norms and order in international society." *International Organization* 68: 143–176.

Allen, J., and A. Cochrane. 2007. "Beyond the territorial fix: Regional assemblages, politics and power." *Regional Studies* 41: 1161–1175.

Altman, David, and Anibal Perez-Linan. 2002. "Assessing the quality of democracy: Freedom, competitiveness and participation in eighteen Latin American countries." *Democratization* 9: 85–100.

Altman, Edward, *et al.* 2012. "Regulation of ratings agencies." In *Regulating Wall Street: The Dodd-Frank Act and the New Architecture of Global Finance*, ed. Viral Acharya *et al.* New York: Wiley.

Alvarez, Mike, Jose Antonio Cheibub, Fernando Limongi, and Adam Przeworski. 1996. "Classifying political regimes." *Studies in Comparative International Development* 31 (2): 3–36.

Amin, A., and N. J. Thrift. 1995. "Territoriality in the global political economy." In *Diffusing Geography: Essays for Peter Haggett*, ed. P. Haggett and A. D. Cliff. Oxford: Blackwell.

Andersson, Staffan, and Paul M. Heywood. 2009. "The politics of perception: Use and abuse of Transparency International's approach to measuring corruption." *Political Studies* 57: 746–767.

Andreas, Peter, and Kelly Greenhill. 2010. "Introduction: The Politics of Numbers." In Peter Andreas and Kelly Greenhill, eds. *Sex, Drugs and Body Counts: The Politics of Numbers in Global Crime and Conflict.* Ithaca, NY: Cornell University Press.

Antaleva, N. 2003. "Georgia: Shevardnadze's Dilemma." *Transitions Online*, September 30.

Apaza, Carmen. 2009. "Measuring governance and corruption through the Worldwide Governance indicators: Critiques, responses, and ongoing scholarly discussion." *PS: Political Science & Politics* 43: 139–143.

Armstrong, David A. 2011. "Stability and change in the Freedom House political rights and civil liberties measures." *Journal of Peace Research* 48: 653–662.

Arndt, Christiane. 2008. "The politics of governance ratings." *International Public Management Journal* 11: 275–297.

Arndt, Christiane, and Charles Oman. 2006. *Uses and Abuses of Governance Indicators*. Paris: Organisation for Economic Cooperation and Development (OECD).

Aron, Raymond. 1944 [2002]. "The secular religions." In *The Dawn of Universal History: Selected Essays from a Witness to the Twentieth Century*, trans. Barbara Bray. New York: Basic Books.

Arruñada, Benito. 2007. "Pitfalls to avoid when measuring institutions: Is doing business damaging business?" *Journal of Comparative Economics* 35: 729–747.

Atkinson, Michael M. 2011. "Discrepancies in perceptions of corruption, or why is Canada so corrupt?" *Political Science Quarterly* 126: 445–464.

Avant, Debora, Martha Finnemore, and Susan Sell, eds. 2010. *Who Governs the Globe?* New York: Cambridge University Press.

Baker, Pauline. 2006. *The Conflict Assessment System Tool (CAST). An Analytical Model for Early Warning and Risk Assessment of Weak and Failing States*. Washington, DC: Fund for Peace.

   2007. "Fixing failed states: The new security agenda." *The Whitehead Journal of Diplomacy and International Relations* 8: 85–96.

Baraka, Amiri. 1962. "Tokenism: 300 years for five cents." *Kulchur* 5, Spring.

Barnett, Michael, and Raymond Duvall, eds. 2005. *Power in Global Governance*. New York: Cambridge University Press.

Barnett, Michael, and Martha Finnemore. 2004. *Rules for the World: International Organizations in Global Politics*. Ithaca, NY: Cornell University Press.

Bauhr, M., and N. Nasiritousi. 2012. "How do international organizations promote quality of government? Contestation, integration, and the limits of IO power." *International Studies Review* 14: 541–566.

Becker, Gary S., and George J. Stigler. 1974. "Law enforcement, malfeasance, and compensation of enforcers." *Journal of Legal Studies* 3 (1): 1–18.

Becker, Lee B., Tudor Vlad, and Nancy Nusser. 2007. "An evaluation of press freedom indicators." *International Communication Gazette* 69: 5–28.

Beetham, David, ed. 1994. *Defining and Measuring Democracy*. Thousand Oaks, CA: Sage Press.

Beliakov, Gleb, Ana Pradera, and Tomasa Calvo. 2007. *Aggregation Functions: A Guide for Practitioners*. New York: Spring; Berlin: Heidelberg.

Benassy-Quere, A., M. Coupet, and T. Mayer. 2007. "Institutional determinants of foreign direct investment." *World Economy* 30: 764–782.

Bennett, D. Scott. 2006. "Toward a continuous specification of the democracy-autocracy connection." *International Studies Quarterly* 50: 313–338.

Berg-Schlosser, Dirk. 2004. "Indicators of democracy and good governance as measures of the quality of democracy in Africa: A critical appraisal." *Acta Politica* 39: 248–78.

Blyth, Mark. 2002. *Great Transformations: Economic Ideas and Political Change in the Twentieth Century*. Cambridge University Press.

Bob, Clifford. 2002. "Merchants of morality." *Foreign Policy* 129: 36–45.
  2005. *The Marketing of Rebellion: Insurgents, Media and International Activism*. New York: Cambridge University Press.

Bogaards, Mattjis. 2007. "Measuring democracy through election outcomes: A critique with African data." *Comparative Political Studies* 40: 1211–1237.

Bollen, Kenneth A., and Pamela Paxton. 2000. "Subjective measures of liberal democracy." *Comparative Political Studies* 33: 58–86.

Borrás, Susana, and Kerstin Jacobsson. 2004. "The open method of co-ordination and new governance patterns in the EU." *Journal of European Public Policy* 11: 185–208.

Boschma, R. A. 2004. "Competitiveness of regions from an evolutionary perspective." *Regional Studies* 38: 1001–1014.

Bowker, Geoffrey C., and Susan Leigh Star. 1999. *Sorting Things Out: Classification and its Consequences*. Cambridge, MA: MIT Press.

Bowman, Kirk, Fabrice Lehoucq, and James Mahoney. 2005. "Measuring political democracy: Case expertise, data adequacy, and Central America." *Comparative Political Studies* 38: 939–70.

Bristow, G. 2005. "Everyone's a 'winner': problematising the discourse of regional competitiveness." *Journal of Economic Geography* 5: 285–304.

Bruckner, T. 2009. "Decision-making and Georgia's perpetual revolution: The case of IDP housing." *Caucasian Review of International Affairs* 3: 172–180.

Bruner, Christopher M., and Rawi Abdelal. 2005. "To judge Leviathan: Sovereign credit ratings, national law, and the world economy." *Journal of Public Policy* 25: 191–217.

Brunnermeier, Markus. 2009. "Deciphering the liquidity and credit crunch 2007–2008." *Journal of Economic Perspectives* 23: 77–100.

Buduru, Bogdan, and Leslie A. Pal. 2010. "The globalized state: Measuring and monitoring governance." *European Journal of Cultural Studies* 13: 511–530.

Bukovansky, Mlada. 2006. "The Hollowness of Anti-Corruption Discourse." *Review of International Political Economy* 13: 181–209.

Burawoy, M. 2001. "Grounding globalization." In *Global Ethnography: Forces, Connections, and Imaginations in a Postmodern World*, ed. M. Burawoy. London: University of California Press.

Büthe, Tim. 2010a. "Private regulation in the global economy: A (p)review." *Business and Politics* 12, 3 (October), Article 2.

2010b. "The power of norms; the norms of power: Who governs international electrical and electronic technology?" In *Who Governs the Globe?* ed. Debora Avant, Martha Finnemore, and Susan Sell. New York: Cambridge University Press.

2012. "Beyond supply and demand: A *political*-economic conceptual model." In *Governance by Indicators: Global Power through Classification and Rankings*, ed. Kevin Davis, Angelina Fisher, Benedict Kingsbury, and Sally Engle Merry. New York: Oxford University Press.

Büthe, Tim, and Walter Mattli. 2011. *The New Global Rulers: The Privatization of Regulation in the World Economy.* Princeton University Press.

Cabinet Office. 2008. *National Security Strategy of the United Kingdom.* London: Cabinet Office.

Call, Charles T. 2008. "The fallacy of the 'failed state'." *Third World Quarterly* 29: 1495–1507.

2011. "Beyond the 'failed state': Toward conceptual alternatives." *European Journal of International Relations* 17: 303–326.

Campbell, D. T. 1975. "Assessing the impact of planned social change." In *Social Research and Public Policies: The Dartmouth/OECD Conference*, ed. G. Lyons. Hanover, NH: Dartmouth College, The Public Affairs Center.

Cantor, Richard, and F. Frank Packer. 1996. "Determinants and impact of sovereign credit ratings." *Economic Policy Review, Federal Reserve Bank of New York* 2: 37–53.

Capoccia, Giovanni. 2005. *Defending Democracy: Reactions to Extremism in Interwar Europe.* Baltimore, MD: Johns Hopkins University Press.

Car, Dev, and Devon Cartwright-Smith. 2010. "Illicit financial flows from Africa." Global Financial Integrity (March), www.gfintegrity.org/storage/gfip/documents/reports/gfi_africareport_web.pdf.

Carroll, L. 1982. *The Complete Illustrated Works of Lewis Carroll.* New York: Avenel Books.

Carruthers, Bruce. 2011. "Turning uncertainty into risk: The case of credit rating agencies." Unpublished manuscript.

Casper, Gretchen, and Claudiu Tufis. 2003. "Correlation versus interchangeability: The limited robustness of empirical findings on democracy using highly correlated data sets." *Political Analysis* 11: 196–203.

Cerny, P. G. 1997. "Paradoxes of the competition state: The dynamics of political globalization." *Government And Opposition* 32: 251–274.

Chang, H.-J. 2002. *Kicking Away the Ladder: Development Strategy in Historical Perspective.* London: Anthem Press.

Cheibub, Jose Antonio, Jennifer Ghandi, and James Raymond Vreeland. 2010. "Democracy and dictatorship revisited." *Public Choice* 143: 67–101.

Christensen, John. 2007. "Mirror, mirror on the wall, who's the most corrupt of all?" Paper presented to World Social Forum, Nairobi, Kenya (January). Available from the Tax Justice Network at: www.taxjustice. net/cms/upload/pdf/0701_Mirror_Mirror_corruption.pdf.

Chwieroth, J. 2007. "Neoliberal economists and capital account liberalization in emerging markets." *International Organization* 61: 443–463.

Cingranelli, David L., and David L. Richards. 2010. "The Cingranelli and Richards (CIRI) human rights data project." *Human Rights Quarterly* 32: 401–424.

Collier, David, and Robert Adcock. 1999. "Democracy and dichotomies: A pragmatic approach to choices about concepts." *Annual Review of Political Science* 2: 537–565.

Collier, David, and Steven Levitsky. 1997. "Democracy with adjectives: Conceptual innovation in comparative research." *World Politics* 49: 430–451.

Cooley, Alexander, and James Ron. 2002. "The NGO scramble: Organizational survival and transnational action." *International Security* 27: 5–37.

Coppedge, Michael, Angel Alvarez, and Claudia Maldonado. 2008. "Two persistent dimensions of democracy: Contestation and inclusiveness." *Journal of Politics* 70: 632–647.

Coppedge, Michael, and John Gerring. 2011. "Conceptualizing and measuring democracy: A new approach." *Perspectives on Politics* 9: 247–267.

Council of the European Union. 2007. "Council conclusions on an EU response to situations of fragility." 2831st External Relations Council Meeting, 19–20 November, Brussels.

Cutler, Tony, and Barbara Waine. 1998. *Managing the Welfare State: The Politics of Public Sector Management*. New York: Berg Publishers.

Daly, Siobhan. 2003. "The ladder of abstraction: A framework for the systematic classification of democratic regime types." *Politics* 23: 96–108.

Davis, Kevin E. 2004. "What can the rule of law variable tell us about rule of law reforms?" *Michigan Journal of International Law* 26: 141–146.

Davis, Kevin E., Angelina Fisher, Benedict Kingsbury, and Sally Engle Merry, eds. 2012. *Governance by Indicators: Global Power through Classification and Rankings*. New York: Oxford University Press.

Davis, Kevin E., Benedict Kingsbury, and Sally Engle Merry. 2012a. "Governance by indicators." In *Governance by Indicators: Global Power through Classification and Rankings*, ed. Kevin Davis, Angelina Fisher, Benedict Kingsbury, and Sally Engle Merry. New York: Oxford University Press.

2012b. "Indicators as a technology of global governance." *Law & Society Review* 46: 74–101.

Davis, Kevin E., and Michael B. Kruse. 2007. "Taking the measure of the law: The case of the Doing Business project." Law and Social Inquiry 32: 1095–1119.

Delanda, M. 2002. *Intensive Science and Virtual Philosophy*. London: Continuum.

Djankov, S., Hart, O., McLiesh, C., and Shleifer, A. 2008. "Debt enforcement around the world." *Journal of Political Economy* 116: 1105–1149.

Donnelly, Jack. 2006. *Realism and International Relations*. New York: Cambridge University Press.

Duffield, Mark. 2001. *Global Governance and the New Wars: The Merging of Development and Security*. London: Zed.

2008. *Development, Security and Unending War: Governing the World of Peoples*. Cambridge: Polity.

Dunn, E. C. 2004. *Privatizing Poland: Baby Food, Big Business, and the Remaking of the Polish Working Class*. Ithaca, NY: Cornell University Press.

Ebrahim, Alnoor. 2003. "Accountability in practice: Mechanisms for NGOs." *World Development* 31: 813–829.

Eichengreen, Barry. 2008. *Globalizing Capital: A History of the International Monetary System*. Princeton University Press.

Elkins, Zachary. 2000. "Gradations of democracy? Empirical tests of alternative conceptualizations." *American Journal of Political Science* 44: 287–294.

Epstein, David L., Robert Bates, Jack Goldstone, Ida Kristensen, and Sharyn O'Halloran. 2006. "Democratic transitions." *American Journal of Political Science* 50: 551–569.

Ericson, R. E. 2009. "Eurasian natural gas pipelines: The political economy of network interdependence." *Eurasian Geography and Economics* 50: 28–57.

Ertman, Thomas. 1997. *The Birth of the Leviathan: Building States and Regimes in Medieval and Early Modern Europe.* Cambridge University Press.

Espeland, Wendy Nelson, and Michael Sauder. 2007. "Rankings and reactivity: How public measures recreate social worlds." *American Journal of Sociology* 113: 1–40.

Espeland, Wendy Nelson, and Mitchell L. Stevens. 2008. "A Sociology of quantification." *European Journal of Sociology* 49: 401–436.

Euben, J. Peter. 1989. "Corruption." In *Political Innovation and Conceptual Change*, ed. Terence Ball, James Farr, and Russell L. Hanson. Cambridge University Press.

European Council on Foreign Relations. 2012. *European Foreign Policy Scorecard 2012.* London: ECFR. Available at: http://ecfr.eu/scorecard/2012.

Fearon, James. 2010. "Do governance indicators predict anything? The case of 'fragile states' and civil war." Draft paper for the Annual Bank Conference on Development Economics.

Ferri, Giovanni, Li-Gang Liu, and Joseph E. Stiglitz. 1999. "The procyclical role of rating agencies: Evidence from the East Asian crisis." *Economic Notes* 28: 335–355.

Finer, Samuel. 1975. "State and nation-building in Europe: The role of the military." In *The Formation of National States in Europe*, ed. Charles Tilly. Princeton University Press.

Fisher, Angelina. 2012. "From diagnosing under-immunization to evaluating health care systems: Immunization coverage indicators as a technology of global governance." In *Governance by Indicators: Global Power through Classification and Rankings*, ed. Kevin Davis, Angelina Fisher, Benedict Kingsbury, and Sally Engle Merry. New York: Oxford University Press.

Fougner, Tore. 2006. "The state, international competitiveness and neoliberal globalization: Is there a future beyond 'the competition state'?" *Review of International Studies* 32: 165–185.

Freedom House. 2008. *Freedom House 2007 Annual Report: Financial Statements, Donors, Board of Trustees.* Available at: www.freedomhouse.org/uploads/special_report/72.pdf.

2010. *Freedom in the World 2010: Checklist Questions and Guidelines.* Available at: www.freedomhouse.org.

Friman, H. Richard. 2010. "Numbers and certification: Assessing foreign compliance in combating narcotics and human trafficking." In *Sex, Drugs, and Body Counts: The Politics of Numbers in Global Crime and Conflict,* ed. Peter Andreas and Kelly M. Greenhill. Ithaca, NY: Cornell University Press.

Georgian-European Policy and Legal Advice Centre (GEPLAC). 2008. *Georgian Economic Trends: Quarterly Review.* Tbilisi, Georgia: GEPLAC.

Gerschenkron, Alexander. 1962. *Economic Backwardness in Historical Perspective: A Book of Essays.* Cambridge, MA: Belknap Press of Harvard University Press.

Giannone, Diego. 2010. "Political and ideological aspects in the measurement of democracy: the Freedom House case." *Democratization* 17: 68–97.

Gleditsch, Kristian S., and Michael D. Ward. 1997. "Double take: A reexamination of democracy and autocracy in modern polities." *Journal of Conflict Resolution* 41: 361–383.

Globerman, S., and D. Shapiro. 2002. "Global foreign direct investment flows: The role of governance infrastructure." *World Development* 30: 1899–1919.

Goertz, Gary. 2006. *Social Science Concepts: A User's Guide.* Princeton University Press.

Goldstone, Jack, Jonathan Haughton, Karol Soltan, and Clifford Zinnes. 2004. *Strategy Framework for the Assessment and Treatment of Fragile States: Executive Summary (revised).* Washington, DC: University of Maryland.

Gorton, Gary. 2010. *Slapped by the Invisible Hand: The Panic of 2007.* New York: Oxford University Press.

Gourevitch, Peter A., David A. Lake, and Janice Gross Stein, eds. 2012. *The Credibility of NGOs: When Virtue is Not Enough.* New York: Cambridge University Press.

Grabel, Ilene. 2000. "The roots of the Asian financial crisis: A story of export-led growth and liberalized capital flows." In *Political Economy and Contemporary Capitalism: Radical Perspectives on Economic Theory and Policy,* ed. Ron Baiman, Heather Boushey, and Dawn Saunders. Armonk, NY: M.E. Sharpe.

Grabher, G. 2009. "Yet another turn? The evolutionary project in economic geography." *Economic Geography* 85: 119–128.

Grant, Ruth, and Robert Keohane. 2005. "Accountability and abuses of power in world politics." *American Political Science Review* 99: 29–43.

Guillaumont, Patrick, and Sylviane Guillaumont Jeanneney. 2009. *State Fragility and Economic Vulnerability: What is Measured and Why?* Clermont-Ferrand: CERDI-CNRS/University d'Auvergne.

Hadenius, Axel, and Jan Teorell. 2005. "Assessing alternative indices of democracy." *Committee on Concepts and Methods Working Paper Series*, #6.

Hafner-Burton, Emilie. 2008. "Sticks and stones: Naming and shaming and the human rights enforcement problem." *International Organization* 62: 689–716.

Haims, Marla, David Gompert, Gregory Treverton, and Brooke Stearns. 2008. *Breaking the Failed State Cycle.* RAND Occasional Paper. Santa Monica, CA: RAND.

Hall, Rodney Bruce. 2003. "The discursive demolition of the Asian development model." *International Studies Quarterly* 47: 71–99.

Hall, Rodney Bruce, and Thomas J. Biersteker. 2002. *The Emergence of Private Authority in Global Governance.* New York: Cambridge University Press.

Hazelkorn, E. 2008. "Learning to live with league tables and ranking: The experience of institutional leaders." *Higher Education Policy* 21: 193–215.

Heidenheimer, Arnold J., and Michael Johnston. 2001. *Political Corruption: Concepts and Contexts*, 3rd edn. Somerset, NJ: Transaction.

Heidenheimer, Arnold J., Michael Johnston, and Victor T. LeVine, eds. 1989. *Political Corruption: A Handbook.* Somerset, NJ: Transaction.

Heimann, Fritz, and Gillian Dell. 2012. *Exporting Corruption? Country Enforcement of the OECD Anti-Bribery Convention, Progress Report 2012.* Transparency International.

Helleiner, Eric. 1994. *States and the Reemergence of Global Finance.* Ithaca, NY: Cornell University Press.

Hermes, N., and R. Lensink, eds. 2001. *Changing the Conditions for Development Aid: A New Paradigm?* London: Routledge.

Hessel, H., and B. J. Hall. 2007. *Investigating Country Risk and its Relationship to Sovereign Ratings in Emerging Europe.* New York: Standard and Poor's.

Hood, Christopher, Ruth Dixon, and Craig Beeston. 2008. "Rating the Rankings: Assessing international rankings of public service performance." *International Public Management Journal* 11: 298–328.

Hout, W. 2004. "Political regimes and development assistance – The political economy of aid selectivity." *Critical Asian Studies* 36: 591–613.

Humphreys, Macartan, and Jeremy Weinstein. 2007. "Policing politicians: citizen empowerment and political accountability in Africa." Paper presented to the 2007 Annual Meeting of the American Political Science Association.

Huntington, Samuel P. 1968. *Political Order in Changing Societies.* New Haven, CT: Yale University Press.

    1989. "Modernization and corruption." In *Political Corruption: A Handbook*, ed. Arnold J. Heidenheimer, Michael Johnston, and Victor LeVine. Somerset, NJ: Transaction.

    1991. *The Third Wave: Democratization in the Late Twentieth Century.* Norman, OK: University of Oklahoma Press.

Ikpe, Eka. 2007. "Challenging the discourse of fragile states." *Conflict, Security and Development* 7: 85–124.

Independent Evaluation Group, World Bank. 2011. *World Bank Country-Level Engagement on Governance and Anticorruption: An Evaluation of the 2007 Strategy and Implementation Plan.* Washington, DC: The World Bank.

Inkeles, Alex. 1991. *On Measuring Democracy: Its Consequences and Concomitants.* New Brunswick, NJ: Transaction Publishers.

International Budget Partnership. 2010. *Open Budget Survey 2010: Open Budgets, Transform Lives.* Washington, DC.

Johnston, Alistair Iain. 2001. "Treating international institutions as social environments." *International Studies Quarterly* 45: 487–515.

Johnston, Michael. 2005. *Syndromes of Corruption: Wealth, Power, and Democracy.* Cambridge University Press.

Jurgen, Morten. 2013. *Poor Numbers: How We are Misled by African Development Statistics and What We Can Do about It.* Ithaca, NY: Cornell University Press.

Kaminsky, Graciela Laura, and Sergio L. Schmukler. 2002. "Short-run pain, long-run gain: The effects of financial liberalization." Policy Research Working Paper Series 2912. The World Bank.

Karatnycky, Adrian. 1999. "The decline of illiberal democracy." *Journal of Democracy* 10 (1): 112–125.

Keck, Margaret, and Katherin Sikkink. 1998. *Activists Beyond Borders.* Ithaca, NY: Cornell University Press.

Kekic, Laza. 2007. *The Economist Intelligence Unit's Index of Democracy.* Available at: www.economist.com/node/12499352.

Kelley, Judith. 2012. *Monitoring Democracy: When International Election Observation Works and Why it Often Fails.* Princeton University Press.

Kelley, Judith, and Beth Simmons. 2015. "Politics by number: indicators as social pressure in international relations." *American Journal of Political Science* 59 (1): 1146–1161.

Kellstedt, Paul M., and Guy D. Whitten. 2009. *The Fundamentals of Political Science Research.* New York: Cambridge University Press.

Keohane, Robert. 1984. *After Hegemony.* Princeton University Press.

Keynes, John Maynard. 1936. *The General Theory of Employment, Interest and Money*. New York: Harcourt Brace.

King, Gary, and Langche Zeng. 2001. "Improving forecasts of state failure." *World Politics* 53: 623–658.

Kipnis, A. B. 2008. "Audit cultures: Neoliberal governmentality, socialist legacy, or technologies of governing?" *American Ethnologist* 35: 275–289.

Kirshner, Jonathan. 2000. "The study of money." *World Politics* 52: 407–36.

Klinz, Wolf. 2011. "On credit rating agencies: Future perspectives." Brussels: European Parliament Committee on Economic and Monetary Affairs.

Knack, Stephen. 2007. "Measuring corruption: A critique of indicators in Eastern Europe and Central Asia." *Journal of Public Policy* 27: 255–291.

Knight, Frank H. 1921 [1971]. *Risk, Uncertainty and Profit*. University of Chicago Press.

Koremenos, Barbara, Charles Lipson, and Duncan Snidal. 2001. "The rational design of international institutions." *International Organization* 55: 761–799.

Krasner, Stephen, ed. 1982. *International Regimes*. Ithaca, NY: Cornell University Press.

1991. "Global communications and national power." *World Politics* 43: 336–366.

Krasner, Stephen D., and Carlos Pascual. 2005. "Addressing state failure." *Foreign Affairs* 81: 153–163.

Kurer, Oscar. 2005. "Corruption: An alternative approach to its definition and measurement." *Political Studies* 53 (1): 222–239.

Lai, K. P. Y. 2006. "'Imagineering' Asian emerging markets: Financial knowledge networks in the fund management industry." *Geoforum* 37: 627–642.

Lake, David A. 2009. *Hierarchy in International Relations*. Ithaca, NY: Cornell University Press.

Lall, S. 2001. Competitiveness indices and developing countries: An economic evaluation of the global competitiveness report. *World Development* 29: 1501–1525.

Lampland, Martha. 2010. "False numbers as formalizing practices." *Social Studies of Science* 40: 377–404.

Lane, J. E. 2000. *New Public Management*. London: Routledge.

Larner, W. 2003. "Neoliberalism?" *Environment and Planning D: Society and Space* 21: 509–12.

Larraín, Guillermo, Helmut Reisen, and Julia von Maltzan. 1997. "Emerging market risk and sovereign credit ratings." OECD Development Centre Working Papers 124, OECD Publishing.

Latour, Bruno. 2005. *Reassembling the Social: An Introduction to Actor-Network Theory.* Oxford University Press.

Lavelle, K. C. 2000. "The International Finance Corporation and the emerging market funds industry." *Third World Quarterly* 21: 193–213.

Lawson, Stephanie. 1993. "Conceptual issues in the comparative study of regime change and democratization." *Comparative Politics* 25: 183–205.

Lee, R. 2003. "The marginalization of everywhere? Emerging geographies of emerging markets." In *Remaking the Global Economy: Economic-Geographical Perspectives*, ed. J. Peck and H. W.-C. Yeung. London: Thousand Oaks.

Levitsky, Steven, and Lucan A. Way. 2002. "The rise of competitive authoritarianism." *Journal of Democracy* 13 (2): 53.

2010. *Competitive Authoritarianism: Hybrid Regimes After the Cold War.* Cambridge University Press.

Lewis, Michael. 2011. *The Big Short: Inside the Doomsday Machine.* New York: W. W. Norton and Company.

Linz, Juan J. 1975. "Totalitarian and authoritarian regimes." In *The Handbook of Political Science*, ed. Fred Greenstein and Nelson Polsby. Reading, MA: Addison-Wesley.

Löwenheim, Oded. 2008. "Examining the state: a Foucauldian perspective on international 'governance indicators'." *Third World Quarterly* 29: 255–274.

MacKenzie, Donald. 2006. *An Engine Not a Camera: How Financial Models Shape Markets.* Cambridge, MA: MIT Press.

Mainwaring, Scott, Daniel Brinks, and Anibal Perez-Linan. 2001. "Classifying political regimes in Latin America, 1945–1999." *Studies in Comparative International Development* 36: 37–65.

Malecki, Edward. 2002. "Hard and soft networks for urban competitiveness." *Urban Studies* 39: 929–945.

2004. "Jockeying for position: What it means and why it matters to regional development policy when places compete." *Regional Studies* 38: 1101–1120.

2007. "Cities and regions competing in the global economy: knowledge and local development policies." *Environment and Planning C – Government And Policy* 25: 638–654.

Markoff, John. 1996. *Waves of Democracy: Social Movements and Political Change.* Thousand Oaks, CA: Sage Press.

Marshall, Monty G., Ted Robert Gurr, and Keith Jaggers. 2010. *Polity IV Project Dataset Users' Manual.* Available at: www.systemicpeace.org/polity/polity4.htm.

Mattli, Walter, and Ngaire Woods, eds. 2009. *The Politics of Global Regulation.* Princeton University Press.

Mawdsley, E. 2007. "The millennium challenge account: Neo-liberalism, poverty and security." *Review of International Political Economy* 14: 487–509.

McCormick, James M. and Neil J. Mitchell. 1997. "Human rights violations, umbrella concepts, and empirical analysis." *World Politics* 49: 510–525.

McGann, James. 2008. "The global 'Go-to think tanks'." Philadelphia: University of Pennsylvania.

McHenry, Dean E. 2000. "Quantitative measures of democracy in Africa: An assessment." *Democratization* 7: 168–185.

Merry, Sally Engle. 2011. "Measuring the world: Indicators, human rights, and global governance." *Current Anthropology* 52: s83–s95.

Migdal, Joel S., and Klaus Schlichte. 2005. "Rethinking the state." In *The Dynamics of States: The Formation and Crises of State Domination*, ed. Klaus Schlichte. London: Ashgate.

Moody's Investor Service. 2007. Global Credit Research, Special Comment, "Sovereign Default and Recovery Rates, 1983–2006."

Munck, Gerardo L. 2009. *Measuring Democracy: A Bridge Between Scholarship and Politics*. Baltimore, MD: Johns Hopkins University Press.

Munck, Geraldo L., and Jay Verkuilen. 2002. "Conceptualizing and measuring democracy: Evaluating alternative indices." *Comparative Political Studies* 35: 5–34.

Nanda, V. P. 2006. "The 'Good Governance' concept revisited." *The Annals of the American Academy of Political and Social Science* 603: 269–283.

National Security Council (NSC). 2002. *National Security Strategy of the United States*. Washington, DC: NSC.

2006. *National Security Strategy of the United States*. Washington, DC: NSC.

2010. *National Security Strategy of the United States*. Washington, DC: NSC.

Ndikumana, Leonce, and James K. Boyce. 2008. "New estimates of capital flight from sub-Saharan African Countries: Linkages with external borrowing and policy options." Working Paper No. 166. Political Economy Research Institute, University of Massachusetts, Amherst.

Newman, Edward. 2007. "Weak states, state failure and terrorism." *Terrorism and Political Violence* 19: 463–488.

2009. "Failed states and the international order: Constructing a post-Westphalian world." *Contemporary Security Policy* 30: 421–443.

Noonan, John T. Jr. 1984. *Bribes*. New York: Macmillan.

Nye, Joseph S. 1967. "Corruption and political development: a cost-benefit analysis." *American Political Science Review* 61 (2): 417–427.

Ó Tuathail, G. 1997. "Emerging markets and other simulations: Mexico, the Chiapas revolt and the geofinancial panopticon." *Ecumene* 4: 300–317.

2008. "Russia's Kosovo: A critical geopolitics of the August 2008 war over South Ossetia." *Eurasian Geography and Economics* 49: 670–705.

O'Donnell, Guillermo. 1993. "On the state, democratization and some conceptual problems: A Latin American view with glances at some postcommunist countries." *World Development* 21: 1355–1369.

OECD (Organisation for Economic Cooperation and Development). 2005. *Fighting Corruption in Transition Economies: Georgia*. Paris: OECD.

2010. *The State's Legitimacy in Fragile Situations: Unpacking Complexity*. Paris: OECD.

OECD Development Assistance Committee. 2007. *Principles for Good International Engagement in Fragile States and Situations*. Paris: OECD.

2008. *Concepts and Dilemmas of State Building in Fragile Situations*. Paris: OECD.

Oliver, Adam. 2012. "The folly of cross-country ranking exercises." *Health Economics, Policy and Law* 7: 15–17.

O'Loughlin, J., G. Ó Tuathail, and V. Kolossov. 2005. "Russian geopolitical culture and public opinion: The masks of Proteus revisited." *Transactions of the Institute of British Geographers* 30: 322.

Oren, Ido. 2002. *Our Enemies and Us: America's Rivalries and the Making of Political Science*. Ithaca, NY: Cornell University Press.

Orwell, George. 1946 [2000]."Politics and the English language." In *The Collected Essays, Journalism & Letters of George Orwell*, Volume 4. Boston: Nonpareil Books.

Papava, V. 2006. "The political economy of Georgia's Rose Revolution." *East European Democratization* 50: 657–667.

Partnoy, Frank. 1999. "The Siskel and Ebert of financial markets? Two thumbs down for the credit rating agencies." *Washington University Law Quarterly* 77: 619–712.

Patrick, Stewart. 2006. "Weak States and Terrorism: Fact or Fiction?" *Washington Quarterly* 29: 27–53.

Peck, Jamie. 2002. "Political economics of scale: Fast policy, interscalar relations, and neoliberal workfare." *Economic Geography* 78: 331–360.

2004. "Geography and public policy: Constructions of neoliberalism." *Progress In Human Geography* 28: 392–405.

Pemstein, Daniel, Stephen A. Meserve, and James Melton. 2010. "Democratic compromise: A latent variable analysis of ten measures of regime type." *Political Analysis* 18: 426–449.

Phelps, N. A. 2007. "Gaining from globalization? State extraterritoriality and domestic economic impacts – The case of Singapore." *Economic Geography* 83: 371–393.

Phelps, N. A., M. Power, and R. Wanjiru. 2007. "Learning to compete: Communities of investment promotion practice in the spread of global neoliberalism." In *Neoliberalization: States, Networks, Peoples*, ed. K. England and K. Ward. Malden, MA: Blackwell.

Phelps, N. A., and A. Wood. 2006. "Lost in translation? Local interests, global actors and inward investment regimes." *Journal of Economic Geography* 6: 493–515.

Pilon, Juliana Geran. 1993. "The measure of freedom." *Journal of Democracy* 4: 127–129.

Pistor, Katharina. 2012. "Re-construction of private indicators for public purposes." In *Governance by Indicators: Global Power through Classification and Rankings*, ed. Kevin Davis, Angelina Fisher, Benedict Kingsbury, and Sally Engle Merry. New York: Oxford University Press.

Porter, M. E., K. Schwab, A. Lopez-Claros, and X. Sala-i-Martin. 2006. *The Global Competitiveness Report 2006–2007*. Geneva: World Economic Forum.

Porter, M. E., K. Schwab, and X. Sala-i-Martin. 2007. *The Global Competitiveness Report 2007–2008*. Geneva: World Economic Forum.

Porter, Theodore M. 1995. *Trust in Numbers: The Pursuit of Objectivity in Science and Public Life*. Princeton University Press.

Porter, Tony. 2009. "Making serious measures: Numerical national indices, peer review and global governance." Paper presented to the 2009 International Studies Association Meeting, New York.

Power, Michael. 1997. *The Audit Society: Rituals of Verification*. Oxford University Press.

2007. *Organized Uncertainty: Designing a World of Risk Management*. New York: Oxford University Press.

Przeworski, Adam, Michael Alvarez, José Antonio Cheibub, and Fernando Limongi. 1996. "What makes democracies endure?" *Journal of Democracy* 7: 39–55.

2000. *Democracy and Development: Political Institutions and Well-Being in the World, 1950–1990*. New York: Cambridge University Press.

Przeworski, Adam, and Fernando Limongi. 1997. "Modernization: theories and facts." *World Politics* 49: 155–184.

Reich, Gary. 2002. "Categorizing political regimes: New data for old problems." *Democratization* 9: 1–24.

Reinhart, Carmen. 2002. "Sovereign credit ratings before and after financial crises." In *Ratings, Rating Agencies and the Global Financial System*, ed. Richard Levich, Giovanni Majnoni, and Carmen M. Reinhart. New York: Kluwer Academic Press.

Revenuewatch. 2010. *Revenue Watch Index 2010.* New York: Revenuewatch Institute. Available at: www.revenuewatch.org/rwin dex2010/pdf/RevenueWatchIndex_2010.pdf.

Rice, Susan, and Stewart Patrick. 2006. *Index of State Weakness in the Developing World.* Washington, DC: Brookings Institution.

Robert Schuman Centre for Advanced Studies. 2009. *European Report on Development – Overcoming Fragility in Africa, Forging a New European Approach.* San Domenico di Fiesole: European University Institute.

Roberts, S. M., S. Wright, and P. O'Neill. 2007. "Good governance in the Pacific? Ambivalence and possibility." *Geoforum* 38: 967–984.

Robson, A. J. 2005. "Complex evolutionary systems and the Red Queen." *Economic Journal* 115: 211–224.

Rona-Tas, Akos, and Stephanie Hiss. 2010. "The role of ratings in the subprime mortgage crisis: The art of corporate and the science of consumer credit rating." In *Markets on Trial: The Economic Sociology of the US Financial Crisis,* ed. Michael Loundsbury and Paul Hirsh. Bingley, UK: Emerald Group Publishing.

Rose-Ackerman, Susan. 1999. *Corruption and Government.* Cambridge University Press.

Rotberg, Robert. 2002. "Failed states in a world of terror." *Foreign Affairs* 81: 127–141.

2014. *On Governance: What it is, What it Measures and its Policy Uses.* Ontario: Centre for International Governance Innovation.

Rothstein, Bo. 2011. *The Quality of Government: Corruption, Social Trust, and Inequality in International Perspective.* University of Chicago Press.

Ruggie, John G. 2004. "Reconstituting the global public domain – issues, actors, and practices." *European Journal of International Relations* 10: 499–531.

Saint-Martin, Denis. 2004. *Building the New Managerialist State: Consultants and the Politics of Public Sector Reform in Comparative Perspective.* New York: Oxford University Press.

Sanderson, Ian. 2001. "Performance management, evaluation and learning in 'modern' local government." *Public Administration* 79: 297–313.

Sanín, Francisco Gutiérrez. 2009. "The quandaries of coding and ranking: Evaluating poor state performance indexes." Crisis States Working Papers Series 2, November 2009. London: LSE Development Studies Institute.

2011. "Evaluating state performance: A critical view of state failure and fragility indexes." *European Journal of Development Research* 23: 20–42.

Sanín, Francisco Gutiérrez, Diana Buitrago, and Andrea Gonzáles. 2013. "Aggregating political dimensions: Of the feasibility of political indicators." *Social Indicators Research* 110: 305–326.

Sarfaty, Galit. 2013. "Regulating through numbers: A case study of corporate sustainability reporting." *Virginia Journal of International Law* 53: 575–622.

Sauder, Michael, and Ryon Lancaster. 2006. "Do rankings matter? The effects of *U.S. News and World Report* rankings on the admissions process of law schools." *Law & Society Review* 40: 105–134.

Schäfer, Armin. 2006. "A new form of governance? Comparing the open method of co-ordination to multilateral surveillance by the IMF and the OECD." *Journal of European Public Policy* 13: 70–88.

Schmitter, Philippe C., and Terry Lynn Karl. 1991. "What democracy is … and is not." *Journal of Democracy* 2: 75–88.

Schoenberger, E. 1998. "Discourse and practice in human geography." *Progress In Human Geography* 22: 1–14.

Schueth, Sam. 2011. "Assembling international competitiveness: The Republic of Georgia, USAID and the *Doing Business* project." *Economic Geography* 87: 51–77.

Schwab, K., and M. E. Porter. 2008. *The Global Competitiveness Report 2008–2009*. Geneva: World Economic Forum.

Schwab, K., X. Sala-i-Martin, and J. Blanke. 2009. *The Global Competitiveness Report 2009–2010*. Geneva: World Economic Forum.

Scott, James C. 1972. *Comparative Political Corruption*. Englewood Cliffs, NJ: Prentice-Hall.

1999. *Seeing Like a State: How Certain Schemes to Improve the Human Condition Have Failed*. New Haven, CT: Yale University Press.

Sharman, Jason. 2011. "Testing the global financial transparency regime." *International Studies Quarterly* 55: 981–1001.

Shaxon, Nicholas. 2007. "Oil, corruption and the resource curse." *International Affairs* 83: 1123–1140.

Sheppard, Eric. 2000. "Competition in space and between places." In *A Companion to Economic Geography*, ed. E. Sheppard and T. J. Barnes. Oxford: Blackwell.

2002. "The spaces and times of globalization: Place, scale, networks, and positionality." *Economic Geography* 78: 307–330.

Sidaway, J. D., and J. R. Bryson. 2002. "Constructing knowledges of 'emerging markets': UK-based investment managers and their overseas connections." *Environment and Planning A* 34: 401–416.

Sidaway, J. D., and M. Pryke. 2000. "The strange geographies of 'emerging markets'." *Transactions of the Institute of British Geographers* 25: 187–201.

Simmons, Beth. 2009. *Mobilizing for Human Rights*. New York: Cambridge University Press.

Sinclair, Timothy J. 1994. "Passing judgment: Credit rating processes as regulatory mechanisms of governance in the emerging world order." *Review of International Political Economy* 1: 133–159.

1999. "Bond-rating agencies and coordination in the Global Political Economy." In *Private Authority and International Affairs*, ed. Claire Cutler, Virginia Haufler, and Tony Porter. Albany, NY: State University of New York Press.

2001. "The infrastructure of global governance: Quasi-regulatory mechanisms and the new global finance." *Global Governance* 7: 441–451.

2003. "Global monitor: Bond rating agencies." *New Political Economy* 8: 147–161.

2005. *The New Masters of Capital: American Bond Rating Agencies and the Politics of Creditworthiness*. Ithaca, NY: Cornell University Press.

Skaaning, Svend-Erik. 2010. "Measuring the rule of law." *Political Research Quarterly* 63: 449–460.

Smith, Roy C., and Ingo Walter. 2002. "Rating agencies: Is there an agency issue?" In *Ratings, Rating Agencies and the Global Financial System*, ed. Richard M. Levich *et al.* Boston: Kluwer Academic Publishers.

Snyder, Jack, and Karen Ballentine. 1996. "Nationalism and the marketplace of ideas." *International Security* 21: 5–40.

Soederberg, S. 2004. "American empire and 'excluded states': The millennium challenge account and the shift to pre-emptive development." *Third World Quarterly* 25: 279–302.

Spruyt, Hendrik. 1994. *The Sovereign State and its Competitors*. Princeton University Press.

Stein, E., and Daude, C. 2001. "Institutions, integration and the location of foreign direct investment." In *New Horizons of Foreign Direct Investment*. Paris: OECD Global Forum on International Investment.

Stone, Christopher. 2012. "Problems of power in the design of indicators of safety and justice in the global south." In *Governance by Indicators: Global Power through Classification and Rankings*, ed. Kevin Davis, Angelina Fisher, Benedict Kingsbury, and Sally Engle Merry. New York: Oxford University Press.

Strathern, Marilyn. 2000a. *Audit Cultures: Anthropological Studies in Accountability, Ethics, and the Academy*. London: Routledge.

2000b. "The tyranny of transparency." *British Educational Research Journal* 26: 309–321.

Sylla, Richard. 2002. "An historical primer on the business of credit rating." In *Ratings, Rating Agencies and the Global Financial System*, ed. Richard M. Levich *et al.* Boston: Kluwer Academic Publishers.